THE RAI

Homer's epics reflect an eighth-century BC world of warrior tribes that were fractured by constant strife; aside from its fantastic scale, nothing is exceptional about Troy's conquest by the Greeks. Using a fascinating and innovative approach, Professor Gottschall analyzes Homeric conflict from the perspective of modern evolutionary biology, attributing its intensity to a shortage of available young women. The warrior practice of taking enemy women as slaves and concubines meant that women were concentrated in the households of powerful men. In turn, this shortage drove men to compete fiercely over women: almost all the main conflicts of the *Iliad* and *Odyssey* can be traced back to disputes over women. *The Rape of Troy* integrates biological and humanistic understanding – biological theory is used to explore the ultimate sources of pitched Homeric conflict, and Homeric society is the subject of a bio-anthropological case study of why men fight.

JONATHAN GOTTSCHALL is Adjunct Assistant Professor of English at Washington and Jefferson College. He co-edited (with David Sloan Wilson) *The Literary Animal: Evolution and the Nature of Narrative* (2005) and has published numerous articles seeking to bridge the humanities-sciences divide.

THE RAPE OF TROY

Evolution, Violence, and the World of Homer

JONATHAN GOTTSCHALL

CAMBRIDGE UNIVERSITY PRESS
Cambridge, New York, Melbourne, Madrid, Cape Town, Singapore, São Paulo, Delhi

Cambridge University Press
The Edinburgh Building, Cambridge CB2 8RU, UK

Published in the United States of America by Cambridge University Press, New York

www.cambridge.org
Information on this title: www.cambridge.org/9780521690478

First published 2008

Printed in the United Kingdom at the University Press, Cambridge

A catalogue record for this publication is available from the British Library

ISBN 978-0-521-87038-2 hardback
ISBN 978-0-521-69047-8 paperback

"[We are men] to whom Zeus has given the fate of winding down our lives in painful wars, from youth until we perish, each of us."

Odysseus, *Iliad* 14.85–87

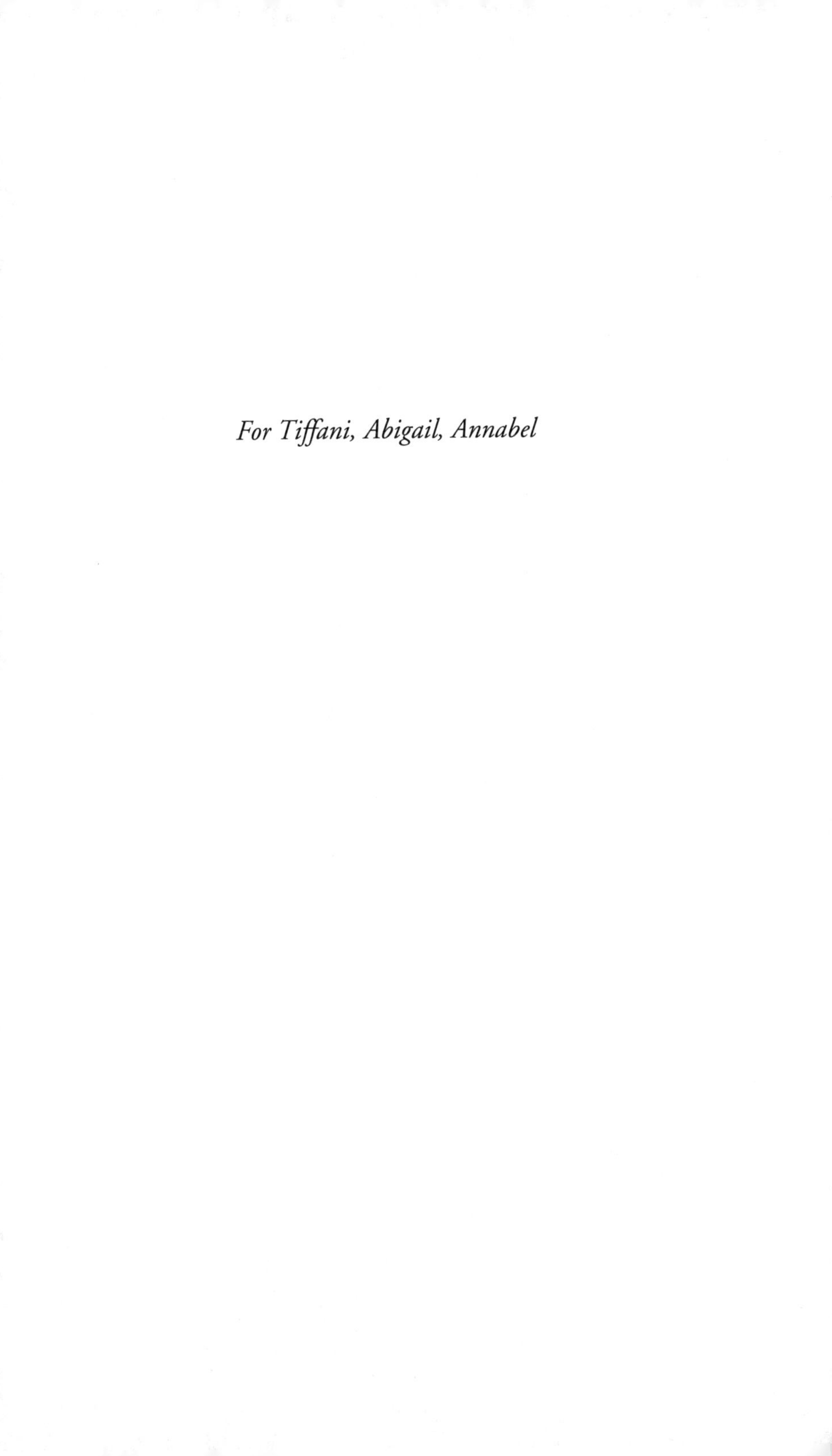

For Tiffani, Abigail, Annabel

Contents

Acknowledgments (or, the fate of Thersites)

A new participant in Homeric debates risks the fate of Thersites. Thersites is scrawny and scraggly, he has no strong allies, and he lacks pedigree and heroic credentials, yet he has the temerity to stand up amidst all the Greeks assembled on the Trojan beach and rail against great Agamemnon for his pride and greed. He can call on a measureless trove of words, and his abuse of Agamemnon is on the mark even if his speech is sometimes shrill and disorderly. Thersites is a churl who dares strive with heroes and, for this, Odysseus shames him with insults and threats, before clubbing him between his bony shoulders with a heavy staff:

> Thersites of reckless speech, clear flowing speaker though you are, curb yourself, and do not try to strive by yourself against chiefs. For I say there is no mortal man who is worse than you among all those who came with the sons of Atreus beneath Ilium . . . But I say to you straight out, and it will be a thing accomplished, if I find you again playing the fool, even as you are now, then may the head of Odysseus rest no more on his shoulders, and let me no longer be called the father of Telemachus, if I do not seize you and strip off your clothes, your cloak and tunic that hide your nakedness, and send you wailing to the swift ships, driven out of the assembly with shameful blows. (2.246–64).

In our last glimpse of Thersites he is dissolving in tears of impotent shame, smarting from his bleeding welt and the ostracism of all the assembled Greeks, who applaud Odysseus' attack with laughter and cheers.

When entering into discussion of "Homeric questions," one finds oneself among 2,500 years' worth of scholarly heroes, and one is exposed to the very real possibility of being – metaphorically speaking – stripped naked, flogged brutally, and reduced to an object of derision: the bolder the argument the greater the risk. The dangers are enhanced in my case by the massively interdisciplinary nature of my undertaking, which has obliged me to attempt to master not only relevant aspects of the truly vast corpus of Homeric scholarship, but also daunting literatures in comparative anthropology and evolutionary biology. Time will tell whether I will suffer the fate of Thersites and be whipped from the assembly of scholars, or whether I will be offered a seat there. But before I take up my scepter and begin to make my case, I'd like to thank those who did what they could to shield me from the fate of Thersites.

Thanks are owed to my interdisciplinary dissertation committee at the State University of New York, Binghamton, who oversaw the completion of a first version of this book: Haim Ofek (Economics), Marilyn Gaddis-Rose (Comparative Literature), David Sloan Wilson (Biology), and Zola Pavloskis-Petit (Classics). I am especially grateful to Zola, and another distinguished classical scholar from Binghamton – Saul Levin – for patiently answering many questions as I worked to improve my Greek. I am deeply obliged to Barry Powell, who generously agreed to read and comment on my manuscript when it showed up – out of the blue – in his email inbox. Marcus Nordlund and Ineke Sluiter offered advice on the manuscript, and Kurt Raaflaub provided a second opinion on technical questions under tight time pressure. My father (Jon), my brother (Richard), and my wife (Tiffani) all commented on the manuscript, and my little girls (Abigail and Annabel) helped me keep my work in perspective. My editor at Cambridge, Michael Sharp, commissioned two fair, thorough, and sometimes bruising peer reviews. The readers (Hans van Wees and an anonymous reviewer) provided expert advice and criticism, and the final version of this book is greatly improved because of their challenges.

Finally, four people must be singled out for truly indispensable contributions. My mother, Marcia Gottschall, a teacher of literature and writing, read different versions of this book almost half-a-dozen times over as many years. Its style and substance owe much to my ability, and ruthless willingness, to exploit this source of cheap, skilled labor. David Sloan Wilson was the first to express confidence in my approach and helped nurture this project through its early phases. Brian Boyd and Joseph Carroll meticulously read and commented on different versions of the book as well as on related scholarly articles. They have also been absolutely dependable sources of moral support, mentorship, and good cheer.

At this point a writer customarily absolves his benefactors for the failings of his work. However, while I accept final responsibility for the shortfalls of *The Rape of Troy*, disapproving readers are also encouraged to blame the persons mentioned above. For without their support there would be no book.

Introduction

The Trojan War finally ends in the Rape of Troy: in the black of night thousands of men and boys are butchered in city streets and homes, and the women and girls are led out across the plain to the sea. They are stowed in the bellies of ships and sped across the Aegean to lives of slavery and concubinage in the Greek homelands. The climax of the war – as foreshadowed in the *Iliad* and described in the *Odyssey* – is a terrifying orgy of sexual and violent passions that serves as the symbolic heart of both poems.

However, aside from the fantastic scale of the Trojan War, little is exceptional in the Rape of Troy. The world of Homer's poems is a mosaic of tribes and chiefdoms, fractured by constant strife. Most Homeric conflicts are nothing like the Trojan War in duration or scope. The typical conflict is closer to a Viking raid: fast ships with shallow drafts are rowed onto beaches and seaside communities are sacked before neighbors can lend defensive support. The men are usually killed, livestock and other portable wealth are plundered, and women are carried off to live among the victors and perform sexual and menial labors. Homeric men live with the possibility of sudden, violent death, and the women live in fear for their men and children, and of sails on the horizon that may harbinger new lives of rape and slavery.

When Homeric men are not fighting neighbors, they are usually competing among themselves. Men vie compulsively and intensely, formally and informally, in dancing and storytelling, games, public debate, martial skill and courage, speed of foot and strength of arm, proficiency in sailing and horsemanship, skill in mowing grain and plowing straight furrows, physical carriage and dress, costly armor and good looks, the size and fierceness of killed foes, the heroic feats of their forebears, the ranks of the gods in their family trees, and their ability to give costly gifts and lavish feasts. In other words, almost any occasion serves for Homeric men to measure themselves against one another. Constant brinkmanship frequently escalated to violence. While most conflicts are defused before lives are lost, Homer suggests a world where small provocations could lead to hot-blooded murders, cool-headed assassinations, and reciprocal killings by vengeful kinsmen.

The Homer scholar John Myres wrote, savoring his understatement, "It is not easy to say anything new about Homer."[1] After more than 2,500 years in which the *Iliad* and *Odyssey* have been the most popular, esteemed, frequently translated, and exhaustively analyzed works of fiction in the world, what is left to discover? The truth of Myres' axiom is epitomized in my opening paragraphs: the pervasiveness and ferocity of Homeric conflict have been a subject of constant, if frequently informal, commentary.

In all that has been written, however, remarkably few different explanations have been advanced for the special fury of Homeric conflict.[2] By far the best treatment of Homeric war and conflict to date is Hans van Wees' *Status warriors* (1992), and his review of the important literature covers just a few scholars and needs just seven pages.[3]

There are relatively few competing perspectives on Homeric conflict because the poems themselves tightly constrain interpretation. Many of Homer's men are as keen as philosophers as they are fearsome as warriors; they cudgel their brains to understand why they so often find themselves far from home, courting death among hostile men, despite the manifest desirability of peace. Most commentators have trusted the words of the warriors themselves, arguing that pitched Homeric conflict is an end product of their hatred of mortality, their desire to attain immortality of reputation through heroic deeds.[4] The bedrock of heroic life is this premise: life is ephemeral, but memory is deathless. The true hero etches his name big, deep, and indelible in the cultural memory banks. If he dares greatly and performs gloriously, his words and deeds will reverberate in immortal song – with his name and accomplishments preserved in the amber of poetic meter, he will never perish. However, other scholars have argued that the quest for poetic immortality provides only a partial explanation, and partially obscures that Homeric men fight for resources, social status and power.

The Rape of Troy does not reject these claims. It analyzes Homeric conflict from the perspective of modern anthropology and evolutionary biology; it is best described as an evolutionary anthropology of conflict in Homeric society. It is based on research showing that the Homeric epics are not only precious as literary art; they are also our most important artifacts of life on island outcroppings and threads of coastal land in and surrounding the Aegean sea almost three thousand years ago. As will be explained later, reconstructing this prehistoric society on the basis of the epics and other patchy evidence is rife with complications. For now it is only necessary to say that when I generalize about "Homeric society," I refer not so much to Homer's fictional *construction* as to a specific scholarly *reconstruction* of the real world from which the epics emerged. This reconstruction is based not only on careful analysis of Homer, but also on study of Hesiod's roughly contemporaneous *Works and Days* and *Theogony*, preserved summaries of lost epics, comparative anthropology, the study of non-Greek oral traditions, linguistics, archaeology, and more.

I have three main arguments. First, I argue that patterns of conflict in Homeric society converge beautifully with those described by anthropologists and ethnographers across a strikingly diverse spectrum of non-state societies. Others have offered that Homeric men compete primarily over one or another scarce social or material resource: subsistence goods, prestige wealth, social status, or immortal fame. My goal is not so much to correct or supplant these arguments as to provide a broader view capable of placing all elements of Homeric conflict within a single explanatory context. I suggest that none of these sources of Homeric conflict – and I would also add fierce and ubiquitous competition over women to the list – can be singled out as *the* root cause. Rather, all forms of Homeric conflict result from direct attempts, as in fights over women, or indirect attempts, as in fights for social status and wealth, to enhance Darwinian fitness in a physically and socially exacting ecological niche. While the sources of Homeric conflict often appear ludicrously trivial – vast wars and homicides over pretty women, a murder over a game of dice, biting insults and dangerous brinkmanship over which man has sharper eyesight – they

are not treated as such because what is truly at stake is access to the scarce, precious things required to sustain and reproduce life.

But none of these pressures are unique to Homeric society. Competition for resources, social status, and mates is common to all societies. So the big question is still unanswered: Why was Homeric society *particularly* prone to intense conflict within and between groups? The scenario I propose in answer is my second main argument, and it is likely to be the most controversial aspect of this book. I argue that patterns of violence in Homeric society are tantalizingly consistent with the hypothesis that Homeric society

suffered from acute shortages of available young women relative to young men. The institution of slave-concubinage meant that women were not equitably distributed across the circum-Aegean world; they were concentrated in certain communities and, within those communities, in the households of powerful men. While Homeric men could have only one legitimate wife, the society was in fact polygynous, with high-status men monopolizing the reproductive capacities of multiple women and low-status men comparatively deprived. This uneven distribution of women across and within communities may have been exacerbated by excess mortality of juvenile females, either through disproportionate exposure of female infants or differential parental care (i.e., weaning girls at an earlier age, providing insufficient nutrition in times of hardship, etc.). This shortage of women, whether it was brought about solely through polygyny or also through differential mortality, created strong incentives for men to compete, as individuals and in groups, not only for direct access to women, but also for the limited funds of social and material resources needed to attract and retain them.

Thirdly, and finally, I claim that this model helps to illuminate the origins of specific features of Homeric philosophy. An oppressive miasma of fatalism and pessimism pervades the *Iliad* and, to a lesser but still palpable extent, the *Odyssey*. While the desirability of peace is obvious, Homeric men – like their fathers and grandfathers before them – feel that they are doomed to perpetual conflict. The blame for this is placed at the feet of awesome supernatural forces – of cruel and capricious gods and uncaring fate. In the final chapter of the book, I argue that incessant Greek conflict can be explained without recourse to the supernatural. A shortage of young women helps to explain more about Homeric society than its relentless violence; it also sheds light on the origins of a tragic and pessimistic worldview, a pantheon of gods deranged by petty vanities, and a people's resignation to the pitiless dictates of fate.

For readers who hold to stereotypes of classics as stodgy and dry (and for those classicists who *are*, in fact, stodgy and dry), my approach may seem odd. However, while many of the details of my perspective are novel in Homeric studies, my approach is far more traditional than it may first appear. In fact, the promiscuous interdisciplinarity of this study places it in an old and illustrious tradition of Homeric scholarship. In the final years of the eighteenth century, when German scholars in particular were laying foundations for the modern study of Homer and all the rest of Greek and Roman antiquity, the goal was to create an *Altertumswissenschaft* – a science of antiquity.[5] As the great nineteenth-century classicist Ullrich von Wilamowitz-Moellendorff explained, the object of this science was to use the power of systematic inquiry to resurrect the dead societies of antiquity in all of their aspects:

> [The subject matter of classical scholarship is] Graeco-Roman civilization it its essence and *in every facet* . . . The task of scholarship is to bring that dead world to life by the power of science – to re-create the poet's song, the thought of the philosopher and the lawgiver, the sanctity of the temple and the feelings of the believers and the unbelievers, the bustling life of market and port, the physical appearance of land and sea, mankind at work and play.[6]

Given that the goal was to revivify and reconstruct *every facet* of classical civilization, this science encouraged – no, demanded – unfettered disciplinary miscegenation.

For Wilamowitz and the architects of *Altertumswissenschaft* this meant drawing on literary scholarship, linguistic study, history, and the study of art, inscriptions, coins, papyrus fragments, and more. But from the beginning of the modern era of Homeric scholarship up to the present moment, insights that were anthropological in fact, if not in name, fueled great advances in the understanding of the epics and the society that engendered them. This tradition stretches back at least as far as Robert Wood's seminal *Essay on the original genius of Homer* (1769),[7] which based sharp observations about Homeric poetry and society on comparisons of modes of life described in Homer with those of Bedouin Arabs in Northern Africa. Similarly, the radical research programs of nineteenth-century Homerists were inspired, in no small part, by cross-cultural studies of oral traditions in Gaelic Scotland, England, Germany, and Finland. Through the course of the nineteenth century Homerists increasingly drew, however haphazardly, on cross-cultural information. Many of these studies bore vitally on one of the biggest and oldest Homeric questions, one that will be taken up yet again in the present study: to what extent does the world portrayed in Homer reflect a real society?

The use of anthropology to illuminate aspects of Homeric society flourished in the twentieth century as anthropology established itself as an academic discipline.[8] In fact, the anthropological prowess of the early twentieth-century Homerist Milman Parry (1902–35) enabled what is arguably the most important advance in the long history of Homeric scholarship. Parry confirmed a radical thesis about the composition of the Homeric poems through extensive fieldwork collecting and analyzing the traditional oral epics of Yugoslavia (see Chapter One). While Parry had no formal training, in a real sense he *was* an anthropologist, and a particularly able one at that. As Parry's son Adam, himself an important Homerist, wrote of his father: "If he had not been able to learn the language as well as he did, and to drink with the singers and their audiences in coffee-house and tavern, if he had not been able to take part in this society and win the respect of its members, he could not have carried on the work itself."[9]

While the anthropological component of this study thus places it in the best scholarly company, its reliance on theory derived from evolutionary biology is unorthodox.[10] Indeed, scholars who have exerted substantial formative influence on my views are on record as considering biology all but irrelevant to warfare in general (e.g., Lawrence Keeley) and Homeric warfare in particular (e.g., Hans van Wees).[11] One burden of this book is to overcome these widespread feelings and convince a skeptical audience that the evolutionary perspective on human conflict generally, and Homeric conflict specifically, is both valuable and neglected.

In the process I hope to bring Homeric studies into contact and conversation with large and vibrant areas of intellectual ferment from which they have been isolated. For all the bold interdisciplinary history of Homeric scholarship, many Homerists, and classicists generally, have been justly accused of failing to make their studies relevant to the interests of outsiders.[12] This is symbolized, above all, in the fact that readers lacking knowledge of Greek and Latin, as well as the main European languages, are effectively barred from a huge proportion of the total scholarly literature because scholars do not bother to translate for non-specialists. Further, going back as far as Aristotle, Homeric commentators have tended to get bogged down in petty wars over small, often linguistic, disagreements, and to neglect the big picture.[13] This "isolationist" streak led Milman Parry to warn, "I have seen myself, only too often and too clearly, how, because those who teach and study Greek and Latin literature have lost the sense of its importance for humanity, the study of those disciplines has declined, and will decline until they quit their philological isolation and again join in the movement of current human thought."[14]

Evolutionary studies of human behavior, psychology, and culture have influenced and invigorated all branches of the human and social sciences over the last several decades. By approaching Homeric questions from an evolutionary perspective, I hope to again demonstrate Homer's perennial relevance to "the movement of current human thought." Insofar as the spirit of *Altertumswissenschaft* still obtains, I am confident that my ideas will receive fair consideration from classical scholars. Insofar as I am able to explain the relevance of my study to the movement of current thought, I am confident of a fair hearing from the two other audiences I am most interested in reaching: general readers and the interdisciplinary community of scholars using evolutionary theory and research to explore and explain the human condition.

Trying to write a book like this – one that breaks new intellectual ground while still remaining accessible and invigorating for non-specialists – is like threading a fine needle with coarse thread. It can be done, but it takes unwavering hands. The most salient result of my attempt to reach diverse audiences is that I can only skim the surface of some deep controversies in Homer studies, evolutionary biology, and anthropology, and that I relegate specialist material to the notes. Arthur Adkins' comment about making his study of Greek values both rigorous and accessible to non-specialists also applies to my effort: "The method adopted may occasionally give the impression that certain inconvenient questions are being quietly throttled in dark corners; but a trial of alternatives has convinced me that it is the best available in the circumstances."[15]

So what *is* the evolutionary perspective that I propose to bring to bear on Homeric conflict? It is studying the behavior of animals following Darwin's powerfully simple rule: the bodies of animals, including human animals, have been shaped by their environments to maximize survival and reproduction, *and so have their psychologies and behaviors.* Darwin's earliest notebooks on his "species theory," started soon after the Beagle returned to England, and more than twenty years before the publication of *On the origin of species,* reveal unequivocally that the theory of natural selection was always as much about brain as body, as much about mind as morphology.[16] For Darwin, demonstrating the evolutionary origins of "the highest psychical faculties of man," like the emotions or our sense of morality, was just as vital as demonstrating how "organs of extreme perfection," like the human eye, were formed through slow gradation.[17] Darwin felt it would be necessary to jettison his whole theory if it failed to account for any aspect of human mental life. We are only now, after many years and many wrong turns, seeing the maturation of an evolutionary science of human behavior and psychology, a science with the potential to address some of the deepest and most persistent questions about why we are the way we are.[18]

But two concerns arise whenever the powerful mechanism of evolutionary explanation is brought to bear on human behavior. The first concern is that evolutionary thinking is insidiously deterministic – that it denies the capacity for change and suggests that we are stuck with the worst aspects of ourselves. But to argue that a biological perspective on human conflict, or on anything else, is valuable is not to suggest that war and other forms of violence are determined exclusively by biology or that we have "instructions" for violence inscribed in our genes. There is no such thing as a complex, biologically determined behavioral trait, and there is no reason to fear that identifying an evolutionary foundation for a behavioral or psychological pattern means we are helpless to change it.

The other main complaint leveled against evolutionary explanations of human behavior is that they are crudely reductive. Critics accuse evolutionists of aggressively conquesting through the disciplines, seeking to place all aspects of human behavior and culture within a biological framework. Indeed, they are not wrong. Placing all of human behavior and culture within the biological purview *is* the ambitious goal of the "adaptationist program." But this does not mean that all other approaches are thus subsumed and rendered irrelevant. Nor does it mean renouncing or demoting "nurture." An evolutionary biology that ignores or de-emphasizes the importance of physical and social environments is, in fact, profoundly *un*-biological. Environments – social and physical – shape, constrain, and elicit the behaviors of organisms. As Matt Ridley writes in *Nature via nurture*, "The more we lift the lid on the genome, the more vulnerable to experience genes appear to be . . . Genes are not puppet masters or blueprints. Nor are they just carriers of heredity. They are active during life; they switch each other on and off; they respond to the environment . . . They are both cause and consequence of our actions."[19]

Therefore, evolutionists who study behavior and psychology, human or otherwise, must pay as much attention to environments as to genes. Accordingly, the present study does not portray Homeric peoples as genetic automatons blindly acting out imperatives coded in their DNA. On the contrary, this study is inclusively biosocial: it describes how a highly specific social and physical environment interacted with the raw material of evolved human nature to produce certain outcomes.

In short, to explain human conflict at the evolutionary level is not to reduce or slight its distinctively human grandeur, horror, or complexity; it is not to demote social and cultural influences that are equally important, and it is not to sanction a grim view of the human capacity for change.

Finally, my effort does not attempt – akin to some of the physicists – to derive a Homeric "theory of everything." Evolution *is* the ultimate theory of everything biological, but of course I do not believe that it holds simple solutions to all of Homer's literary and historical mysteries. At the same time, however, my approach has not exhausted the potential scope for an evolutionary analysis of Homer or other traditional humanities topics. The promise of a new research program is defined at least as much by its ability to inspire interesting questions as by its ability to answer them.[20] I address some of these questions in the final chapter, but this still leaves a lot of ground unexplored. For example, this book is strictly about Homeric competition (what Adkins called the "competitive virtues"); but an equally interesting evolutionary exploration could focus – contrary to Adkins – on the salience of cooperative virtues in Homer.

After 2,500 years of sifting the evidence, real advances in Homeric studies can come from only two places: discoveries of new evidence or applications of new perspectives that allow us to see existing evidence in a fresh way. Anthropological theory and data have provided just such a perspective, and evolutionary biology can too – it can bring previously fuzzy phenomena into sharper focus and provide more satisfying explanations for some important dynamics of the epics. John Myres was just off the mark when he said that it is not easy to say anything new about Homer. It is, in fact, easy to say things that are new about Homer; it is harder to say things that are both new *and true*.[21] Bringing the combined apparatuses of evolutionary biology and anthropology to bear on the question of Homeric conflict allows us to see some things that are new as well as true. These lenses reveal a powerful coherence in the society depicted in the poems and inexorable logic in patterns of conflict.

To be more specific, I believe that commentators have rarely appreciated the extent to which Homeric disputes trace back to conflicts over women. *Of course*, scholars have recognized that many conflicts touch on rights to desirable women. They have usually suggested, however, that winning women is merely a proximate goal masking more important motives: Greeks and Trojans fight not over Helen but over honor; Achilles and Agamemnon fight not over an alluring young woman but over prestige; Odysseus and the suitors fight not over his lovely wife but over wealth and political power. In short, critical explanations of violence in the epics strongly downplay Homer's incessant point: women are a major source of conflict among men.[22] *The Rape of Troy* does not deny that Homer's heroes compete obsessively over honor, power, status, and material goods. In fact, this competition is absolutely central to its case. Nonetheless, an evolutionary perspective suggests that commentators have typically had things backwards. For Homer's heroes, as for ordinary men, women are not a proximate route to the ultimate goals of honor, political power, and social dominance. On the contrary, honor, political power, and social dominance are proximate routes to the ultimate goal of women.

CHAPTER I

Rebuilding Homer's Greece

From the earliest period of Greek letters, Homer has been mined for information on the lifeways of prehistoric Greece. But controversy surrounding Homer as a source of historical information also goes back to the start – to Herodotus and Thucydides, both of whom were skeptical of some of his facts. This chapter argues that the Homeric epics can be used as primary sources for reconstructing an anthropologically coherent picture of Greek social life at the time the Homeric poems are believed by many to have reached what is basically their current shape, probably sometime around the eighth century BC (for discussion of dating controversies, see Appendix). I will call this the Late Dark Age model of Homeric society, and will outline its basic features in the next chapter. But I must first discuss views of the historical relevance of Homer that dominated earlier thinking, and which still have influence today. Specifically, I must consider the argument – ascendant in the nineteenth century and popular for much of the twentieth – that the epics are jumbles of facts, social practices, linguistic details, and items of physical culture from across an expanse of distinct and diverse time periods and geographical areas. In strong versions of this model, frequently called the "mosaic" or "mélange" model, Homer loses virtually all legitimacy as a source of historical information.[1] I must also discuss a model that emerged with Heinrich Schliemann's sensational discovery of the royal tombs of Mycenae, and his claim to have found the historical Troy. This "Mycenaean" model suggests that Homer *is* a valuable and reliable source of information about Greek history and social life. However, it suggests that the epics primarily reflect Greek life at the time the Trojan War might actually have been fought, near the close of the grand Mycenaean era (c.1200 BC). Along the way it will be necessary to discuss some highlights in the history of Homeric scholarship, including Milman Parry's paradigm-annihilating answer to the famous "Homeric question."

THE HOMERIC QUESTION

The so-called Homeric question goes back in its most basic form to the beginnings of Greek literature. The ancients speculated about who Homer was and when he composed his poems; they bickered about which of the many hymns, epics, and fragments attributed to him were authentic and which were not; and partisans from different regions staked competing claims to Homer's place of birth. The question, however, did not take its modern form until the end of the eighteenth century. The *question* is actually a series of extraordinarily difficult and tightly intertwined *questions* concerning the origin, dating, transmission and, most importantly, authorship of the *Iliad* and *Odyssey*.[2] The birth of the modern Homeric question is conventionally dated to 1795 because, in that year, the German philologist F. A. Wolf (1759–1824) published his *Prolegomena ad Homerum* – a high point in the history of classical scholarship, and the most important book on Homer ever written. The *Prolegomena* brought fresh and powerful ideas to bear on an old controversy, and argued with unparalleled rigor and persuasiveness that the Homeric epics were the product of an illiterate age. Wolf was not the first to claim that Homer was an *aoidos* (singer) like Phemius and Demodocus in the *Odyssey* rather than a writer like Virgil. He was inspired by the English scholar Robert Wood who stated his "opinion, as a matter of conjectore [*sic*] . . . that the art of Writing, though probably known to Greece when the Poet lived was very little practiced there; that all knowledge at that time was preserved by memory, and with that view committed to verse, till an alphabet introduced the use of prose composition."[3] And, in turn, the Jewish historian Josephus reached a similar conclusion about seventeen centuries earlier: "They say that not even Homer left his poems behind in writing, but that they were transmitted by memorization, and put together [later] out of the songs, and that they therefore contain many inconsistencies."[4] But before Wolf's meticulous and sustained argument the idea of an oral Homer was a heretical, minority view. Soon after the *Prolegomena* was published it became the orthodox stance and has remained that way ever since, despite the occasional outcries of dissidents.

Wolf's *Prolegomena* dictated and defined the course that all subsequent Homeric scholarship would take. This is because embracing an oral Homer demanded a truly radical re-examination of what the Homeric poems *were.* The key problem lay in the frailties of human memory. The *Iliad* is a poem of immense length and complexity: a teetering stack of 15,693 lines of demanding dactylic hexameter verse (about 400–650 pages in modern English translations) that would take about 24 hours to recite out loud;[5] the *Odyssey*, at over 12,000 lines, is also very long and just as complicated. Robert Wood knew that this presented the oral theory with a grave challenge: "As to the difficulty of conceiving how Homer could acquire, retain, and communicate all he knew, without the aid of Letters; it is, I own, very striking."[6] Wood, groping for a way out, resorted to the "well known" fact of the elephantine memories of preliterate peoples; Homer's feat only seemed superhuman to people whose powers of memory had atrophied through heavy leaning on the crutch of literacy.[7]

For Wolf, as for the great majority of Homerists ever since, this explanation was manifestly insufficient and unsatisfying. The notion of any man, even a great and inspired genius, caching almost forty-eight hours of complicated, polished, often sublime poetry in his head simply defied belief. Wolf's solution to the problem of memory was much different than Wood's, and more plausible. Despite his theory's radical implications – despite the ravages it would one day wreak on poems scholars usually approached with awe – his logic was so relentlessly clean and simple that it immediately won the preponderance of opinion. Wolf's argument was based on the conviction that no human being could have composed in his head, much less memorized and recited, works of such prodigious length, complexity, and artistic virtuosity. At the same time, evidence clearly suggested that the poems emerged from a preliterate age. How to solve the conundrum? Wolf's solution was brilliant not in its perfect originality but for the new logical momentum he gave to existing, though marginal, ideas.[8] Wolf argued that Homer (or perhaps many

*Homers**) composed and left behind him a series of short lays which were, at some later and literate date, collected, organized, trimmed, shuffled, and pressed together into something like the *Iliad* and *Odyssey* we have today.

Wolf's bold thesis elegantly accounted for aspects of the Homeric compositions that had always been troubling and confusing. Scholars had long struggled to reconcile the prevailing vision of Homer as the paragon of poetic genius with his numerous lacunae, anomalies, contradictions, repetitions, rambling digressions, anachronisms, and awkward shifts in style and tone. At a stroke, Wolf provided a satisfying explanation for it all. The sometimes queer and episodic nature of the plot was obviously the result of a not quite successful attempt to force another lay into the larger narrative, like a puzzle piece that almost fits. The inconsistencies, shifts in tone and linguistic idioms, and outright contradictions could also be explained on the theory that the epics were "Frankenstein's monsters," brought to life from the parts of different songs. Under Wolf's theory almost every problem that puzzled scholars could be attributed to incompatibilities between lays and editorial ham-handedness – what Wilamowitz would identify as the crude seams in "patchwork poetry."[9]

ANALYSTS VERSUS UNITARIANS

Wolf and his theory won immediate and nearly universal acclaim, despite the protests of some ardent and vociferous holdouts. His followers, mainly Germans like their charismatic leader, came to be known as analysts, and they took it upon themselves to vivisect the Homeric corpus. By identifying gaps, fissures, and gossamer connective tissues between different pieces of the poems, analysts sought to isolate the different lays, to tell which lays came from which historical periods and, in many cases, to excavate the authentic Homeric nucleus around which the vast bulk of the poems had accreted. The heart of

* For the sake of clarity and consistency with tradition, I refer to Homer as a single individual who composed both the *Iliad* and *Odyssey*. Whether the *Iliad* and *Odyssey* were actually composed by the same person – or whether Homer was merely *un idea* (as Vico put it in *The Scienza Nuova Secunda*, 1730) or an "anthropomorphization of the epic tradition" (as in Foley 2004, 186) – is not critical to my arguments.

their position, so bruising to the holdouts, who came to be known as unitarians, was that the epics were not the inspired products of a single transcendent genius. Rather, they were the accomplished, but still ungainly, product of collaboration across untold generations of singers, as well as later compilers, redactors, and interpolators.

From 1795 until the early decades of the twentieth century Homeric scholarship consisted of a running battle between unitarians and analysts over the answer to the Homeric question. The analysts sliced Homer into more and more, smaller and smaller, chunks. The German philologist Karl Lachman (1793–1851), for example, sought to prove that the *Iliad* was a clump of no fewer than eighteen separate songs on the same general theme.[10] The unitarians, while clearly battered in the nineteenth century and nearly driven from the field, fought back by pointing out what they took to be stronger unities of language, tone, plot, society, and theme. Unitarians savaged analysts for the way they undertook reckless surgeries on the Homeric corpus – wholesale multiple amputations, really – on flimsy and subjective grounds on which no two analysts could agree. The positions of analysts and unitarians grew less dogmatic in the era following World War I, with analysts admitting evidence of overarching Homeric design and unitarians admitting the possibility of historical strata and interpolations.[11] Yet there were still appreciable differences in emphasis even between moderate unitarians and analysts. Where the eyes of analysts tended to see systematic inconsistencies and anomalies, the eyes of unitarians saw consistent signs of single authorship.

The controversies waxed and waned and grew tedious: neither side could muster the arguments or evidence to decisively win the day. This stalemate lasted until an American graduate student named Milman Parry (1902–35) came out of nowhere to discover what many take to be the essential solution to the Homeric question while he was still in his mid-twenties. As a signal of his preeminence in the pantheon of modern Homeric scholarship, as well as the specific character of his contribution, Parry has been called "the Darwin of oral literature."[12]

MILMAN PARRY: THE DARWIN OF ORAL LITERATURE

Parry has been compared to Darwin on the grounds that he uncovered the evolutionary history of the epics in the same way that

Darwin revealed the evolutionary history of all life. This comparison, while true, does not go far enough. Like Darwin, Parry can be called the most brilliantly innovative thinker in the history of his field. The only difference is that Darwin's preeminence is incontestable and Parry's is not – in modern times an argument can be made for Wolf and in ancient times for the Alexandrian scholiast Aristarchus (c.217–c.145 BC). Both Darwin and Parry addressed and, to a large though not perfect extent, solved the riddles recognized as premier in their respective fields: Darwin on the origin and modification of species; Parry on the biggest and most enduring questions concerning the foundational works of Western literature. While Darwin lived a long and productive life, not publishing *The origin* until he was fifty and continuing to do productive science until he died at the age of seventy-three, Parry had his great insight in his early twenties, and he had brilliantly tested and confirmed his arguments in the "living laboratory" of a still thriving tradition of Yugoslavian oral epic by the time he was killed by a gunshot at the age of thirty-three.* Moreover, Parry's contribution was, in its own sphere, as radical as Darwin's. By the time Parry's theory was assimilated, Homer had been transformed into a traditional popular singer improvising entertainments through his reliance on "tricks of the trade" that had been passed down the generations by a long line of oral poets.

Yet Parry's greatness – and the Darwinian nature of his contribution – does *not* rest mainly on his proof that the epics are end products of a long and gradual evolutionary process. Homer comes down to us after untold generations in the oral tradition, and more than 2,000 years of meticulous, error-prone hand copying. It was not until 1488 that the epics were ossified by the printing press. Mutations in the texts, small and large, purposeful and accidental, accumulated over this time. Over 1,500 different papyrus fragments of the *Iliad* and *Odyssey*, from the third century BC up until the seventh AD, betray a discomfiting amount of textual variation.[13] Thus the fact that the Homeric corpus had changed significantly over time was a fundamental tenet not only of the analysts, but also of the great Homeric

* While Parry's death was ruled an accident, classicists have argued, often bitterly, about whether it may have been a suicide linked to depression over possible denial of tenure at Harvard.

scholiasts of the Hellenistic age (men like Aristarchus). After Wolf published the *Prolegomena*, virtually everybody – every analyst at least – was a confirmed evolutionist. Parry's real distinction was the same as Darwin's. It did not mainly consist in winning the day for evolution (Darwin had predecessors and contemporaries with their own evolutionary theories), but in discovering the *mechanism* of the evolutionary process; Parry discovered the compositional process that produced the Homeric poems.

The specifics of Parry's contributions are fairly well known and well understood so I will only briefly summarize them here. Parry demonstrated conclusively, first by meticulous linguistic analysis, and then by brilliantly innovative fieldwork in a living oral tradition, that Homer was an oral poet. The critical difference between Parry's oral Homer and previous conceptions was that Parry's Homer composed his poems "not *for*, but *in*, performance."[14] The poet was *not* reciting a memorized, set text that had been previously arranged in his head. Rather he was creating the poem on the fly, improvising at dizzying speed along familiar lines. In short, experiencing Homer on the page is a lot like reading the transcript to a folk singer's performance. What is missing is the same: instrumental music, performer histrionics, strong drink, smoke, improvisation, and the role of the audience.[15]

The singer accomplished this seemingly miraculous feat by mastering an ancient tradition of oral formulaic poetry. He relied on a great store of sophisticated traditional techniques, especially swarms of memorized stock phrases, lines, and even whole scenes, that were lovingly constructed to meet the demands of improvised hexameter verse. Thus Parry's main contribution was to provide a brilliant and empirically buttressed answer to the problem that puzzled Robert Wood and launched the analytic movement: "As to the difficulty of conceiving how Homer could acquire, retain, and communicate all he knew, without the aid of Letters; it is, I own, very striking."

Parry verified his argument through careful study of a flourishing tradition of Yugoslavian oral poetry, which functioned precisely as Parry predicted it would. While the length of the Yugoslavian line was shorter than the Homeric line, Yugoslavian singers regularly improvised heroic songs of between 3,000 and 8,000 lines, and the most accomplished singer Parry encountered, Advo Medovecić, once sang a song of over 12,000 lines. Since then, in the explosion of research on oral poetics inspired by Parry and his collaborators, many other traditions have been identified where oral-improvised poems can reach monumental length.[16]

By introducing a poet who created his story anew each time he sang it, Parry obliterated "the problem of memory" that was the main pillar of the analytic movement: their arguments collapsed on themselves, and analysis, in its old form, soon ceased to exist. The anomalies and internal inconsistencies on which the analysts set such great store now received a more cogent and empirically robust explanation as artifacts of the sometimes messy process of improvised oral composition. However, the defeat of the analysts did not mean victory for the unitarians. Unitarians tended to portray Homer as a transcendent, quasi-divine genius who created his epics in flashes of inspiration. Parry's metrical and comparative studies destroyed this romantic myth, revealing a singer who was probably not striving for originality. Rather he was an expert craftsman who relied on a set of tools and conventions that were the gifts of his artistic tradition. While the poet of the *Iliad* and *Odyssey* must have been outstandingly talented, the epics could be seen as end products of intense collaborations among many oral poets across untold generations. As Darwin's researches are sometimes said to have "killed" a certain version of God, Parry's work annihilated the unitarians' transcendent Homer, leading the most devoted unitarians to resist Parry's findings almost as energetically as biblical creationists have resisted Darwin's.

However, Parry's work did vindicate the unitarians in one vital respect. Unitarians and analysts tended to very different conclusions concerning Homer's value as a historical source. The former were committed to a single author of the *Iliad* and *Odyssey*. This man lived at a specific time in history, in a specific cultural and social environment, and his poems would naturally convey the texture of that environment. The analysts did not believe in a single poet of the *Odyssey* and *Iliad*, or in two poets or three; they believed the epics to be slurries of shorter songs produced by many singers across communities and generations. Obviously one could not put great faith in the epics as historical sources because realities from different eras and places were slapped one on top of the next, like the layers of a cake. Some analysts believed that it was possible to define where one historical or cultural layer started and another stopped. As Porter writes, "The Homeric texts themselves began to appear as something like an archaeological site, with layers of history built into them in a palpable stratigraphy."[17] But analysts often disagreed on the best way to distinguish and date layers, and were generally more skeptical of the poems as historical sources.

The overall result of Parry's discoveries was to provide limited support for the unitarian perspective, but not to vindicate any naïve view that the epics represented uncomplicated reflections of social and historical realities. Fieldwork in Yugoslavia and in other oral traditions shows that originally oral epics do indeed convey valuable information for the social and cultural historian. However, comparative work did not vindicate the "fundamentalist faith" of some unitarians in the historical value of the Homeric scriptures.[18] At this point, it is necessary to introduce the greatest and most fervid of all the Homeric fundamentalists, Heinrich Schliemann.

HEINRICH SCHLIEMANN'S MYCENAEAN HOMER

When Heinrich Schliemann began digging at Hissarlik on the western coast of Asia Minor (modern-day Turkey), most scholars believed that the *Iliad* and *Odyssey* were unhistorical fantasies, bearing little meaningful relationship to any real world that had ever existed.[19] The year was 1870, and Schliemann was a faithful unitarian holdout against the analyst mainstream. He was also the most colorful figure in the long history of Homeric scholarship: a pitiless businessman who made several fortunes; a self-educated prodigy with proficiency in a dozen languages; an "odd little man"[20] who, toward the end of his life, increasingly used Ancient Greek as a living language; an egoist who fabricated a romantic myth of himself in his autobiographical writings and inscribed his tomb with the words *heroi schlimannoi* (for the hero Schliemann); and a self-promoting scoundrel who double-crossed collaborators and almost certainly falsified some of his data.[21] He was also a talented and preternaturally energetic archaeologist and Homerist who has exerted lasting influence, for good and ill, on both fields.

At Hissarlik, Schliemann set out to redeem the old view held by most Greeks throughout antiquity: that the *Iliad* and *Odyssey* were accurate chronicles of historical realities; that there was a real Trojan War; that Greeks fought for fame and lucre over long years on foreign shores and then went home, experiencing more adventure and hardship along the way. Under Schliemann's direction, the mound of Hissarlik beetled with unskilled diggers, and he soon reported to the world, breathlessly, that he had found the charred remains of a grand citadel destroyed in prehistory by hostile men – that he had found Priam's Troy, and it was just where Homer said it would be.

Later Schliemann made sensational discoveries on the Greek mainland, most notably at Mycenae, where his finds corresponded, he claimed, to Homer's description of a rich Mycenaean kingdom, ruled by Agamemnon, the head of the Greek army deployed against the Trojans. Impressed with Schliemann's findings, as well as those of other archaeologists,[22] Homerists grew increasingly confident that the epics presented a reasonably accurate reflection of life in the palace cultures of the Late Greek Bronze Age (c.1600–1200 BC). Of course, the poems attracted straggling anachronisms in the long course of their transmission, and one had to account for epic exaggerations and fantasy, but these details could be carefully moved aside to reveal a precious socio-historical time capsule from the Late Bronze Age.[23]

During this period the Greek world was divided into large numbers of small bureaucratic states. The civilization is called "Mycenaean," because Mycenae was among the richest, most powerful, and most influential centers of the era, but the designation is highly misleading for its suggestion of strong political centralization. In fact, the Late Bronze Age states were fiercely independent. They evolved sophisticated and pugnacious warrior cultures at least as much to defend against one another as against non-Greeks;[24] there was no politically or territorially expansive kingdom ruled from Mycenae. However, despite political fragmentation, and despite frequent embroilments in internal and external military conflicts, the Late Bronze Age states attained high civilization: each state was led by a *wanax* (king) and administered by lesser officials; they developed a system of writing (Linear B) to track complex bureaucratic dealings; they were bold tradesmen, who plied the waves to barter in foreign lands; wealth piled up and was invested in heavy fortifications and rich palatial complexes. Schliemann boldly claimed that the *Iliad* and *Odyssey*, aside from the heroic exaggerations and the supernatural components, reflected true Mycenaean history. While many quibbled with Schliemann's details, up until the 1950s most scholars (at least those who believed that the epics meaningfully reflected a real Greek society) accepted his view.

This orthodoxy began a radical shift in the 1950s as the archaeological record filled out, the confusing Mycenaean syllabary was finally deciphered, and the profound differences between the relatively simple world described in the epics and the complex, highly centralized, and strictly hierarchical Mycenaean civilization became impossible to overlook. The basic irreconcilability of Homer's portrait and the Mycenaean picture was further confirmed in cross-cultural studies of oral epic – inspired by Parry and his collaborator Albert Lord – which demonstrated that Homer was an improvising oral poet, and that such improvisation always involves updating inherited material to make it relevant to contemporary context.[25] While oral literature often deals with events set in the distant past, the social and cultural landscape reflects conditions near to the time the tale is told: "heroic epic is historical in appearance but contemporary in meaning."[26]

Comparative study suggested that while oral epic was a valuable source of social history, it was an entirely unreliable source for history in the sense of names, dates, places, and significance of events. Comparativists found startling distortions even in poetry that dealt with relatively recent events.[27] Homeric scholarship was forced to concede the staggering unlikelihood that an even remotely coherent portrait of the Mycenaean world could have been preserved for the nearly half-millennium between the disintegration of Mycenaean civilization and the roughly eighth century BC time frame when most believe the narratives reached their present form. Rather, the poems, while perhaps originating in the Mycenaean era, would have evolved through the centuries in step with shocking upheavals in the socio-cultural environment (see below). To return to my Darwinian comparison, unlike rigid written narratives, malleable oral tales are continuously being adapted to the environments in which they circulate.

Finally, a generation of Homerists emerged, led by Moses Finley, who realized that the customs and lifeways described in Homer had more in common with the tribes and chiefdoms described in anthropology than the state societies of the Mycenaean era. For these reasons, Homeric scholars over the last half-century have gradually arrived at the conclusion that Schliemann and other advocates of the Mycenaean theory were wrong. Finley's dismissal of the Mycenaean model, which was boldly iconoclastic in the 1950s, is now the clear consensus: "The Homeric world was altogether post-Mycenaean and the so-called reminiscences and survivals [of life in the Mycenaean era] are rare, isolated and garbled. Hence Homer is not only not a reliable guide to the Mycenaean tablets; he is no guide at all."[28]

Most Homerists, however, did not revert to the belief that the epics were almost valueless as historical sources. Rather, with notable exceptions, most remained convinced that the world described in the *Iliad* and *Odyssey* possessed an *unus color*, a picture of institutions, customs, rites, and beliefs that possessed the coherency of a real world. As Moses Finley wrote, "A model [of Homeric society] can be constructed, imperfect, incomplete, untidy, yet tying together the fundamentals of political and social structure with an appropriate value system in a way that stands up to comparative analysis, the only control available to us in the absence of external documentation."[29] Homerists simply adapted their view of what type of world, and what period of Greek history, was principally reflected in the epics. Most now believe that while Homer sang of a distant age of great heroes that is perhaps loosely based upon centuries-old memories of Mycenaean grandeur, the Homeric epics actually reflect the material culture, political realities, and social conditions of life in the period when the poems reached what is basically their current shape. However, precisely *when* this event occurred is intensely debated. The overwhelming balance of recent opinion suggests that the poems reached a relatively fixed state somewhere between roughly 800 and 650 BC. My own opinion, which is consistent with some distinguished authorities and inconsistent with others, is that Homer's society is most plausibly identified with the first half of this range (for further discussion of dating controversies see the Appendix). The Homeric poems reflect life in the last moments of the Greek Dark Age.

DARK AGE GREECE

Sometime in the late thirteenth and twelfth centuries BC the materially rich, politically complex, and culturally sophisticated Mycenaean world suffered an awful calamity, considered by some historians to be the worst catastrophe in all of ancient history.[30] The ultimate causes of the collapse are not precisely known; contributing factors may have included sweeping invasions by northern hordes or by "Sea Peoples," internal upheaval, natural disasters, and destabilizing innovations in modes of warfare. What we do know is that within the space of about 100 years virtually every major Mycenaean center, along with many of the smaller villages, was devastated.[31] In the terrible century, the great citadels were burned and abandoned, depopulation owing to death and/or migration was appalling (estimated at between 60 to 90 percent for most regions), the number of inhabited settlements plunged by 80 percent or more, rivers of trade evaporated, road networks linking Mycenaean states crumbled away, vastly reduced populations took up residence in isolated villages, knowledge of reading and writing were forgotten, sophistication in arts and crafts decreased, monumental stone architecture ceased to be produced, wealth disappeared, health and longevity declined, and cultural exchanges between Greeks and foreigners diminished. True, there were shocks of light in the Dark Age – for instance, Athens, Lefkandi on Euboea, and Eleteia in Phocis achieved a fairly high cultural level. But, on the whole, the Greek world had entered into a period of cultural decline, isolation, illiteracy, and regional irrelevance, and would not see illumination for several hundred years.

Most importantly, the complex system of politically centralized, bureaucratic government, along with the institution of the *wanax*, came to an end. Dark Age Greeks clustered in small, poor villages often of less than 100 souls. The largest settlements, like Athens and Argos, might have boasted 1,000 or 2,000 residents. Political organization was more fluid: sharp Mycenaean hierarchies gave way to semi-egalitarian structures that blurred distinctions between the leaders and the led. In place of the *wanax* there was now the *basileus*, a figure bearing much closer resemblance to what anthropologists refer to as a "big man" or chieftain than a king.

The belief that Homer reflects realities of Greek life somewhere around the end of the Dark Age, with the best cultural analogs drawn not from the Mycenaean palace cultures but from the prestate cultures described in world ethnography, has transformed both the study of the epics and the understanding of the Dark Age. The age is called "dark" not only because of its relative primitiveness, but also because scholars are deprived of illuminating historical and archaeological data.[32] Historians of Ancient Greece now agree, rather uniformly, that the Homeric epics are our most important sources of information on Late Dark Age social life.[33] Homer paints a largely coherent picture of Greek attitudes, ideology, customs, political arrangements, ethics, manners and mores that is consistent with the archaeological record and fully intelligible in the context of anthropological research on societies at similar levels of cultural complexity.

In fact, evidence from the epics, carefully supplemented by information from other sources and by a measure of educated speculation, allows us to construct a working ethnography of Homeric era Greeks. Homerists have given up their dream of reconstructing a history of prehistoric Greeks based upon the epics.* As Moses Finley wrote, the *Iliad* and *Odyssey* "are a collection of fictions from beginning to end."[34] But these fictions provide a precious window into Late Dark Age *social* history – a history that archaeological evidence is good at supplementing but bad at providing on its own.[35] Finley's argument, on which many have since elaborated, was that the fictional nature of Homer's narratives, while creating insurmountable barriers for the traditional historian, presented only surmountable impediments for the social historian.[36]

Viewed from the perspective of the social historian, Homer's epics are a record of what Greek people valued, what they feared, what they

* Recent archaeological work, combined with analyses of Hittite and Egyptian documents, has, however, provided better evidence of an historically valid kernel to the Trojan War (for overviews see Fields 2004; Latacz 2004). New excavations, under the directorship of Manfred Korfman, reveal that Troy VI/VIIa (c.1700–1250 BC) was surrounded by a large and previously undiscovered lower city. Estimates of the city's area have jumped by a full order of magnitude (to 200,000 sq. meters) and her population has increased by approximately thirteenfold (to 5–10,000 inhabitants). This has transformed Troy VI/VIIa into a prosperous, influential city not unworthy of Homer's description. The city, with its impressive inner and outer fortifications, sat near the entrance to the Hellespont and is believed to have controlled access to trade in the Black Sea. Perhaps the most likely scenarios for conflict between Achaian invaders and Trojan defenders center on a dispute over this trade route. However, while this research boosts the plausibility that the Trojan cycle of epics may be based on memories of a historical event, it does not increase the plausibility of the Mycenaean model of Homeric society. All of our comparative evidence indicates that oral literature reflects contemporary social dynamics. Common sense and comparative research suggest that the Homeric poems could not have retained a meaningful portrait of an extinct society over 500 years of oral transmission.

hoped for, what they despaired of, and how they managed both the mundane details and the extraordinary happenings in their social and political lives. The Homeric corpus, as Eric Havelock notes, "*allows us to glimpse the mentality* of those who created it."[37] From the epics we can see that the Greeks were a warlike people; we can trust that their political organization was loose but not chaotic; we can tell that theirs was a muscularly patriarchal world, and we can observe the basic workings of an agrarian economy; we can see what animals they raised and what crops, how they mixed their wine and treated their slaves and women; we learn highly specific rules of good conduct for women, men, girls, boys, the young, the old, guests, hosts, slaves, masters, warriors, friends, chiefs, bard and audience; we witness the proper way to butcher a boar at a feast, the way to singe it, carve it, spit it, season it, and prepare the portion for the gods; we learn which cut of meat to serve a man of high status, and we learn who should be served first if guests are of unequal age. And we learn much more. The arguments of this book are based on the conviction that the *Iliad* and *Odyssey* are not "merely" stories, but troves of important social and cultural artifacts from a lost age, fossilized in dactylic hexameter, and available for careful excavation.

The upcoming chapter, "A short ethnography of Homeric society," synthesizes research on Homeric society that has been conducted mainly in the last fifty years. The details of this chapter flow in the deep parts of the scholarly mainstream. However, this is not to imply that these views – which serve as a main foundation for the rest of the book – are uncontroversial, uncontested, or definitive. On the contrary, modelers of Homeric society face the difficult task of trying to produce a reliable portrait of a vanished society on the basis of clues that are scattered, enigmatic, and contradictory. Thus, like all models, mine relies significantly on educated speculation and large numbers of subjective judgments.

This may make the attempt to construct a progressively more reliable model of Homeric society seem hopeless. But pessimism would be quite unwarranted. The last two centuries *have* seen the emergence of a progressively more reliable and durable reconstruction of life in the Homeric period. For instance, scholars have all but ruled out the two leading models of Homeric society prior to 1950:

the mélange and Mycenaean theories. At the same time, reconstructions of Homeric society based on the eighth and early seventh centuries have withstood many challenges. These advances were based on a confluence of new evidence: archaeological findings, including the discovery of a prosperous "heroic" society at Lefkandi on the island of Euboea (c. tenth and ninth centuries BC); the decipherment of Linear B by Michael Ventris (with the assistance of John Chadwick), which would eventually lead to the collapse of the Mycenaean model; a blossoming of cross-cultural work on oral narrative; and the increasing sophistication of anthropological modeling. And these advances grew, in turn, from earlier achievements, like the rediscovery of the tenth-century Venetus A manuscript of the *Iliad*, which inspired Wolf's study. In the same way, we can hope that new tools and evidence will one day emerge that will allow us to evaluate more confidently and decisively the claims of this book.

CHAPTER 2

A short ethnography of Homeric society

> The proper study [of the heroic element in epic poetry] is . . . anthropological and historical, and what Doughty tells us about cattle-lifting among the Bedouins is more enlightening, if we are reading Nestor's tale of a cattle raid into Elis, than is the mere knowledge that the theme occurs elsewhere in ancient poetry.
>
> (Milman Parry)[1]

An ethnography of Homeric Greeks must begin with a description of their homelands, which, to an extraordinary degree, shaped their political and social lives. On a map of the Homeric world the center would be the Aegean and her liberal sprinkling of small islands. The periphery would be composed of coastal lands – by the edge of the Balkan Peninsula to the west, by settlements on Asia Minor to the east, by scattered villages on the mainland to the north, and by Crete and the open waters of the Mediterranean to the south. To the west, the Greek mainland was traced with ragged limestone mountains and cut by valleys into smallish tracts of arable land. Eighty percent of the territory was mountainous, and travel between the farmable regions was discouraged by scarce mountain passes and an absence of navigable rivers.

Thanks to the topography of their world, Homeric era Greeks, like those living before and after them, lived in semi-isolation from each other – separated by walls of mountains and expanses of tossing waves. As with all other periods of Greek history up to the end of the fourth century BC, when Macedonian conquerors finally unified Greece at spear point, geographical separation begat political separation. The very term "Greek" is, in fact, a convenient though misleading abstraction. Like the term "Mycenaean," it suggests a degree of political cohesion that was utterly foreign to Greek peoples throughout antiquity. The word suggests that the Greeks were a unified people, a coherent nation, like "Norway" or "Japan." But for thousands of years, from the time when the lands were first inhabited until the reign of Alexander, "Greece" was not a nation or a unified people; it was a collection of separate but related peoples inhabiting a geographical region. They shared a commonly intelligible language (though it was divided into many different dialects), culture, and religion, but they were fiercely independent and called truces in their internecine wars only for the sake of fleeting alliances against common enemies. Even the heroic defense against Persian imperialism was a temporary and tenuous response to an immediate threat of conquest and thralldom; almost as soon as the Persian threat was neutralized, Greeks again turned their navies and phalanxes upon each another.

Only the sea held them together. As the geographer Strabo wrote, "The sea presses in on Greece with a thousand arms," and most settlements were located within a day's walk of the shore. The broad and relatively hospitable highways of the Aegean – where mariners' eyes were rarely deprived of the comfort of land – ensured that Greeks could travel and trade, and that cultural and linguistic differences never yawned so wide that they forgot their cultural and ethnic kinship. The people of the Late Dark Age did not yet know the word "Greek" or "Hellenes" – neither name had yet been coined – but they had terms that expressed their sense of cultural relationship: *Achaians, Argives, Danaans, Pan-Achaioi.* But the key fact is that Greek *geographical fragmentation* – peoples scattered across scores or hundreds of settlements, divided by mountains and expanses of sea – begat *political fragmentation.* If the Greeks were a family, they were a highly dysfunctional one, acknowledging and sometimes celebrating their kinship, while struggling for position and snarling at one another across mountain passes and waves. The end results of the fragmentation of the Greek world are aptly assessed by Finley Hooper:

> In brief, the story of Ancient Greece is not the story of a nation. Rather it is the story of a people who ... remained politically a family of small independent states, sometimes cooperating against an outsider but usually venting their tempers on one another. Taken singly, especially at Athens, their contributions to Western thought and art were invaluable, yet taken

together these little states with their petty jealousies and intrigues wore themselves down into a condition of disgrace and helplessness.[2]

TRIBES, CHIEFDOMS, OR KINGDOMS?

Until the last few decades, reconstructions of Homeric society were implicitly or explicitly based on the models of European monarchies, Mycenaean kingdoms, feudal baronies, or Classical Era city states. Thus translations of the *Iliad* and *Odyssey* typically refer to the *basileus* with regal, un-Greek terms like "Prince" or "King," commentators casually refer to Homeric heroes as "aristocrats," and unwary readers are apt to conclude that the meaning of the term *polis* in Homer (a town and its surrounding territory) is the same as the meaning of the term in later Greek history (city-state). English translations of the poems are, in fact, highly misleading for those who cannot read Greek because they bristle with terminology and concepts that are utterly foreign to Homeric society. One cannot read the *Iliad* or *Odyssey* in translation without internalizing a mangled picture of Homer's world. This is partly because Homer wants it that way: by filling his poems with supernatural occurrences and vastly exaggerated splendor he was communicating to ancient audiences that the epic heroes lived in a fundamentally different type of world. But it is also because translators fill the narratives with inappropriate words like "king," "monarch," "queen," "prince," "princess," "lord," "peasant," "commoner," "noble," for which there are no clear analogs in the Homeric world. Most readers leave the translations imagining a wealthy world of stable monarchies ruled by powerful kings; and this vision is a great distortion.[3]

Among the most important advances in recent Homeric scholarship is the realization that the best models of Homeric society may come not from European or Greek history books, but from the annals of cross-cultural ethnography. Over the last several decades consideration of anthropological evidence has resulted in important revisions of nearly everything about Homeric society. Patterns of social and political behavior that seemed garbled when considered alongside state societies[4] gained sudden coherence when considered alongside the tribes and chiefdoms of anthropology.

For example, confusing and idealized depictions of Homeric combat were once considered prime evidence for the unhistorical nature of Homer's world. Yet Hans van Wees' reconstructions of the Homeric battlefield, based partially on analogies with forms of combat in Highland New Guinea, show that a coherent description of warfare lies just below the epic veneer.[5] Generally the two sides formed up at some distance apart, while opportunistic *promachoi*, front-fighters, ranged forward to fling javelins or rocks at vulnerable opponents before ducking back to the comparative safety of the main throng of comrades. They fought in open order and only bunched into phalanx-like formation in special and dire circumstances. Hand-to-hand fighting with swords or thrusting spears was comparatively rare; simple rocks, flung by hand, were at least as prominent and effective as swords. Archers and some slingers hid in the throng and exacted their tolls from a relatively safe distance. Similarly, some Homerists have dismissed the constant and lavish gift-giving among Homeric men as an unrealistic figment of heroic idealism. But this custom was intelligible to Homerists who recognized it as a common means of cementing friendship and mutual obligation in prestate societies.[6]

The bulk of current opinion suggests that the Homeric world was divided *mainly* into simple or low-level chiefdoms with many of the institutions of the early *polis* in place, although in rudimentary form.[7] The people lived in small, isolated settlements called *poleis* (singular, *polis*). A *polis* was not a city-state; depending on context, the word referred merely to a small village, or to the village as well as its small agricultural plain. There were a lot of them, perhaps scores or even hundreds.[8]

The people filled their bellies by coaxing harvests of barley, wheat, olives, grapes, and other crops from rough and stingy soils; they hunted and fished; they grazed herds of cattle, sheep, and goats on the hillsides, and they raised pigs and fowl. Their animals gave them wool, hides, manure, labor, fat and protein. While the poems, especially the *Odyssey*, emphasize the consumption of huge quantities of meat, this is an artifact of epic exaggeration and of Homer's focus on special occasions – on feasts, ceremonies, entertainments of guests, and the barbecues of campaigning warriors. In reality, the Greek diet would have been much more balanced, as is reflected in the Homeric truism that wheat and barley are "the marrow of men's bones."

A superficial reading of the epics would suggest a background picture of fantastic splendor and highly concentrated wealth – a perception that would only be enforced, when read in translation, by the constant allusions to kings, queens, princesses and other non-existent royals. However, most Homer scholars see this as a purposeful exaggeration, and an attempt to create "epic distance" as Homer looks back from his relatively degraded age and imagines a lost world of great prosperity – a world that must have seemed all the more plausible for those members of Homer's audiences who might have strolled the ruins of Mycenaean palace complexes. Once the trappings of epic splendor are stripped away, however, we are left with a poor, small-scale, agrarian world. Geddes' stark assessment is shared by many other Homerists:

> The archaeological evidence certainly suggests that everyone was rather poor during the centuries when the epic poems were recited. And Homer confirms this when he tries to explain the fabulous wealth of his kings and he sounds naïve ... Nausicaa drives the mule cart to the river to wash her father's clothes, and the daughter of the Laestrygonian king carries water. Alcinous himself stows the gifts for Odysseus under the benches of the ship, and Odysseus has somewhere learnt to cut grass and plough. His "palace" has a dung heap by its front door and a dirt floor and is accessible to an alarming number of farm animals, geese, and pigs. Goats and cattle are tethered under the portico. It appears therefore that Homer did not know about great men in real life; that in his experience there were not huge concentrations of wealth in the hands of the few at the expense of the mass of the poor. In classical times there is little evidence for large land owners in Attica either, but for small holdings, and in spite of his attempt to imagine fabulous wealth there is nothing to suggest that Homer knew otherwise in his day.[9]

LEADERSHIP

The leadership of each settlement was highly informal compared with that in the Mycenaean era and in the ages that would follow. Each settlement was headed by a group of influential males. They were known as *basileis* (singular, *basileus*). Each settlement had a paramount *basileus*, a sort of *primus inter pares*, who exerted stronger influence than the other big men (e.g., *Odyssey* 8.390–91). We can think of the *basileus* as a chief whose position of dominance was tenuous and limited. He owed his position, and the perquisites that attached to it, *mainly* to a generally recognized sense of his personal leadership capacity rather than his hereditary status.[10] In Homeric society there is as yet no yawning division, no clear break, between personal merit and social rank. In Homer there are no cowardly or dissipated chiefs who feed subordinates into the mouth of battle while they shelter safely in the rear.[11] No chief wields the scepter solely because his father did; rather, every *basileus* is portrayed as a man of merit, a *promachos* (front fighter), one who is an outstanding warrior, counselor, or both.

And how could it be otherwise? In a pre-state society lacking structures of institutionalized power – standing armies, police, formal law codes, royal bodyguards – how would the inept son of a paramount *basileus* retain power when surrounded by strong, competent, well supported, and intensely ambitious compeers?

This is to deny that Homeric *basileis* were kings in the common sense of the word – men with unchallengeable rights to pass dictatorial power to their sons. It is not to deny a very significant hereditary element to leadership. The son of a powerful man was clearly well positioned, by tradition and nepotism, to rise to eminence (e.g., *Iliad* 20.178–83). But sons of leaders apparently did not win position solely by default of birth; rather, the position of paramount *basileus* seems to have been one for which other *basileis* could legitimately compete. This is clearly expressed by Telemachus: "There are many other Achaian chiefs in seagirt Ithaca, both young and old. One of these, it may chance, will have this honor [of becoming paramount *basileus*], since noble Odysseus is dead" (*Odyssey* 1.394–98; see also below, Chapter Four). Another *basileus* responds in agreement: "Telemachus, this matter surely lies on the knees of the gods, who of the Achaians will be chief in seagirt Ithaca." (1.400–01).

The model of a rigidly class-based world dominated by powerful kings is further weakened by the absence of technical language that decisively indicates differences in rank or birth.[12] For instance, there is no term capable of differentiating between the paramount *basileus* and the other *basileis*. The closest Homer comes are the terms *basileuteros* and *basileutatos*, which are not titles but descriptive terms meaning, roughly, *chieflier* and *chiefliest*. This suggests to some scholars that leadership is not so much an office that a Homeric man holds, but a characteristic of which he can have degrees.[13] Likewise, descriptors such as *aristoi* (the best, noblest, bravest), *agathoi* (good, noble, brave), and *kakoi* (bad, cowardly, base) – which have often been seen as suggesting rigid social stratification – can just as defensibly be interpreted as referring simply to the talents and qualities of the person in question; they do not necessarily signify a default hereditary condition.[14] For instance, the exchange among Agamemnon, Thersites, and Odysseus (see acknowledgments) has frequently been treated as a microcosm of class conflict, with Agamemnon and Odysseus representing the aristocrats and Thersites the commoners. However, we are never told that Thersites is a commoner, and he himself suggests that he has captured and ransomed Trojan prisoners – activities associated with front fighters, not the lightly armed mass of ordinary warriors.[15] In fact, nothing in the scene confirms that the disputants come from different hereditary classes. None of the withering criticism of Thersites signals out his birth or class – it focuses exclusively on his physical ugliness, his churlish personality,[16] and his feebleness as a warrior.

The word *basileus* is most frequently translated as "king" and the word *anax* as "lord" or "master." Some have treated the two words as signaling a difference of status, with the *anax* holding higher authority than the *basileus.* This is probably because the word *anax* is most frequently applied to Zeus, among gods, and Agamemnon, among men. However, what, if any, clear distinction in status exists between the two titles is famously ambiguous. Finley argues that the two terms are basically interchangeable and synonymous.[17] Likewise, Bowra adamantly denies that there is a difference of status between the two titles: "In Homer there is no distinction at all between the two words. Not only is the same person called by the two titles in different places (e.g., Agamemnon is *anax* in *Iliad* 1.7 but *basileus* in 1.231), but the two words are combined and applied to the same person in *Odyssey* 20.194, *basilēi anakti*, and there can be no doubt that, so far as meaning is concerned, they are interchangeable."[18] Indeed, while Agamemnon is frequently referred to as *anax*, the word *basileus* is still applied to him more than to any other character in the *Iliad.* In fact, most of the main chiefs – Achilles, Odysseus, Priam, Alcinous, and so on – are called *both anax* and *basileus* in different contexts.[19]

Arguments like these have led some to insist that inherited class distinctions were absent or, at most, indistinct in Homeric society; if there was an aristocracy, it was one of merit not birth.[20] However, just because the Homeric world lacked an aristocracy in our sense of the word, does not mean that it was egalitarian. To the contrary, Homeric society was stratified along social and economic lines, with the *aristoi*, the best, enjoying perquisites and looking down on the rest.[21]

In sum, the *basileus* was no autocrat or despot. Great Agamemnon is continually insulted, defied, and even threatened with grievous harm by other chiefs; on the voyage home from Troy, Odysseus' commands are repeatedly flouted, resisted, or overruled by his men; Alcinous and Odysseus share authority with many other local *basileis* (*Odyssey* 1.394–95; 8.390–91); when a *basileus* kills a man from his community he must desperately flee revengers just like anyone else (*Iliad* 17.569–76; *Odyssey* 20.40–43); and Hector must reluctantly bend to the will of the council when it settles on a conservative defense of Troy (*Iliad* 15.718–23). That the *basileus'* powers of persuasive speech are second in importance only to his military prowess is an important indicator of his limited power: lacking dictatorial rights he must persuade, relying on charisma and a subtle tongue. Furthermore, recent analyses have illustrated that the decision-making process of the *basileus* is significantly constrained by the collective power of the people as represented in the council and the assembly – structures that would one day evolve to form the foundations of the city-state.[22] Decisions that affect the collective are made collectively, not by kingly fiat. No public decision is made without public debate in the assembly, forty-two of which feature in the *Iliad* and *Odyssey*.[23] While the chief *basileus* exerts strong influence in the assembly, public decisions are usually reached by consensus, and a *basileus* was liable to severe consequences if, in ignoring the people's voice, he caused them harm.[24] In short, while some passages can be used to support a kingship model, many Homerists now agree that, on the whole, the poems present a coherent picture of simple chiefs with more influence than power.[25]

But strength was vital. *Basileis* are said to "rule by might," and those who lack strength, usually because they are too old, too young, or lack support from kinsmen and allies – men like Peleus, Laertes, and Telemachus – are apt to see their influence diminish and their interests threatened.[26] This is not to suggest, as it has sometimes been argued,[27] that Homeric men rule solely or mainly through physical domination, like Zeus with his thunderbolts and "invincible hands." This caricature misrepresents the leadership strategy of the *basileus* and underestimates the power of the led. However, it is significant that most *basileis* rely on formidable networks of kin and allies, and that virtually all of them are physically imposing. In fact, the leaders of Homeric groups – whether of war bands or towns – are almost invariably described as the biggest, strongest, and most warlike members of the group. Simply by scanning for the largest men in a crowd it is possible to pick out the leaders (e.g., *Iliad* 3.160–242). In Homer, as in many ethnographical societies, the "big men" are just that.[28]

VIOLENCE

From the Mycenaean period forward, Greek history is a chronicle of constant warfare, with periods between large wars filled, not with peace, but with smaller wars. Occasionally the chronicle is stirringly uplifting, as when a small force of Athenian farmers donned hoplite gear, formed phalanxes, and drove voracious Persian imperialists into the bay of Marathon. Far more often, however, the chronicle is dismal: the ferocious military genius of the Greeks was usually directed against other Greeks, and as soon as Darius and Xerxes were defeated, as soon as the last waves of Persian invaders were drowned in the straights of Salamis or routed on the fields of Plataea, Greek navies and phalanxes turned again on each other; the heroic resistance of the Persian wars gave way to the exhausting futility of the Peloponnesian conflict, in which Athenians, Spartans, and their allies fought each other for long decades, gaining nothing but weakness. It was the futile and internecine Peloponnesian war, not the heroic Persian resistance, which was more representative of Greek conflicts.

The Greeks had a fatalistic view of war, seeing it as an ineradicable feature of the human condition.[29] Plato wrote that "Every state is in a natural state of war with every other, not indeed proclaimed by heralds, but everlasting."[30] This Hobbesian assessment, in which every Greek *polis* is locked in conflict, *omnium contra omnes*, is exaggerated in fact but true in spirit. As Finley wrote of the Homeric world, the people lived in an environment of permanent hostility, "split into many communities more or less like Ithaca.

Among them, between each community and every other one, the normal relationship was one of hostility, at times passive, a kind of armed truce, and at times active and bellicose."[31]

Most Greek peoples – from the Mycenaean kings to the Homeric warlords to the zenith states of Classical civilization – were at war as often as they enjoyed peace. As the ancient historian Victor David Hanson states, war was central to Greek life: it was "arguably the major theme of all Greek historical, philosophical, literary, and theatrical writing," and most of the immortal Greek intellectuals were also experienced combat veterans.[32] It is a singularly revealing and emblematic fact that virtually every Greek settlement of any size, from the Mycenaean period forward, was perched on or around a commanding hill top, often fortified, where denizens could retreat, regroup, and beat off attacks with leverage.

While the Greek Dark Age lacks both the rich archaeological evidence for endemic warfare characteristic of the Mycenaean age and the literary and historical evidence of subsequent epochs, substantial evidence allows us to reconstruct a coherent portrait of warfare at the end of the Dark Age. The epics reveal an extremely warlike society whose people saw a state of unremitting, low-intensity warfare as inescapable (see below, Chapter Eight). This fatalistic view is exemplified in Odysseus' words, which comprise the epigraph to this book: "[We are men] to whom Zeus has given the fate of winding down our lives in painful wars, from youth until we perish, each of us" (*Iliad* 14.85–87). Capable warriors were the most highly respected members of the community, and were awarded special perquisites (e.g., *Iliad* 12.310–21; *Iliad* 8.161–64). A good fighter could be considered a good man (*agathos*) regardless of his personal shortfalls. By the same token, an unskilled or uncourageous warrior could be considered a bad man (*kakos*) no matter how exemplary his other qualities.[33] Fathers taught their sons the skills of war from an early age because war could be economically productive, because self-defense was imperative, and because no one respected a man who could not fight. Virtually every man of status we encounter in the poems – with the possible exceptions of bards, diviners, and priests – is a current or former warrior. Men lived in a state of prickly readiness for conflict: rising from slumber they slung on their swords before tying on their sandals, and they never left home without their spears.

Set-piece battles were rare. Like much else in the Homeric epics, *if* Homer's description of the Trojan War is based on historical events, those events have been vastly embellished. The more representative conflicts were reciprocal, fundamentally acquisitive raids where enterprising bands of risk-takers conducted fast, snatch-and-grab attacks. They were greatly aided by shallow-drafted ships, well-suited to amphibious assault. Like Viking craft, they could be rowed directly onto beaches, disgorge their warriors, and be quickly launched if a hasty retreat proved necessary. In successful raids, resisting males were typically put to the sword, and the settlement was denuded of all things both portable and valuable: food, tools, weapons, hides, treasure, livestock, and women who would become slaves and concubines.

In short, the Homeric background picture reveals a world where violence fed on itself through raids and retributive attacks; the epics provide every indication that Greek peoples of the Late Dark Age were involved in nearly constant low-level raiding and feuding with other Greeks, punctuated by rare larger-scale wars.

Moreover, the competitiveness of Homeric men frequently led to violence *within* communities. In Homer's world there were no formal laws or institutions for enforcing them.[34] While there were clearly defined social rules and customs that everyone recognized and tried to enforce, these rules and customs could be violated if one possessed the strength – both in physical muscle and social networks – to get away with it (see *Odyssey* 18.130–42; see below, Chapter Seven). This is because enforcement of justice was likewise a largely personal matter: it was up to the individual to defend himself against aggressors (e.g., *Odyssey* 2.60–64, 16.71–72, 21.131–33; *Iliad* 24.368–69); there were no police to call upon and the weak could not easily punish the strong. While the epics do contain references to situations where "judges" – almost certainly ordinary *basileis* rather than members of a formal judiciary – settled disputes, it is clear from myriad instances of vigilantism that this was not yet the dominant custom.* Disputes were sometimes settled by compensation payments and, when a man was wronged, he could try to appeal to

* There are references to courts at *Odyssey* 12.439–41 and *Iliad* 18.497–508. The *Iliad* reference comes in the context of the description of Achilles' shield, and it represents a judicial proceeding that is so strange that we would almost not recognize it as such. Several judges

more powerful outside parties for arbitration, including taking his case directly to the assembly.[35] However, edged weapons held magnetic allure – "For of itself does the iron draw a man to it" (*Odyssey* 16.294) – and many disputes were resolved through use of them. A chilling example is presented in the preemptive murder of Orsilochus:

> [I killed him] because he meant to rob me of all my booty from Troy, for the sake of which I had suffered pains of heart out on the waves and in the hard wars of men, all because I would not gratify his father by following him in the land of the Trojans, but instead I led men of my own. So, with a comrade I waited for him in ambush, I hit him with my bronze-tipped spear as he came in from the fields. The heavens were very dark that night and no one could perceive us, no one could see me wrench his life away from him. (*Odyssey* 13.258–71)

The ethic of retribution is not an eye for an eye, but more like two eyes for one, as is indicated on occasions where men are tempted to extreme violence by relatively minor insults and injuries (e.g., *Odyssey* 17.233–37, 20.304–08; *Iliad* 23.84–88). Indeed, Homeric men were expected and encouraged to avenge wrongs and were disgraced if they did not; revenge was a cultural imperative and the revenger, far from facing community disapproval, was lionized.[36] The significant extent of lethal violence within communities is suggested by the stream of roving fugitives we encounter or hear about in the poems – men who killed rivals and then left home to flee vengeful kinsmen.

The causes of strife among Greek communities were many and various. Immediate motives included the desire to neutralize enemies, to seek retribution for attacks, to garner military prestige, to circumvent death by achieving poetic immortality, to gain wealth, and to capture women to serve as slaves and concubines. A similar complexity of motives characterizes strife within communities. All of these motives have been discussed in previous analyses. Yet, as Hans van Wees writes, "the fundamental causes of war and conflict in the epic world are rarely studied in any depth."[37] Demonstrating how, from an evolutionary

consider the claims of a defendant and plaintiff and render their decisions. The judge who is deemed, by the spectators, to have rendered the wisest judgment is then given a large reward. This is, then, a description of a ruling contest. Moreover, we are left to imagine how the best decision would be implemented; there is no evidence of an official apparatus for enforcing the judge's decision – no marshals, police, or officers of the court.

perspective, these many proximate causes of intense and pervasive conflict among and between groups of Greek males were ultimately rooted in reproductive rivalry is the main objective of this book.

Before I turn to this task, however, I must first establish the theoretical and empirical base from which I will be working. The last three decades have seen great advances in our understanding of the root causes of male violence. I now turn to an overview of this work.

CHAPTER 3

Why do men fight? The evolutionary biology and anthropology of male violence

The question posed in this chapter has vexed people across cultures and centuries. In all societies known to history and anthropology, violence has been a significant problem. Yet, even in warlike cultures, peace is generally considered preferable to war, and harmony preferable to strife. This was understood well by Homer's near-contemporary Hesiod, who wrote that "hateful" Strife imposes awful suffering on men: "Painful Toil, Forgetfulness and tearful Pain, Battles, Combats, Murders, Quarrels, Lying Words, Disputes, Lawlessness and Ruin" (*Theogony* 226–30). Yet, despite the fact that "no mortal loves her . . . they are forced by the gods' designs to pay honor to heavy Strife" (*Works and days* 15–16). Similarly, in Herodotus' *Histories* (c.425 BC), the Persians ask the captured Lydian King, Croesus, why he has attacked them. He responds: "The god of the Hellenes is responsible for these things, inciting me to wage war. No one is so foolish as to choose war over peace. In peace sons bury their fathers, in war fathers bury their sons."[1]

Like sentiments are common in anthropological annals. Among the Yanomamö of Venezuela and Brazil, who were dubbed "the fierce people" for their warlike ways, even the boldest warriors professed a preference for peace, and hatred for the fear and privation of endless war.[2] Similarly, in tribal New Guinea, where rates of violent death were among the highest recorded anywhere, war was considered "a rubbish way of doing things."[3] As one Papuan tribesman put it,

> War is bad and nobody likes it. Sweet potatoes disappear, pigs disappear, fields deteriorate, and many relatives and friends get killed. But one cannot help it. A man starts a fight and no matter how much one despises him, one has to go and help because he is one's relative and one feels sorry for him.[4]

Like sentiments circulate in Homer's epics, despite the undeniable bellicosity of the men. While Homeric warriors can enjoy the adrenal surge of combat (see *Odyssey* 14.216–28), and while they realize that their status as elite warriors brings them privileges beyond the hopes of ordinary men, there is little question that peace and the pleasures of home, wives, and children (e.g., *Iliad* 2.291–96; *Odyssey* 6.180–85) are preferable to "terrible warfare" (e.g., *Iliad* 22.64). Perhaps incongruously for a warrior world, the most despised god in their pantheon is "hateful Ares," the war god, a "plague to man" (*brotoloigos*). Zeus abhors Ares, his own son, and calls him to his face, "most hateful to me of all the gods" (*Iliad* 5.889–90).

Yet for all the universal condemnation of violence, no society has succeeded in rooting it out – not New Guinean bands, not Yanomamö tribes, not Homeric chiefdoms, and not modern societies. Moreover, while the New Guineans and Yanomamö are notorious for their pugnacity, anthropology has revealed no aboriginally peaceful peoples, much less the prelapsarian world of primitive harmony envisioned by Rousseau and his many followers. The best candidates for this vision, like the !Kung San of southern Africa, famously dubbed "the harmless people" by an ethnographer,[5] had homicide rates several times higher than the most violent American cities. And the !Kung's homicide rates *were* low in comparison with many other simple societies. For instance, among the Waorani of the Ecuadorian Amazon 60 percent of all male deaths over five generations were violent.[6] While the Waorani represent an extraordinary case, a comprehensive survey recently concluded: "All of the available evidence indicates very high killing rates in all known simple hunter-gatherer societies"[7]

The argument that war is a squawking newborn in man's repertoire of evils, that modern man is fallen from primitive grace, is totally unsupported by compelling historical, archaeological, anthropological or literary evidence. All evidence indicates that lethal intergroup conflict has been part of the human condition for at least tens of thousands of years. In fact, the observation of regular and destructive "wars" between neighboring groups of chimpanzees suggests that something like war has been part of our lineage for millions of years, perhaps extending back to the common ancestor of chimpanzees and humans.[8]

Finally, contrary to the claims of mid-twentieth-century military historians and social scientists, "primitive" war is not less horrible or destructive than "civilized" war.[9] While modern wars are more destructive in the absolute numbers of people killed, deaths as a percentage of population have been far fewer.[10] Analyzing mortality statistics drawn from ethnographical studies, the military historian Lawrence Keeley estimates that death rates in modern wars are approximately *twenty times* lower than death rates in prestate wars.[11]

Why are human societies violent despite the fact that, as Keeley phrases it, "war is universally condemned and peace is everywhere preferred"?[12] Most explanations have invoked the important roles of social, cultural, and economic forces. For instance, violence in modern American society is often blamed on a "culture of violence," referring to a pervasive complex of values, historical legacies, and media forces that glorify and sanction violence of all kinds. In bringing the apparatus of evolutionary biology to bear on this problem, I do not seek to demote, much less to deny, the role of such influences. However, an evolutionary perspective is indispensable for understanding important aspects of human violence. Purely socio-cultural explanations may adequately address why violence is particularly rare or frequent in given societies; they cannot explain why predictable patterns of violence should prevail in *all* societies, even in those with highly limited intercultural contact.

In other words, strictly socio-cultural analysis is best at addressing variance across cultures and societies, not uniformity. The New Guineans could not have "contracted" their pugnacity from westerners because they were not contacted until the 1930s, and their first ethnographers, as well as native informants, uniformly testified that intense conflict stretched back as long as anyone could remember.[13] The same goes for Aboriginal Australians and Tasmanians who, despite their extreme cultural isolation, developed a bloody tradition of raids and counter-raids.[14] Ten-thousand-year-old paintings depicting freeform battles between men armed with bows and arrows decorate Australian caves.[15] Similarly, there is incontrovertible evidence for frequent, widespread, often sanguinary, warfare in the Americas prior to western contact.[16]

It would, of course, be extremely unparsimonious to devise thousands of culturally particular scenarios to account for violence across human societies. I repeat, cultural analyses are invaluable for helping us understand variation in violence across societies and, for these case studies, invoking an evolutionary perspective may be helpful but – so long as one does not propound the false dichotomy of nature versus nurture – it is not necessarily required. But strictly cultural explanations are powerless to explain human universals; to explain universal phenomena requires a theory of shared human nature, and the only scientifically viable one emerges from evolutionary biology.

THE EVOLUTIONARY BIOLOGY OF MALE VIOLENCE

From an evolutionary point of view, the leading cause of violence is maleness (Robert Wright)[17]

There is no stronger predictor of a person's likelihood of committing different forms of violence than their sex. As the psychologists Martin Daly and Margo Wilson explain, "There is a cross-culturally universal sex difference in human use of physical violence, whether it be fist fights or homicides, warfare or the slaughter of non-human animals. There is no evidence even suggesting that this sex difference is contravened anywhere."[18] In fact, things can be understood with greater precision: violent acts are overwhelmingly perpetrated by young males, especially unmarried ones.[19] This is apparently true of Homeric society, where we are reminded that hot-headed young men – like the suitors of Penelope or the Phaiacian youths who goad and insult Odysseus (*Odyssey* 12.440) – stir up trouble and provoke fights.

But before attempting to answer the question, "why do men fight?" it is useful to first expand it. Lethal aggression within a species, contrary to the canons of mid-twentieth-century ethology,[20] is nothing like a human monopoly. On the contrary, in most well-studied species mortality rates from violent intraspecies competition are *far higher* than those documented among humans.[21] And in the overwhelming majority of species so far studied, males are the more competitive, aggressive, and violent sex; they are more likely to kill conspecifics and they are, in turn, more likely to be killed.[22] So, before focusing on human males we should ask a bigger question: why are males across the animal kingdom, and especially among mammals, more violent?

Evolutionary biology is not an exact science like physics or astronomy. It is a historical science like geology or cosmology: the evolutionary process usually cannot be observed directly; it must be inferred from various streams of evidence. Yet, as Ernest Mayr writes, these inferences can warrant enormous confidence "because 1) the answers can very often be predicted and the actual findings confirm them, 2) the answers can be confirmed by several different lines of evidence, and 3) in most cases no rational competing explanation can be found."[23] Just such a case of enormous confidence is represented in the evolutionary answer to the riddle of male violence.

The reason males are typically more violent – which was anticipated by Darwin (1871) and formalized by the Harvard biologist Robert Trivers (1972)[24] – is to be found in the different amounts males and females typically invest in reproduction. Like many great ideas in evolutionary biology this one is simple in hindsight, though it holds the distinction of completing Darwin's theory of sexual selection by revealing exactly how it operates.[25] As Trivers phrased it, in all sexual species, "The relative parental investment of the sexes in their young is the key variable controlling the operation of sexual selection. Where one sex invests considerably more than the other, members of the latter will compete among themselves to mate with the former. Where the investment is equal, sexual selection should operate similarly on the two sexes."[26] In other words, the investment of the sex investing more represents a precious resource for the sex investing less – a resource well worth competing over.

The biological definition of a female is the member of the species with larger sex cells; the male is the member with smaller sex cells. Females have large, nutritious and expensive eggs; males have small, cheap sperm. Therefore Trivers' theory predicts, just on the basis of gamete size, that females will be more discriminating in choosing mates because reproduction is usually more costly for them. On the other hand, males will *attempt* to mate more promiscuously both because sex is cheaper for them, and because they have the *potential* to produce many offspring with multiple females. I emphasize the words "attempt" and "potential" because if every male adopts a relatively promiscuous strategy, and if some males succeed, then other males will not reproduce at all. The majority of sexually reproducing species are, therefore, characterized by *a fundamental shortage of female reproductive capacity relative to male demand.* In economic terms, even when sex ratios are equal, and most times they very nearly are, male demand for female reproductive capacity significantly outpaces supply. This ratchets up the "value" of female reproductive capacity and the costs that males are willing to "pay" for access to it, measured in the currency of risky competition and/or other costly physical and behavioral traits.

In short, males typically face higher risks of total reproductive failure and higher hopes of extraordinary reproductive success. This creates strong incentives to compete for mates. Males who are better able to compete for access to scarce female reproductive capacity, in whatever form the competition takes, pass on genes more effectively than rivals.

This is, of course, a description of sexual selection: the gradual development of traits that give advantage in mate competition.[27] Sexual selection also shapes female characteristics, the more so in species (like ours) where males invest significantly in reproduction. However, the power of sexual selection is almost invariably weaker on females because male reproductive capacity is rarely in short supply; females have little incentive to enter costly competitions for a commodity (i.e., sperm) that males are already competing to give away. The general situation, then, is a veritable glut of male reproductive capacity relative to female demand. This drives down the "value" of male reproductive capacity in the market of female "buyers" and depresses the price they will "pay" for access to it, measured in the currency of risky competition and/or other costly physical and behavioral traits.

These factors give rise to a pattern of "effective polygyny." In this type of mating system some males monopolize the reproductive capacities of more than one female and other males necessarily die without issue. The more polygynous the species, the steeper are the costs and benefits of the reproductive contest and the more intense is the male competition. To relate a classic example, the most successful male elephant seals can win harems of fifty cows, and sire up to 200 pups in their lifetimes.[28] Thus for every successful bull there are dozens of chafing bachelors with everything to gain and nothing to lose from intense competition. Since victory in elephant seal competitions comes down to size, strength, and ferocity, the bulls are enormously large (the comparatively diminutive females are sometimes crushed in mating), and their clashes are spectacular.[29]

As Trivers elegantly demonstrated, the most compelling evidence for his theory of parental investment is found in the anomalies: in the few animal species where males actually invest more in reproduction than females (including several species of pipefish seahorses, the Mormon cricket, and the poison-arrow frog), sexual selection results in reversed sex roles: males tend to be coy and sexually selective, females are more promiscuous and compete aggressively for the male's investment.[30] Thus Trivers showed that many of the attributes typically associated with the terms "male" and "female" are *not essential properties of "maleness" or "femaleness" but properties of low or high parental investment.*

For mammalian males the minimal costs of reproduction are a bit of time and some sperm. For females the minimal costs include all of the calories required to sustain long periods of internal gestation and lactation, all the opportunity costs of forgone mating opportunities during that period of time and, in about 95 percent of mammalian species, all the costs of fostering young. Therefore we should expect the typical pattern of effective polygyny to be exaggerated among the mammals. And it is: females tend to be highly discriminating in selecting mates and male competition can be particularly intense. Because female mammals invest so heavily in reproduction, that investment is, for males, a precious resource worthy of competitive risk-taking. Of course, females also compete with one another for the best mates, especially in species, like ours, where male investment in reproduction adds up to much more than sperm. However, theory predicts and field studies demonstrate that, given the lower "value" of the male's investment, females are generally less willing to pay the high price of violently competing for it.[31]

In short, Trivers' theory of parental investment provides an elegantly parsimonious answer to the question, What are male animals fighting over? *The answer is that they are mostly fighting over females.* Of course, like most generalizations this one comes at the cost of some degree of oversimplification. Males also compete for food, territory or, if they are social animals, they will compete for rank. But these competitions are often proxy fights for reproductive opportunities: males fight for females or they fight for the territories, social dominance, or other resources required to attract and retain them. While it can be more difficult to see, this logic applies as much to coalitional conflicts as to individual conflicts. In social species where males fight one another in groups – like lions, dolphins, and chimpanzees – the coalitions are significantly, and sometimes exclusively, motivated by the goal of gaining access to another group's females.[32]

***

> We may conclude that the greater size, strength, courage, pugnacity, and energy of man, in comparison with woman, were acquired during primeval times, and have subsequently been augmented, chiefly through the contests of rival males for possession of the females. (Darwin, *The Descent of Man*)[33]

We are finally prepared to answer the question posed at the outset of this chapter, Why do men fight? Why is competition between and among human females so much less likely to escalate to the level of serious physical violence – to impromptu fist fights, formal duels, murders, and wartime killings – than competition between and among human males? And why is this pattern truly universal, lacking even a single substantiated counter-example in all the history of the world? Unlike the above discussion of non-human animals, this question is beset by the many social, cultural, and cognitive complications that arise whenever we consider *Homo sapiens*. However, while these complications are important, and have served as the basis for many valuable studies, they do not obscure the fact that we are a relatively straightforward example of an effectively polygynous species. Humans are not among the exceptional 5 percent of mammals that are either monogamous or polyandrous; biologists read a variety of straightforward indicators as clear evidence of our mildly polygynous evolutionary history. These indicators include the larger size and superior upper-body musculature of men, their superior cardio-vascular capacities, the fact that more males are conceived and born, their slower maturation and faster senescence, their higher rates of mortality from natural and external factors, and their different behavioral and psychological attributes.[34] Moreover, genetic evidence has recently surfaced for human effective polygyny and its universal result: sexual selection operating more intensely on males. This research is summarized by Steven Pinker:

> Geneticists have found that the diversity of the DNA in the mitochondria of different people (which men and women inherit from their mothers) is far greater than the diversity of the DNA in the Y chromosomes (which men inherit from their fathers). This suggests that for tens of millennia men had greater variation in their reproductive success than women did.[35]

In short, while humans are surely not like highly polygynous gorillas or elephant seals, our bodies, behaviors, and genomes announce that we are not like effectively monogamous gibbons either.

In humans, female reproductive capacity is in short supply for all of the typical reasons listed above, but there are also some unique exacerbating factors. First, there is the evolutionary puzzle of the menopause, which tightly constricts the supply of female reproductive capacity. Male fertility lasts much longer than female, and older men compete with the younger, often successfully, for access to the limited numbers of post-pubescent, pre-menopausal women. This situation contrasts starkly with other primates, most interestingly chimpanzees, where it is the mature females, with proven fertility and higher social rank, who are considered most desirable; young females are markedly less attractive to chimpanzee males. Second, raising human offspring to maturity is uniquely costly. These costs are so onerous, in fact, that human males are among a small minority of mammalian males who actually share the burden. Yet, there is no question that females bear most of the burdens of childcare across human societies,[36] further ramping up their investment in reproduction and providing more incentive for males to compete for that investment. In short, a *real shortage of female reproductive capacity, relative to male demand, is endemic to the human condition.*

In this shortage lies the answer to why men fight. On the basis of our status as effectively polygynous mammals, biologists would predict that human males would be more prone to intense competition, up to and including violent competition, than females; they would also predict, as Darwin did in *The Descent of Man*, that much of this competition would be over females or over the resources required to attract them. On the first prediction – males will be more competitive and violent – there is simply no doubt. There is overwhelming and redundant evidence from a confluence of different fields that men perpetrate most of the violence across cultures. While it is possible to cite evidence for female warriors and killers, there is literally no shred of evidence in the great annals of history, anthropology, or archaeology for a society that violates this pattern, though there are some interesting examples, like the Amazons, in the annals of mythology.[37] Verifying the second prediction is more complicated: are men fighting over women?

Looking first at the question of interpersonal violence, and leaving coalitional violence for later, the answer would seem to be a resounding "no": men sometimes fight over women, yes, but as often they fight over material or social capital – over money, insults, or other things. Yet from a Darwinian perspective the answer to this question is a qualified "yes": sexual selection has shaped men to compete for women *and* for concrete material resources *and* for intangible social resources because they are all *reproductive resources.*

In the final analysis, men compete for status and wealth because – in the environments of our ancestors – these resources reliably converted to reproductive advantage. Across species and human societies there is a powerful correlation between a male's ability to control social and material resources and his reproductive success. This is a foundational tenet of the study of animal behavior, based on robust correlations between access to social and material resources and high reproductive success.[38] It is also a governing tenet of evolutionary studies of human behavior, where exactly the same correlations have been documented in scores of diverse societies. In her classic study, *Despotism and differential reproduction* (1986), Laura Betzig documents strong correlations between status and reproductive success in a cross-cultural study of the world's first civilizations. Betzig writes, for example, that "principal persons" among the Inca were allotted fifty young women; leaders of vassal nations, thirty; heads of provinces with more than 100,000 people were given twenty; governors of at least 100 people were given eight; petty chiefs received seven; and smaller chiefs received five. Similarly, Eleanor Herman's *Sex with kings* (2004) demonstrated that the typical European monarch capitalized on practically unlimited access to mistresses and casual affairs, and, as a result, "most European courts were littered with royal bastards."[39] Daly and Wilson's review of the relevant literature concludes as follows:

> *Homo sapiens* is very clearly a creature for whom differential social status has been associated with variations in reproductive success. Men of high social rank have more wives, more concubines, more access to other men's wives than men of low social rank. They have more children and their children

survive better. These things have consistently been the case in foraging societies, in pastoral societies, in horticultural societies, and in state societies.[40]

The biological anthropologist Bobbi Low reaches a similar conclusion in her survey: "In more than one hundred well-studied societies there are clear formal reproductive rewards for men associated with high status: high ranking men have the right to more wives, and they have more children than others."[41] The only known exceptions to the positive correlation between male social status and reproductive success are found in modern societies. In these societies high-status men have more sexual partners but fewer children; the cultural novelties of reliable contraception and legally enforced monogamy have negated the correlation.[42]

The claim that clashes between human males, like those of other animals, boil down to reproductive conflict, will strike some readers as recklessly reductive. It seems to deny the unique social determinants of violence in given cultures, determinants that are responsible for all the impressive variation in levels of violence across societies. But the arguments of this chapter do not make social and cultural analysis any less indispensable, and they do not conflict with claims that conflict in a given milieu may be influenced by a "culture of violence," economic inequality, or racial or ethnic prejudice. This book attempts to integrate biological and socio-cultural analysis, not to enshrine one over the other. The evolutionary approach cannot replace approaches operating at different analytic levels; the best it can do is complement them.* For example, the evolutionary perspective on male violence does not conflict with the claim that high rates of violence perpetrated and absorbed by minority populations in American inner cities result from a history of racial discrimination and economic marginalization. An evolutionary orientation may

* I agree with the military historian Lawrence Keeley, who writes: "Though many partisans in these debates [over the nature and causes of prestate war] imply that the warfare of a particular region – or even all warfare – has a single cause, no complex phenomenon can have a single cause. There are efficient, formal, material, and final causes, as well as necessary and sufficient conditions . . . The complexity of the concept of cause means that seemingly contradictory views are often actually complementary because they focus on different categories. The anthropological debates about the causes of warfare may represent a classic case of unacknowledged complementarity" (1996, 17).

complement this explanation,[43] but it cannot replace it. However, the evolutionary account clashes directly with the claim that violence is a cultural innovation with none but the most tenuous and inconsequential links to biology. It clashes with the claim that war is a novel pathology characteristic of human societies only since the Neolithic revolution and the discovery of agriculture. And it clashes with the claim that males are more violent only because cultures arbitrarily condition them to be that way. These claims have been effectively falsified by evidence for the cross-cultural ubiquity of predictable patterns of male violence, by legions of precedents from non-human animals, and by the harmony of these data with predictions derived from evolutionary theory.

The claim that interpersonal male violence is the result of direct or indirect reproductive competition is controversial enough, but what explains our more complicated and horrible propensity for warfare? The tendency of human males to join groups and fight against other groups is without ubiquitous non-human parallels. Male coalitional violence is relatively rare in animals. In the most warlike creatures of all, ants and termites, the warriors are mainly female.[44] Can human warfare be viewed as a form of coalitionary reproductive competition? Do coalitions of males compete for scarce reproductive resources in the same way that individuals do? The next section attempts to address these questions, limiting itself to the matter closest at hand: coalitional conflicts in non-state societies.

"WOMEN! WOMEN! WE FIGHT OVER WOMEN!"

With savages . . . the women are the constant cause of war. (Darwin, *The Descent of Man*)[45]

The anthropologist Napoleon Chagnon, living among and studying the warlike Yanomamö people of Venezuela and Brazil, strode out of the jungle and into a remote village with a sinister commando knife slapping his thigh. The headman of the village, Sasawa, thought it was a magnificent tool – for hunting, for farming, for fighting – and ardently begged Chagnon to give it to him. Chagnon declined because the tribesmen were always pestering him for his possessions, and the knife had great sentimental value in addition to its practical utility. His father carried it as a soldier during World War II.

Sasawa's fascination was not diminished by Chagnon's rebuff: he asked him all about the knife and where it came from. The anthropologist answered in terms Sasawa could easily understand: his people's warriors carried these knives when they embarked upon a great raid against their enemies. Sasawa, like virtually all able-bodied Yanomamö men, was a warrior himself so he was naturally curious:

> "Who did you raid?"
> "Germany."
> "Did you go on the raid?"
> "No, but my father did."
> "How many of the enemy did he kill?"
> "None."
> "Did any of your kinsmen get killed by the enemy?"
> "No."
> "You probably raided because of women theft, didn't you?"[46]

When Chagnon answered this last question in the negative, Sasawa was confused and he conferred excitedly with other village men who had clustered around. They all seemed to doubt his answer. While the men then asked about secondary and tertiary *casus belli* like witchcraft and theft of food, they seemed to have difficulty grasping how so dire a conflict as World War II could have *nothing* to do with women. After all, the polygynous tribesmen attributed their constant warfare with neighboring villages to disputes over possession of women. Warriors from hostile villages were perpetually raiding one another, abducting new wives while exacting revenge for previous attacks. Moreover, frequent hostilities between males of the same village were most often attributable to disputes over women.

Once, Chagnon made the mistake of asking a Yanomamö man why they were always fighting. The tribesman was appalled by his ignorance and exclaimed: "What? Don't ask such a stupid question! It is women! Women! We fight over women!"[47] On another occasion he asked a group of men whether they were fighting over meat and game animals – as suggested by the then fashionable "protein deprivation hypothesis" of tribal conflict – or women. One of the warriors responded, "Even though we do like meat, we like women a whole lot more!"[48] Chagnon had to ask such "stupid" questions because when he entered Amazonia it had not occurred to him that men should kill one another in droves over women – at the time of Chagnon's survey roughly 30 percent of Yanomamö men died violently.[49]

This also stunned many of his readers. In fact, some have suggested, most recently Patrick Tierney in *Darkness in El Dorado* (2000),* that Chagnon overstates the role of women in Yanomamö violence, and that their conflicts are ultimately based in competition for food and western goods.[50] However, even Chagnon's critics do not dispute that conflict over women is salient among the Yanomamö. To do so, they would have to confront not only Chagnon, but also the avowals of the Yanomamö themselves and the testimony of generations of explorers, traders, anthropologists, and missionaries. And even if it were discovered that Yanomamö conflict had little to do with women after all, it would not negate the mass of evidence linking warfare and access to women in other preindustrial societies circling the globe. For instance, when anthropologists traced the roots of violence among the "harmless" !Kung, roughly 75 percent of all murders resulted from feuds over women; the most common cause of sub-lethal violence was suspicion of adultery.[51]

On the basis of his observations and data, Chagnon was persuaded to accept the tribesman's answer as basically the right one: the Yanomamö were fighting over women. Chagnon never claimed that the Yanomamö fought only over women. Indeed, he emphasized that raiding parties were seldom motivated only by the desire to capture women, although warriors never passed up opportunities to abduct and rape young women. There is little argument among anthropologists that Yanomamö raiders were primarily motivated to revenge past wrongs. Yanomamö wars were like "Hatfield and McCoy" feuds. Warriors did not meet in force to clash decisively; rather, small war parties conducted reciprocal hit-and-run raids over

* Tierney leveled many serious charges against Chagnon related to his moral behavior and the quality of his science. Formal investigations by the American Anthropological Association (http://www.aaanet.org/edtf/final/vol_one.pdf, http://www.aaanet.org/edtf/final/vol_two.pdf) and The University of Michigan (http://cogweb.ucla.edu/Debate/UMichOnChagnon.html) have absolved Chagnon of Tierney's most serious charges. Most commentators on this academic scandal have concluded that Tierney's attack was reckless; others have accused him of deliberate fraud (http://www.anth.ucsb.edu/ucsbpreliminaryreport.pdf).

the course of years or decades.[52] However, Chagnon argued that the reproductive preoccupation of Yanomamö warfare was reflected not only in the ubiquitous abductions of women, but in the fact that bad blood between villages "almost invariably" traced back to disputes over women.[53] The wrongs that needed avenging emerged from conflicts between suitors, adultery, rape, failure to deliver a promised bride, and so on. Within villages the frequent arguments, club fighting duels, melees and murders were also most commonly instigated by disputes over women. Chagnon argued that Yanomamö conflict could be understood, at its deepest level, as reproductive conflict: the Amazon was a Darwinian crucible where men competed, singly and in groups, for women and for the social prestige needed to attract and retain them.

The extent to which Yanomamö violence traces back to disputes over women is not exceptional in prestate societies. For example, at Crow Creek in South Dakota, archaeologists uncovered the site of a massacre that occurred about 150 years before the arrival of Columbus. About 60 percent of the town's 800 occupants were killed, scalped, and mutilated. Judging from forensic analysis of the remains, the survivors were mainly young women, presumably taken as captives.[54] In short, strife over women is perhaps the most frequently attested cause of all forms of male–male conflict in prestate societies.[55] As the anthropologist Azar Gat writes:

> The evidence across the range of hunter-gatherer peoples (and that of primitive agriculturalists) tells the same story. Within the regional group (tribe) women-related quarrels, violence, so-called blood feuds, and homicide were rife, often as the principal category of violence. Some incidents were caused by suitors' competition; some by women's abduction and forced sex; some by broken promises of marriage; most, perhaps, by jealous husbands over suspicion of infidelity. Between groups, the picture is not very different and is equally uniform. Warfare regularly involved stealing women who were subjected to multiple rape, or taken for marriage, or both.[56]

As the primatologist Sarah Hrdy notes, anthropology and ethnography provide such steadfast support for these conclusions that they are no longer much contested.[57]

So, to answer the question posed at the end of the last section: yes, there is a sense in which the propensity of men in prestate societies to fight in coalitions can be usefully interpreted as a form of reproductive competition. To the victors go the spoils, and the spoils include a host of fitness-enhancing benefits: material goods, warrior prestige, diminished conflict over regional resources, and sexual access to a new population of women.*

AN EVOLUTIONARY PERSPECTIVE ON HOMERIC CONFLICT

In the first two chapters I argued that the *Iliad* and *Odyssey* can be used to reconstruct a reasonably reliable portrait of Aegean life at the end of the Greek Dark Age. Now that I have laid theoretical and empirical foundations from biology and anthropology, the way is clear to address the other main claims of this book, which are:

- That patterns of conflict in Homeric society are congruent with patterns widely encountered in world ethnography.
- That this conflict can be understood, at the evolutionary level, as a product of competition within and between groups for scarce resources that convert to reproductive advantage.
- That these pressures were greatly intensified by shortages of young women brought about by de facto polygyny and, possibly, excess mortality of juvenile females.
- That a surplus of unmated young males resulted in viciously circular patterns of violence.
- That these unremitting cycles may help to illuminate both the tragic elements of the Homeric worldview and the frequently cruel and capricious natures of the gods and fate.

* Other authors have made similar, though not identical, arguments for the more complex conflicts of state-level societies. See, for example, Ghiglieri 1999; Darwin 1871; Tooby and Cosmides 1988; Wrangham and Peterson 1996. These arguments are plausible: to the victors in conflicts between states go many of the same spoils as go to the victors in prestate conflicts. However, it is also important to stress that a behavior that was well adapted to the band and tribal environments of our ancestors may be anachronistic, even maladaptive, in the radically different environments of the modern world. Human psychological propensities and modern human environments may frequently be "mismatched." As an example of this mismatch principle, evolutionists are fond of citing human greed for fat and sweets. These nutrients promoted health in ancestral times when they were usually in short supply and when our energy expenditures were much higher. However, in modern, sedentary populations, our greed for these nutrients, combined with their ready availability, is largely responsible for an obesity epidemic that now ranks as the second leading cause of preventable death in the United States (Mokdad et al. 2000).

One of Chagnon's mistakes, especially in his early writings, was in giving his audiences the sense that conflict in prestate worlds was about reproduction in the narrow sense (competing for women only) rather than the broad sense (competing for resources that convert to reproductive advantage).[58] That is, Chagnon gave the impression that Yanomamö disputes focused on women, and therefore if conflicts were proven to be over, say, food, land, or material possessions, these conflicts would be non-reproductive, non-biological. The intention of this book is not only to demonstrate the reproductive significance of Homeric conflict over women, which I believe most readers will readily accept, but to show how pitched rivalry among Homeric men for social status and wealth is only a slightly less direct form of reproductive competition.

But before making this broad case I must discuss Homeric reproductive competition in its narrowest and most obvious sense. I begin with fights over women.

CHAPTER 4

What launched the 1,186 ships?

> Was this the face that launched the thousand ships and burnt the topless towers of Ilium?
>
> (Christopher Marlowe, *Doctor Faustus*)

There is a hint of incredulity in the voice of Faustus, resting his eyes for the first time on Helen. Was *this* the face that launched the ships, that spawned a genocidal massacre, that robbed a generation of its best men, and brought terror and misery into the lives of its women? By what chain of events could such a cause lead to such effects?

Faustus' tacit question has troubled the minds of many others who have written on the Trojan theme, from the beginnings of Greek letters to the present day.[1] The Ancient Greeks eased the incongruity with a story of a pact among Helen's numerous suitors: no matter who won Helen's hand, the others would swarm to his aid if she were ever abducted.[2] According to this legend, the main chiefs who led men against Troy did so to honor the pact. However, there is not a single reference to this story in all of Homer, so it is considered by many to be a post-Homeric attempt to fill a perceived gap between cause (adultery) and effect (world war and genocide). In fact, while some ancient commentators evidently considered wars over ("mere") women to be odd and even fantastic,[3] they were not considered so by Homer or his characters. They express no surprise at fights and wars over women, no need to make sense of them, and no need to explain them away. On the contrary, when the Trojan elders see Helen approaching they breathe to themselves: "It is no cause for blame that Trojans and well-greaved Achaians should for such a woman suffer long pains; she is dreadfully like immortal goddesses to look upon" (*Iliad* 3.155–56).

When more recent commentators note the yawning divide between a single act of adultery and a decade of war culminating in near-total cultural annihilation, they tend to argue that the war was only technically over Helen. While the war may have originated in an act of adultery, what is really at stake is the honor of the fighters and the spoils inside Troy's walls. This is mostly true of commentary on other Homeric disputes over women. From this perspective, female bodies become a different battlefield on which Homeric men strive for power, status, honor, or wealth. One recent treatment pithily embodies this common perspective: the epics are characterized by "competition between men conducted through women"; "traffic in women [is] a medium of contended honor among men."[4] Van Wees' description of the seduction of Helen is also paradigmatic: Paris gave "*the insult* that launched a thousand ships [emphasis mine]."[5] There is nothing original in my claim that Homeric men fight over women; no commentator has ever denied that Homeric men contend over women. But the trend has been to underemphasize the important role women play in these disputes, *as women*.

As discussed in the next chapter, commentators have not been wrong to suggest that disputes over women often conceal greed for power, wealth, and prestige. Competition for these resources is as central to my vision of Homeric society as is direct competition for women. In this chapter, however, I will show that Homeric men compete ubiquitously over women, and that these women are valued primarily as ends in themselves, rather than as means to different ends like wealth and status. Moreover, I contend, in opposition to the assumptions of some, that the women are valued for primarily sexual reasons, as opposed to economic reasons or as potent symbols of the defeat and humiliation of enemies.[6] I argue that direct competition for women is a main cause of warfare and interpersonal male violence in the Homeric world. Like roads circling back to Rome, almost all of the main conflicts of the *Iliad* and *Odyssey* trace back to disputes over women.

INTERPERSONAL CONFLICT

Because of Helen the Greeks grouped at Aulis and sailed for Troy. But the first disputed woman mentioned in the *Iliad* is not Helen but

Chryseis, daughter of Apollo's priest Chryses. The girl was captured in a raid and presented to Agamemnon as his *geras* (*gera*, plural). *Gera* are special prizes, frequently young and beautiful women, awarded to *basileis* after successful raids. Agamemnon is deeply taken with Chryseis' body and mind (*Iliad* 1.113–15), and he will not return her to her priestly father. With lecherous relish he tells the supplicating priest: "I will not set her free. Before that, old age will overtake her in my house in Argos, far from her fatherland, as she moves back and forth at the loom and joins me in my bed" (*Iliad* 1.29–31). The priest prays to Apollo and the infuriated god fells a multitude of Greek warriors with arrows of plague. After a seer reveals the source of Apollo's rage, Agamemnon relents and returns the girl to her father.

However, he negates this good decision by crudely asserting his power as paramount chief and demanding another prize. It would be a great dishonor, he claims, for every *basileus* but him to enjoy a prize. When Achilles objects that there are no prizes left, upbraiding him for his greed, Agamemnon retaliates by forcing Achilles to relinquish his own prize – Briseis, the fair-haired (2.689) and fair-cheeked girl (1.184). With difficulty, Achilles represses a powerful impulse to kill Agamemnon where he stands. But, in protest, he withdraws from the war for Troy. From this conflict, the drama of the *Iliad* flows, setting in motion events that lead to the slaughter of countless Greeks, the near dissolution of their alliance, and the deaths of Patroclus, Hector, and eventually Achilles himself.

Clearly Achilles and Agamemnon are here engaged in dangerous competition for social dominance with roots in earlier years of the Trojan conflict. Achilles resents Agamemnon always claiming the greatest portion of war spoil while he bears the main burden of the fighting. Agamemnon thinks that Achilles does not know his place, and boasts that he will personally seize Briseis so that Achilles will "learn well how much greater I am than you, and another man will shrink before declaring himself my equal and vying with me face-to-face" (1.185–87). Many commentators have used these passages, not without justification, to frame the conflict over Briseis as a dispute over power and honor. Donlan's assessment is typical: "The struggle, *agōn*, between Agamemnon and Achilles is *all about* 'honor' [emphasis mine]."[7]

However, this reading suggests that Briseis' status as a sexually desirable young woman is almost beside the point. It is not. The dispute between Achilles and Agamemnon escalates so quickly and dangerously because of the special character of Agamemnon's effrontery. Agamemnon might have saved face by seizing a different type of *geras* from Achilles, a prized animal or some gaudy treasure. But instead he punishes Achilles in the most humiliating and emasculating way imaginable: by threatening to personally visit his tents and snatch, by force if necessary, a woman Achilles repeatedly claims to love and desire (e.g. *Iliad* 9.335–44). Achilles refers to her as a de facto wife, and there is good reason to believe that he intended to formalize their union after the war (19.295–99). There are no cultures in which Agamemnon's action would not be considered among the gravest possible provocations. It is hard to imagine that the disputes between Agamemnon and Achilles, or between Menelaus and Paris, could have been carried so far if the main points of contention were, instead of stunningly beautiful women, other things coveted by Homeric men, like beautiful armor or gleaming tripods. While Achilles sometimes speaks as though the dispute is only about an insult to honor, just as prominently he is shown pitifully mourning the beloved darling of his heart (e.g., *Iliad* 18.444–46).

The sexual dimensions of the dispute are confirmed in Agamemnon's eventual attempts at reconciliation. He makes two important overtures. First, he promises Achilles direct compensation consisting of great treasure, increased power, and no fewer than twenty-eight women. All of these women have great beauty in common: seven women of Lesbos, renowned for their beauty; his pick of the twenty fairest Trojan captives once the city falls; and one of Agamemnon's own daughters, whichever Achilles prefers. Second, he solemnly swears: "I never laid a hand on the girl Briseis, either desiring her for my bed or for any other reason; she remained undefiled in my huts. If this is sworn falsely may the gods give to me many pains, as they give to all men who sin against them by falsely swearing" (*Iliad* 19.258–66; see also 9.131–34). My intention is not to downplay the important political dynamics in Agamemnon's and Achilles' confrontation. Rather, I emphasize that the political and sexual threads cannot be disentangled. It cannot be justly claimed that one component of their dispute is more important than the other: the political dispute escalates dangerously precisely because it hinges on rights to a desirable woman that one of them loves.

AGAMEMNON'S "GIFT ATTACK"

But Achilles, at least initially, *rejects* Agamemnon's fabulous offer. Does not Achilles' rejection of this Darwinian windfall – a harem of beautiful women and power and riches to boot – count heavily against my case that the behavior of Homeric men complies with evolutionary logic? While it cannot be denied that Agamemnon's offer should provide Achilles with very powerful incentives,* I believe that once Agamemnon's offer is fully contextualized, its salience as counter-evidence recedes to very little.

There are a variety of good reasons why Achilles may have turned down the compensation offer. First, there is the fact that Agamemnon does not actually offer compensation; he offers a conditional bribe. He pledges to deliver up the bounty when (1) Achilles returns to the fight, and (2) when Achilles admits how far he stands below him (while Achilles is never told about this undoubtedly deal-breaking second condition, commentators have argued that, "Achilles knows he is being asked to submit").[8] Donlan, placing the dispute in rich anthropological context, has called Agamemnon's offer a "gift attack." The paramount chief ignores the rule that wrongs must be righted not only with gifts, but also with a genuine, public apology.[9] Agamemnon saliently fails to give Achilles anything like the public apology to match his public insults (Achilles seethes about Agamemnon sending ambassadors to his huts, not daring "to look me in the face," *Iliad* 9.372–73). And, even without the outrageous second condition, the lavishness of Agamemnon's bounty is an insult in itself: his conspicuous display of unmatched wealth and power, of *aretē* in gift-giving, accentuates Achilles' subordinate status.[10] Donlan concludes that Achilles' "gift duel" with Agamemnon

* Achilles' initial refusal to accept compensation also poses difficulties for other models. For instance, if it is argued that Achilles is almost exclusively motivated by the desire to defend his honor, we might expect his outrage to dissolve when offered treasures and powers that would immensely increase his power and prestige. Why doesn't it? We might also expect him to avoid the heavy social costs he incurs for selfishly leaving his friends to be slaughtered in droves (e.g., *Iliad* 16.203–06). Why doesn't he? As my treatment suggests, I believe that, properly contextualized, these difficulties recede. My point is that this whole episode is shot through with ambiguities and that Achilles' initial rejection is problematic from multiple vantage points; that is why this episode has been the subject of unremitting scholarly contention.

culminates in the former's "stunning victory" – Achilles eventually gets his compensation *and* his apology, while bleeding his rival of great prestige.[11] In initially snubbing the offer, Donlan argues, Achilles is rejecting a first offer from a position of bargaining dominance. He can take this strong position because (1) Agamemnon was clearly more in the wrong and (2) Achilles is indispensable; Agamemnon has no option but to bring him back to the fray.

Second, it is possible, if not likely, that Achilles' famous Book Nine epiphany – his realization that the benefits of war do not outweigh its dire costs – is genuine.[12] If so, Agamemnon's offer would have cold appeal for Achilles because of the condition attached to it: returning to the fight. Achilles knows he has two fates: if he stays in Troy and fights he is doomed but he will die gloriously; if he goes home he will live happily and long, but without fame. Achilles knows that accepting the bounty is tantamount to certain death. By the time Troy falls and the bulk of Agamemnon's largesse comes due Achilles understands that he will already be dead.

Third, I have claimed that Briseis – as a woman Achilles adores, not a token of prestige wealth – is an important point of contention between Agamemnon and Achilles. If so, there is reason to doubt that Agamemnon can offer satisfactory reparation. Agamemnon promises to return her and he swears a great oath, accompanied by a sacrifice, that she remains unfouled by his lusts. The gravity and publicness of Agamemnon's oath suggests how important Briseis' purity is to Achilles and also to his reputation. But why should Achilles trust Agamemnon's word? After all, there is only one other oath-sacrifice in Homer, and it is promptly violated by the Trojans (*Iliad* 3.264–301; see also Hera's very solemn, very dishonest oath at *Iliad* 15.34–46). In a warrior world, could a woman ever mean as much to a man after being publicly possessed by his greatest rival? Part of the answer to this question may be given by Achilles when he finally does accept Agamemnon's compensation. Of the formerly beloved girl he says: "I wish that among the ships Artemis had slain her with an arrow on the day when I chose her after I had sacked Lyrnessus. Then not so many Achaians would have bitten the immeasurable earth . . ." (*Iliad* 19.59–61).

Finally, all of this is complicated by the most important ambiguity of all: *Does Achilles truly and finally reject and renounce compensation*?

In Book Nine each of three envoys of Agamemnon seeks to persuade Achilles to accept the bounty. Achilles rejects the first plea, that of Ajax, in certain terms. But by the end of the scene he has changed his mind; he announces that he will remain at Troy after all, though he will withhold from fighting until Hector reaches his own encampment (*Iliad* 9.649–55). By Book Sixteen (56–86), as Hector rages through the Greek camp, and *before* the death of Patroclus, Achilles clearly indicates that he *is* ready to renounce his anger and that he *does* eagerly hope to be compensated – with gifts, glory, and the return of Briseis. In Book Nineteen he accepts the full recompense – along with Agamemnon's tardy apology – in an offhand manner, without any relish. But this is because his whole psychology has been transformed by the death of Patroclus.

The primary conflicts of the *Odyssey* share roots with those of the *Iliad*: *men attempting to gain sexual access to women claimed by other men*. This theme is introduced in the *Odyssey* in numerous references to the deadly love triangle among Clytemnestra, Aegisthus, and Agamemnon ("Aegisthus, beyond that which was ordained, took as his own the wedded wife of the son of Atreus, and slew him when he returned," 1.35–36). But the primary conflict of the poem arises from the suitors' meddlings with women that Odysseus claims as his exclusive sexual property, his wife and his female slaves.

Commentators usually argue that Odysseus' conflict with the suitors is not so much over a desirable woman as it is over wealth and, especially, political power.[13] But Penelope is not a queen and her husband would not automatically inherit Odysseus' position of leadership or his wealth. Even if she were more like a queen in our sense of the word, we would not expect her new husband to become king since there is a grown prince around. While the lead suitors, Eurymachus (15.521–22) and Antinous (22.48–53), desire *both* to marry Penelope *and* to supplant Odysseus, it is nowhere clear that the one is a means to the other.[14] In fact, while Antinous seeks to clear the way for his political ascent by killing Telemachus, there is no clear indication that he views marriage to Penelope in the same way (see *Odyssey* 22.48–53).[15] Thus the case that the suitors pursue Penelope because they hope to rule Ithaca is weak.[16]

And there is less evidence still that the suitors are motivated by hopes of riches. We are told explicitly and repeatedly that the wealth of Odysseus' household belongs to Telemachus, and will stay with him when Penelope goes to keep the house of a new husband. While the suitors do eventually hatch a plan to steal Odysseus' wealth by killing Telemachus, they have been pursuing Penelope for almost four years and they do not devise this plot until the final days of their lives.

In sum, there is no good evidence that desire for wealth or power primarily motivates the dogged suitors. There is no strong evidence that marriage to Penelope is a route, direct or indirect, to Odysseus' position of leadership. And, far from getting rich by marrying Penelope, it is repeatedly emphasized that the lucky suitor will have to pay a spectacularly high bride price – outbidding more than 100 rich, determined, and rivalrous men (see below, Chapter Five).

So why do they court her? Penelope is a woman who has no peer "in the Achaian land, neither in sacred Pylos, nor in Argos, nor in Mycenae, nor yet in Ithaca itself, nor in the dark mainland" (21.107–9). Could it be that the suitors simply see Penelope as a highly desirable potential wife?[17]

This possibility has usually been overlooked on the assumption that Penelope must be too old to inspire such ardent desire, especially in younger men like the suitors. But if we conservatively assume that Penelope was married in her mid-teens (Nausicaa, at peak ripeness for marriage, appears to be about this age, and girls throughout Ancient Greek history typically married in the mid-teens, perhaps younger if their families were rich)[18] and experienced her only pregnancy soon afterwards, she would be in her mid to late thirties during the primary time period covered by the *Odyssey*. And, since the suitors have been pursuing her for nearly four years, it means that she was probably only in her early thirties when the courtship began.

But to do the arithmetic is to miss the point entirely. Homer is not totting up the years. Homer plays it loose with chronology. For instance, while visiting the underworld Odysseus is told that Telemachus has taken his place among men and has won their respect; yet, at the time, Telemachus was barely a teenager. Similarly, however old Penelope is supposed to be, Homer provides us with a mental image that forbids us from seeing her as anything but a paragon of beauty.[19] His portrait of Penelope – exactly like his portrait of well-ripened Helen in the *Iliad* – includes no creeping lines of age or gray streaked hair, rather her face and form are likened to Aphrodite's and Artemis' (e.g., *Odyssey* 18.208–14). And the poem emphasizes her desirability by showing that no fewer than 108 men from four different islands strive for her hand – far more than the legend says courted Helen.[20] That their desire goes far beyond worldly pragmatism is emphasized when Penelope dons beautiful clothes, primps and perfumes her hair, and makes a rare appearance before them : "The suitors' knees went loose, lust bewitched their hearts, and all of them prayed to lie down beside her in bed" (*Odyssey* 18.212–13; see also 1.365–66). When one of the lead suitors says to Penelope, "you surpass all women in beauty and stature" (*Odyssey* 18.249), he is not just flattering her; his description is consistent with the way Penelope is portrayed throughout the poem.

The only exceptions to Penelope's portrayal as an exceptionally attractive woman are based on her own self-descriptions. But she claims that her looks were instantly annihilated on *the very day* that her husband left for Troy (e.g., *Odyssey* 18.178–81; 18.251–53). She is suggesting, then, that her decline resulted from intense grief and worry, not age. And, in any case, Penelope protests too much: her statements are clearly at odds with how she is perceived and described by Homer and his other characters. Odysseus' reaction to the suitors is visceral. He is not only angry that they are literally devouring his wealth (in Homer's world wealth was principally measured in livestock), or over their bad manners, but because they lust for Penelope, hoping *his* wife would bear *their* children (*Odyssey* 22.324). He charges them with sexual, not political, usurpation. When Menelaus hears of the suitors' outrages, his words confirm that he sees things the same way: the suitors "hope to lie in the bed of a stout-hearted man" (*Odyssey* 4.333–34; see also 17.124–25).

The young wooers also take ample liberties with Odysseus' slave women. They commit three main offenses, which are usually described formulaically: devouring Odysseus' wealth, wooing his wife, and raping and seducing his slave women (e.g., *Odyssey* 22.34–38). Thus two of the suitors' three main offenses are trespasses against women Odysseus claims as his own (see next section). That both are commonly mentioned in the same breath suggests that the liberties with the slave women and the courting of Penelope are considered trespasses of similar magnitude. In fact, when Odysseus reveals himself to the suitors, they seem almost as concerned about their freedom with his slave women as with his wife. When Leodes begs in vain for Odysseus' mercy, he mentions not Penelope but his respectful treatment of Odysseus' slave women (*Odyssey* 22.312–19). Leodes' concern is well placed since Odysseus burns with anger over the liaisons of suitors and slaves. Odysseus is gripped with rage as he watches the women sneak off to fornicate with suitors, tittering girlishly all the way:

> There Odysseus lay awake planning evil in his heart for the suitors. And the women slipped out from the hall (those who would lie with suitors, mingling in love) laughing with one another and making merry. But his heart stirred in his chest: much he debated in mind and heart whether to charge them, bringing death to each one, or to let them mingle with the imperious suitors one last time. His heart snarled within him. As a dog bestrides her young puppies and growls at an unrecognized man, eager to fight, so Odysseus' heart growled inside him, indignant at their evil deeds. (*Odyssey* 20.5–16)

Eventually, he quenches his rage not only by massacring the suitors but also by gratifying his urge to kill the twelve wanton slave women. He instructs Telemachus and two male servants to crowd the women into a corner and execute them all: "Smite them with your sharp swords and take all the life out of them, and cause them to forget the lust they had underneath the suitors, mingling in secret" (*Odyssey* 22.442–45).

Why is Odysseus so angry? One possibility is that he is simply outraged by inappropriate behavior, in much the same way that he is appalled by the bad behavior of his male servant Melanthius. Another possibility is that his anger emerges from a specific sense of violated sexual ownership. This would better explain the fact that Odysseus' anger is intensely focused on the *sexual* improprieties of his slave women. It is significant, I think, that his killing rage does not extend to specifically target, say, the slave women who precipitated the whole crisis: the women who perfidiously betrayed Penelope's ruse of unweaving the shroud. While Odysseus faults the condemned women for the general sin of "behaving shamefully" he focuses above all on one offense: lying down under suitors.[21]

Telemachus does as his father asks and executes the women. But he has been closely observing them too; Odysseus mentions that "no folly of women in the house escapes his notice" (*Odyssey* 19.87–88).

Rather than giving the condemned women the relatively quick and merciful death by sword dictated by his father, he again invokes their fornications (*Odyssey* 22.464) before hanging them in sequence, stringing them up by their necks, one by one.

It is not a coincidence that the Greeks, including Homer, intimately linked Ares and Aphrodite (as siblings and lovers), and that their children, Terror and Fear, "rout the tight battle lines of men in chilling war" (*Theogony* 932–36). Wherever beautiful Aphrodite goes, berserk Ares rages in her frothy wake. The union symbolizes the belief that sexual passion can overflow into violence and even war. This theme is exemplified in the conflicts over Helen, Briseis, Clytemnestra, Penelope, and Odysseus' slave women. Copious references to past disputes over women, in both epics – not to mention in preserved summaries of other epics now lost (see below) – show that these conflicts are representative and cannot be dismissed as isolated incidents (*Iliad* 6.160–70; 9.553–61; *Odyssey*, 11.576–81, 8.302ff., 11.660–68, 21.330–40).[22] Finally, the theme is emphasized in the abundant evidence that battles and wars were always fought, in large part, over the defending men's women.

RAIDING FOR WOMEN IN HOMER

The conflicts over Helen, Briseis, and Penelope are only the brightest threads in an immense, billowing tapestry depicting competition over women. The Trojan War is not only fought over Helen; it is fought over Hector's Andromache and all the nameless women of common Trojan men. Likewise, the *Odyssey* clearly reflects a world in which wars were fought, in large part though by no means exclusively, for possession of the other sides' women.

While female slaves are extremely valuable for their productive labor, this section will array evidence for a fact that is usually overlooked or treated in passing: Homeric men risk fighting desperate, determined men with edged weapons largely in hopes of claiming specifically sexual access to new women. In short, much violence between groups of Greek men stems from the same source as violence between individuals: attempts to gain sexual access to women claimed by other men.

That warriors are significantly motivated by the hope of capturing women is clear throughout both epics. This motive is explicit in Nestor's pep talk to the demoralized Greek warriors, reminding them of victory's spoils: "Don't anyone hurry to return homeward until after he has lain down alongside a wife of some Trojan" (*Iliad* 2.355). And the Trojan men constantly goad their flagging valor by reminding themselves of the terrors their wives will experience if Troy should fall. The war boasts of Hector provide a valuable Trojan perspective on the motives of the Greek warriors: "Not through me giving ground will you mount our towers or carry away our women in your ships! Before that I will give you your doom!" (*Iliad* 8.164–66). Later he vaunts over the corpse of Patroclus and says, "Patroclus, surely you imagined you would lay our city waste and you would rob from the Trojan women their day of freedom, taking them in your ships to your dear fatherland – you fool!" (*Iliad* 16.830–33; similar passages include *Iliad* 15.494–99; 17.220–24; 18.261–65; 21.582–89).

The centrality of female spoil is clear not only in the Trojan conflict, but also in a large number of references to wars that were fought in the past. For instance, Achilles' short history of his career as a warrior is particularly explicit but not unrepresentative: "I have spent many sleepless nights and bloody days in battle, fighting men for their women" (*Iliad* 9.325–27). Later Achilles mourns over Patroclus' corpse and refers to all the captive women in their camp, women "we fought to win by our might and our long spears whenever we sacked the rich cities of mortal men" (*Iliad* 18.338–42; see also *Iliad* 18.265; 20.191–94).

Though the *Odyssey* is not a war poem, it also contains numerous references to conflicts in which acquiring the enemy's women was at least as important as stealing his wealth. For instance, sailing back from Troy with his formerly "hollow ships" already stacked to the gunwales with Trojan wealth and women (*Odyssey* 3.153–54; see also *Iliad* 9.364–67), Odysseus still pauses to rob the Cicones of the same (*Odyssey* 9.39–42). Likewise, when he travels to the underworld he is shocked to encounter the shade of Agamemnon. He asks his former leader how he met his end:

> Most glorious son of Atreus, lord of men, Agamemnon, what fate of death, bringing long woe, broke you? Did Poseidon overcome you on your ships,

stirring up a dreadful wind? Or did hostile men harm you on dry land while you were cutting away their cattle and beautiful flocks of sheep, or fighting for their city and women? (*Odyssey* 9.397–403)

This passage suggests the possibility that there were two main types of raids: those targeting livestock on the peripheries of settlements and those focused on the women and spoils inside. Moreover, like other passages in the poems, it indicates that capturing women was not a fortuitous side effect of war, but a main, consciously held objective.

While references to slave women almost always mention their menial skills, they were valued at least as much for their reproductive as for their productive capacities. Descriptive emphasis is usually on beauty – an indicator of youth, fertility, and, possibly, genetic quality[23] – and the most valued slaves are not the sturdy, experienced and skilled older women, but beautiful, maidenly slaves like Chryseis and Briseis, who share Greek beds as well as Greek chores. This is illustrated in Agamemnon's fabulous offer of reparations to Achilles which include seven surpassingly beautiful women of Lesbos and the twenty Trojan women "who are loveliest of all after Argive Helen" (*Iliad* 9.140). In the *Iliad*, high-status Greeks hoard captured women in their tents. Sexual relations are explicitly depicted or implied. Achilles keeps many serving girls in his huts (*Iliad* 23.550) and quickly fills the empty place in his bed left by Briseis with another lovely captive, fair Diomede (9.664–68). Moreover, as we will see below, Agamemnon is resented by the rank and file for claiming the most and best of the captured women (*Iliad* 2.226–28). When Agamemnon tries to inspire the archer Teucer to kill a man, he offers "a woman to mount your bed with" (*Iliad* 8.291) as a prize. Even ancient Nestor is given a slave woman as a war prize – Hecamede, who is notable not so much for her skill at work as for her youthful beauty (*Iliad* 11.624–27; see also *Odyssey* 7.7–11). On the home front, slaves perform indispensable work but, as suggested by Odysseus' (and Telemachus') furious response to the slave women's dalliances, they are also considered to be the master's sexual property. Odysseus' apparently possessive reaction is not consistent with the hypothesis that the slave women were sought exclusively or primarily for their labor. If this were so we might expect Odysseus to encourage them to circulate their favors so as to augment his labor force. Instead he behaves just like an enraged cuckold.

BASTARDS

In many prestate societies there is a correlation between military and reproductive success. Most famously, Chagnon found that Yanomamö *unokais*, men who had killed, had roughly twice as many wives and three times as many children, on average, as men of the same age who were not *unokais*; Chagnon also cited anecdotal evidence that *unokais* had more affairs and produced more illegitimate children.[24] The most prolific *unokai* was Shinbone who had forty-three children by his eleven wives. Thanks in no small part to his prolific son, Shinbone's father had, by his fourteen children, 143 grandchildren, 335 great-grandchildren, and 401 great-great-grandchildren at the time of Chagnon's last census.[25] In one village, 90 percent of the residents were descendants of Shinbone's father, which is not nearly so impressive as the recent finding by geneticists that 8 percent of a large population of Asian men – or approximately 0.5 percent of all people on earth – are likely the direct descendants of Genghis Khan.[26] This would seem to lend support to the thirteenth-century Arab historian Rashid al-Din, who quoted the great Mongolian *unokai* as saying: "Man's greatest good fortune is to chase and defeat his enemy, leave his married women weeping and wailing, ride his gelding, use the bodies of his women like night-shirts and supports, gazing upon and kissing their rosy breasts, sucking their lips which are as sweet as the berries of the breast."[27]

Chagnon's conclusions were immensely controversial. In the face of anthropological consensus, he argued that aggressive behavior advanced male reproductive interests in certain contexts. However, his correlations have since been accepted by many anthropologists, not just for the Yanomamö, but also for a number of other societies where martial success correlates with above-average reproductive success, including the Masai, Samburu, Ayoreo, Quicha, Dodoth, and Jivaro.[28] In fact, cross-cultural studies suggest that warrior prowess has been a reliable route to high reproductive success in a high proportion of band and tribal societies; large-scale statistical analysis of data from hundreds of band and tribal populations suggests that young men are willing to adopt the risks of war in large part *because* it is a reliable route to gaining wives and other mates.[29] As discussed later in this chapter, a similar phenomenon seems to have been at work in historical wars where very high rates of rape, often earning the designation "mass rape," have been ubiquitous.

Homeric society appears to be a striking example of this general cultural pattern. On the one hand, as discussed in the next chapter, outstanding warriors had an easier time attracting consenting mates. The son of Castor, for example, is a shining example of the way that Homeric men parlay military success into reproductive success. He "led away a wife from wealthy people on account of my prowess: I was not weak nor did I flee from fights" (*Odyssey* 14.211–13). On the other hand, women captured in war would obviously have borne their captors' children. While this is explicitly true of Troy's Priam, who has 62 children by his wife and various "women of the palace halls" (*Iliad* 24.596–97), Homer does not go out of his way to list the illegitimate offspring of all the warriors. Homer and his characters are casual about illegitimacy.[30] Far from facing sharp stigma, many bastards bask in their fathers' love and good graces. So, the fact that Homer does not make a "big deal" out of the illegitimate children of warriors does not mean that they did not exist.

On the contrary, there is good reason to believe that, except for the occasionally sterile warrior, like Phoenix, virtually every elite man would have illegitimate offspring.* Another probable exception is represented in Odysseus' father, Laertes. Despite paying an outlandishly high price for the beautiful slave girl, Eurycleia, Laertes never shared her bed for fear of his formidable wife (*Odyssey* 1.429–33). As numerous commentators have pointed out, this scene is one among many which clearly indicates that sexual relations were the norm between masters and slaves. Homer tells us of Laertes' restraint because it was unusual.

The Greek warrior's lifestyle of rapine and plunder allowed him to amass large collections of women. Odysseus, a relatively minor *basileus*, has 50 female slaves *before* he leaves for Troy. Richer and more influential *basileis* would presumably have even more. While it seems unlikely that men in the Late Dark Age could have held such

* Incidentally, we learn at *Iliad* 9.453–95 that Phoenix's sterility originated in a conflict with his own father. His father fell in love with a young female slave and his distraught mother persuaded Phoenix to seduce her in order to destroy their bond. When his father discovered them, he furiously cursed Phoenix with sterility.

large numbers of slaves, ethnographical evidence clearly shows that even the "big men" of small-scale tribal societies – men like Shinbone – routinely monopolized multiple women.[31] So even if these figures exaggerate the slave holdings of Dark Age *basileis*, as they probably do, the point still stands. Homer is often explicit about the sexual uses to which captured women are put. But other times he chooses not to dwell on the obvious – that the women will be concubines and will bear illegitimate children.

However, the epics do provide plentiful evidence of these children in a quiet proliferation of concubinal bastards. In the *Odyssey*, for instance, we glimpse the bastard son of Menelaus, Megapenthes, on his wedding day. His doting father has ordered feasting and festivity. We hear of the bastard son of Castor who, when his father died, had to literally fight for the resources and respect that his legitimate half-brothers tried to deny him. At times we hear listings of the illegitimate offspring of gods and great men (e.g., *Odyssey* 11.225–332, 14.312–28). Bastards frequently comprise main branches of distinguished family trees, and they constantly traverse Homer's battlefield narrative in the *Iliad*. Some, like Teucer, Medon, Eudorus the Myrmidon, or Tlepolemus (the last is one of scores of bastards tradition attributed to Heracles), are high-status individuals. Achilles' son, Neoptolemus, who spearheads the sack of Troy, must also be a bastard because we know Achilles is not married. And, like Megapenthes and the son of Castor, his bastardy does not prevent him from marrying the daughter of a wealthy and powerful man – Hermione, daughter of Menelaus (*Odyssey* 4.8–14). Characters feel much stronger attachment to full siblings "born from the same womb" than to those half-siblings who emerged from different wombs (e.g., *Iliad* 19.293; 24.46–47).

In sum, according to Daniel Ogden's study of Greek bastardy, the *Iliad* and *Odyssey* "paint a broadly coherent picture of bastardy ... [delineating] a society in which bastards born of concubines were honored and integrated into a man's legitimate family, but permitted a lesser share in inheritance, and a society in which bastards could marry women in the best families ... and were unquestionably free."[32] Further, the term *nothos*, in the Homeric poems, always denotes "bastard" in the specific sense of a child of a concubinal relationship, and never in the sense of a fatherless child of an unmarried woman.[33] Perhaps this provides insight into the rage of Odysseus and his execution of the women who mingled with suitors. Since Homeric men invest substantially in bastards, often raising them like their legitimate offspring, they are in danger of being cuckolded by their slave women.*

THE EPIC CYCLE AND EARLY GREEK MYTH

In the absence of historical or archaeological documentation of these claims, where can we turn for external support? One potentially corroborating source is the entire Cycle of epic poetry of which Homer's poems were initially only a small part.[34] All of these epics – six poems (not including the *Iliad* and *Odyssey)* telling the story of the wars for Thebes and for Troy, including their origins and long aftermaths – are now lost, being preserved for us only in lean summaries by later writers. The earliest sources attributed these poems to Homer, but later tradition assigned the poems to different authors.[35] Scholars have traditionally argued that the Cycle was later than Homer, derivative of Homer, and of vastly inferior artistic quality.[36] They have acknowledged that the Cycle summaries may be valuable sources of information for different aspects of the authentic Homeric tradition of epic storytelling. However, evidence from the Cycle has been treated with great caution because there has been no reliable method for determining which aspects of the Cycle derive

* I have been asked: If Odysseus is motivated by reproductive concerns, why would he destroy twelve wombs? This is a good question. One possibility is that Odysseus is sending an overt warning to the 38 surviving women of the household. Whatever the answer, his behavior smacks familiarly of the most commonly attested motives for male on female homicide (and other forms of violence) across cultures. Cross-cultural data suggest that men are most likely to kill women for infidelity or abandonment (Daly and Wilson 1988; for literature review see Buss 2000, 117–21). Odysseus' angry response can therefore be interpreted as reflecting "an evolved sexually proprietary masculine psychology that is panhuman" (Wilson and Daly 1993, 110). This psychology evolved in response to a history of paternity uncertainty and the devastating genetic costs of cuckoldry. But men kill straying mates in only a small percentage of cases. I therefore agree with Wilson and Daly (1993) that murder is not the adaptation, anger is. Male psychology has been engineered to greet infidelity with extreme anger – with all of its menace of violence – in order to deter infidelity (see Wilson and Daly 1993, Daly and Wilson 1992). Sometimes, as in the case of spousal killings, these psychological mechanisms can nonetheless result in clearly "counterproductive" outcomes (1993, 120).

from the authentic tradition and which aspects only *appear* authentic because they were slavishly modeled on Homer's example.

This is not the place to debate the complicated question of the evidentiary value of the Cycle. Suffice it to say that arguments for an invariably late and derivative Cycle have been steadily eroding, and may now be collapsing under the influential arguments of Jonathan Burgess.[37] Drawing converging lines of argument, Burgess undermines all of the reasons why rigorous scholars have usually avoided drawing on the Cycle as evidence for Homeric poetry or society. Burgess shows that it is at least as likely that Homer and the rest of the Trojan Cycle were formed in basically the same epoch, and drew on an identical tradition of pre-Homeric storytelling. To allow Burgess to speak for himself: "There has been unnecessary hesitation in using the Cycle to explore the pre-Homeric tradition. I believe it presents a good picture of the material and tone of the tradition from which the Homeric poems are derived."[38]

The picture that emerges from the tatters of the Cycle is one of strife in foreground and background narratives: of murders, wars, raids, and abductions and rapes of women. For instance, in the *Cypria* – which narrates the origins of the Trojan War up to the dispute between Achilles and Agamemnon – we learn that the three Sidonian women Paris brings back along with Helen (*Iliad* 6.289–92) were taken in an opportunistic raid, not purchased. And Nestor tells another one of his didactic yarns – a familiar story about how Epopeus seduced the daughter of Lycurgus and had his city sacked as a result. Most interestingly we learn that the Trojan War was the second war over Helen. She had previously been abducted by the Athenian hero Theseus. Her two brothers, the Dioscuri, retrieved her, sacking Athens and abducting, in turn, Theseus' mother, Aithra. The brothers, we also discover, gain their own wives by abducting the daughters of Leucippus from Messene. That the story of the first war for Helen was known to Homer – and was thus an authentic part of the pre-Homeric tradition – is suggested by the fact that the same Aithra mentioned above, daughter of Pittheus, is Helen's serving woman in the *Iliad* (3.143–44).[39]

If we accept, along with Burgess, that the Cycle is a good guide to the tradition that produced Homer, the least we can say is that its narratives are consistent with the arguments of this chapter. And similar dynamics feature in early Greek myth – those narratives of heroes and gods that can be traced back at least as far as the early Archaic Age.[40] To read the earliest myths is to be numbed by catalogs of wars, conflicts over women, and the endless sexual depredations of gods and powerful men. Like the *Iliad* and *Odyssey*, the Cycle and early Greek myth suggest a world where intergroup and interpersonal conflicts – frequently over women – were pervasive.

THE RAPE OF TROY

When thou comest nigh unto a city to fight against it, then proclaim peace unto it . . . and if it will make no peace with thee, but will make war against thee, then thou shalt besiege it: And when the Lord thy God hath delivered it into thine hands, thou shalt smite every male thereof with the edge of the sword: But the women, and the little ones, and the cattle, and all that is in the city, even all the spoil thereof, shalt thou take unto thyself. (Deuteronomy 21)

The great war between Greeks and Trojans ends in the Rape of Troy: in massacre of men, mass rape and abduction of women, wholesale theft, and the city's incineration. These events are not the rare savageries of a particularly long and bitter war. Rather, when the Greeks sack a city the pattern is virtually always the same: city looted and destroyed, men killed, women carried off into concubinage and bondage (e.g., *Iliad* 19.287–300; 6.414–27; *Odyssey* 14.262–65). The symbolic relationship between the toppling of citadels and the violation of women within is expressed in the words *kredemnon luesthai* (to loosen a veil), which can mean either to sack a city or to breach a woman's chastity.[41]

Troy's fall is the central event of the Homeric epics. I have dubbed this event the Rape of Troy partly to emphasize the incident's affinities with another incident of mass rape, mass murder, and mass theft: the Rape of Nanking, China. In a reign of terror lasting from December 1937 to March 1938, members of the Japanese imperial army brutally massacred tens of thousands of Chinese men and raped between 20,000 and 80,000 women. This parallel, drawn across almost 3,000 years, is meant to suggest that, while the rapes of Troy and Nanking entailed barbarism on epic scales, a similar dynamic has recurred throughout human history in conflicts featuring radically different types of societies.

A far from comprehensive list of countries that have been identified as loci of mass rapes conducted by military or paramilitary forces just in the twentieth century includes Belgium and Russia during World War I; Russia, Japan, Italy, Korea, China, the Philippines, and Germany during World War II; and in one or more conflicts, Afghanistan, Algeria, Argentina, Bangladesh, Brazil, Burma, Bosnia, Cambodia, Congo, Croatia, Cyprus, East Timor, El Salvador, Guatemala, Haiti, India, Indonesia, Kuwait, Kosovo, Liberia, Mozambique, Nicaragua, Peru, Pakistan, Rwanda, Serbia, Sierra Leone, Somalia, Turkey, Uganda, Vietnam, Zaire, and Zimbabwe.[42] And the list must be constantly updated. As I write, the world is in angst over mass murders and mass rapes of black Africans by Arab militias in Sudan's Western Darfur region.

There is no reason to believe that wartime rape was less common or brutal prior to the twentieth century. Most well-documented historical wars include examples of widespread military rape. For instance, mass rape is well documented in the wars between Jews and their enemies described in the Bible (e.g., Deuteronomy, 21; Isaiah, 13:16; Lamentations, 5:11; Zechariah, 14:2), in Anglo-Saxon and Chinese chronicles, in medieval European warfare, during the crusades, in Alexander's conquest of Persia, in Viking marauding, in the conquest of Rome by Alaric, in the petty wars of Ancient Greeks, and so on ad infinitum.[43]

Moreover, firm evidence indicates that the roots of mass rape extend deep into human prehistory.[44] The words of Ongka, a big man of the Kawelka people of Papua, New Guinea, are not exceptional in ethnographical accounts of prestate wars:

> When we fought in earnest, with lethal weapons, we went to the help of our friends also. We burnt houses, slashed banana trees, tore the aprons off women and raped them, axed big pigs, broke down fences; we did everything. We carried on until the place was empty of resources . . . When we left our women behind and went out to fight, they were in danger. Men came to find them, chasing them down to the edges of streams until they seized hold of them, especially if their bodies were good to look at. Twenty men might lay hold of the same woman, pulling her around for a day and night and then letting her go.[45]

In fact, the promise of sexual access to out-group women has often been identified by anthropologists, ethnographers, and native informants[46] as a primary instigator of conflict in prestate societies.

Evolutionary theorists have recently debated the origins of sexually coercive behavior in humans and other animals. In their controversial book, *A natural history of rape* (2000), Randy Thornhill and Craig Palmer argue that strictly socio-cultural explanations for rape, including wartime rape, are inadequate.[47] Moreover, they array a case, based on evolutionary theory, rape statistics (especially the fact that the great majority of rapes target women at the ages of peak fertility), and comparison with other species where sexual coercion is common (including non-human apes and other primates), that sexual desire is a common motivation for human rape and that this desire ultimately traces back to the evolved sexual psychology of human males.

Thornhill and Palmer's argument is *not* that men are necessarily adapted to commit rape in certain contexts. While they do tentatively advance the theory that men may possess biological adaptations that are specifically designed to promote rape in certain cost-benefit environments, they place equal stress on the possibility that rape is simply a side effect (or by-product) of adaptations for consensual sexual activity. For example, the abdominal clamp of the scorpion-fly is the classic example of a rape-specific adaptation. It appears to exist for one reason only: to restrain unwilling females long enough to inseminate them. In orangutans – where about one third of matings are coerced – males may also be specifically designed to rape. Males come in two distinctive morphs, a larger sort that competes for willing females, and a smaller sort that is more apt to mate coercively (their smaller size helps them pursue females through the trees and helps them avoid conflicts with the large males).[48] However, in other species where rape is known – like dolphins, certain sharks, or gang-raping Mallard ducks – the evidence for rape-specific adaptation is less secure.[49] Coercive sexual behavior may be an accidental by-product of adaptations for consensual sexual behavior. The most obvious example of this type of by-product is represented in coerced *inter*-species matings among some marine mammals.[50] Since pregnancy cannot result from rape between species, "such acts clearly constitute side effects, probably a by-product of the low threshold of male sexual arousal that is calibrated to ensure that opportunities with potential mates are not missed."[51]

The main value of evolutionary exploration of rape is not, therefore, to provide a final answer to the vexed question of whether or not men possess psychological adaptations that are designed for roughly the same purpose as the scorpion fly's abdominal clamp. Tests that can distinguish clearly between the two biological theories of rape – adaptation and by-product – have yet to be devised. (It should be pointed out, however, that most evolutionists who have written on this issue – including *Natural history*'s co-author Craig Palmer – provisionally favor the by-product explanation.) Rather, the most immediate value of evolutionary explorations of rape has been to raise formidable challenges to "anything but sex" theories of rape's motivations.

Before moving on to discuss other aspects of Homeric conflict, I must make a related point about raiding for women as depicted in Homer. In arguing that Homeric warriors are motivated to raid partly to gain sexual access to out-group women, I confront a powerful social science orthodoxy which says that, for all the multiple and complicated motives rapists may possess, rape and other forms of sexual coercion cannot be "about sex."

This orthodoxy, which now possesses all the rigidity of dogma, has recently and firmly entrenched itself in the study of wartime rape. In the last ten to fifteen years, in the wake of mass rapes in Bosnia-Herzegovina, Rwanda, Kosovo, and other places, scholars and activists have worked hard to document, explain, and seek solutions for the phenomenon. Contributors to this literature agree almost uniformly that, while rape generally, and wartime rape specifically, may emerge from a plurality of causes, sexual desire is rarely (if ever) a significant motivating force. Rather, fighters rape to vent their hatred for women and to lord power over them; they rape to emasculate and humiliate enemy men; they rape as a strategy to demoralize the enemy; and they rape in service of genocide – in order to block a people's ability to replenish itself through sexual reproduction.[52] To the extent that a biological component is acknowledged, most writers follow Susan Brownmiller's dismissive argument that rape is "biological" only in the sense that an "accident of biology" (male size and strength and the nature of human sex organs) gave males the "structural capacity" to rape and females the "structural vulnerability" to be raped.[53]

As I have argued in another forum, "not sex" theories of wartime rape cannot parsimoniously account for all of the anthropological and historical evidence.[54] Each of the dominant "not sex" theories fails on the grounds of theory–data fit or parsimony. Since rape is seen as the result of specific socialization practices particular to specific types of societies, feminist rape theory generates the expectation that rape in the context of war (and peace) should only prevail in a limited subset of societies.[55] It doesn't: rape and its proscription are cross-culturally universal.[56] The attractive and currently dominant "strategic rape theory," which suggests that rape is a tactic executed by soldiers in service of a larger military strategy, also fails as a generalizable theory: there is (1) little evidence for it and (2) at least as much evidence that rape by soldiers can severely compromise strategic objectives.*

More to the point, theories that dismiss sexual desire as a motive for wartime rape do not account for what we see in Homer. While Homer depicts none of the strong-arm rapes that are the constant subject of Greek mythology, his warriors are almost all serial rapists. Before Briseis is possessed by Achilles, all of her protectors are slain in a single day – her father, her three brothers, and her husband (the last by Achilles himself). It is difficult to see her congress with Achilles (at least initially) as consensual, despite the emotional ambiguity Homer layers into their relationship. The same goes for all of the master's female slaves, who would have had little space to evade amorous advances.[57] There is no indication in Greek mythology that rape is fueled by anything but the desire for sexual gratification. In the myths, rape usually occurs when a woman – always young and beautiful, usually steadfastly virtuous – awakens, but will not willingly gratify, the lust of a powerful god or man.[58] Rape, along with various forms of trickery, is presented as a way of having intercourse with an unwilling woman, very often after non-coercive strategies

* Strategic rape theory is based on the many disastrous consequences that mass rape has on enemy populations. However, supporters of strategic rape theory may be confusing the *consequences* of wartime rape with the *motives*. Just because these consequences may include demoralized populaces or fractured families does not mean that these were the reasons the rapes were perpetrated in the first place. Moreover, strategic rape theory overlooks evidence from conflicts where widespread rape proved strategically disastrous. For more detailed arguments and references see Gottschall 2004.

have failed. Similarly, there is little indication in Homer that warriors couple with captured women for any reason but sexual gratification. For instance, as commentators have been demonstrating for generations now, the Homeric epics are largely free of the misogynous taint we see in Hesiod and subsequent Greek literature; there is no evidence that they rape in order to vent their contempt for women.

I do not wish to suggest that rape in war or peace is monocausal. Greeks warriors may rape for multiple reasons. In fact, that the Greeks rape partly for revenge against the Trojan men is at least implied in Nestor's pronouncement that each man should rape a Trojan woman in requital for his sufferings over Helen.* Thus, while there may be a sense in which female bodies serve as another type of battlefield upon which men hash out their disputes, and while there may be a sense in which raping enemy women is "the ultimate insult,"[59] the clearly prevailing sense is that all forms of sexual coercion depicted in Greek epic and mythology are mainly motivated by simple sexual desire.

* But we should hesitate before declaring the generality of a revenge motive. The majority of Greek "wartime" rapes would have occurred in the context or aftermath of raids. While some raids are carried out in pursuit of vengeance for past attacks (e.g., the Cattle Raid of Nestor, *Iliad* 11.669–761), in other cases there is no evidence that the raids – frequently targeting strangers – were motivated by animus of any sort, and much evidence that they were motivated by the simple desire for gain (see for instance, the series of raids carried out by the son of Castor in the *Odyssey*, the twenty-three raids led by Achilles in the *Iliad*, and the livestock raids planned by Odysseus at the end of the *Odyssey*).

CHAPTER 5

Status warriors

In Book 19 of the *Iliad* Trojans and Greeks agree on a short truce to bury and mourn their dead. Achilles organizes splendid funeral games for fallen Patroclus. The best athletes will compete in archery, combat sparring, wrestling, foot racing, boxing, and charioteering, and Achilles will provide great prizes for the victors: fine women, horses, and precious wrought metals. The chariot race is the premier contest; the winner takes away, in addition to a gorgeous slave woman and a beautiful tripod, the respect and envy of the other men. The racers muster and set off, driving their horses far across the plain before circling back. Men lacking driving skills or fast horses stand and watch. As the chariots come back into view Idomeneus joyfully calls out that Diomedes is winning. Squinting through the billowing dust the lesser Ajax noisily disagrees: he insults the older man, suggesting that his eyesight has dulled with age; he calls him a notorious loud-mouth and blusterer; and he announces that Eumelus, not Diomedes, is winning. Idomeneus responds with cutting insults of his own, and Achilles must intercede before the contention over eyesight escalates beyond control (*Iliad* 23.469–98).

The epics teem with like incidents, where trivial disagreements and perceived slights fuel fast escalations to the brink of serious violence. In fact, this dispute is only the first of three potentially serious conflicts over the outcome of the chariot race. In the second dispute, Antilochus bridles against Achilles' attempt to give his prize, a pregnant mare, to Eumelus, threatening to fight any man who attempts to seize her; and then Menelaus harshly challenges Antilochus over his dirty racing tactics. Elsewhere in the epics there are copious references to men who have murdered rivals, and have been forced to leave home to escape the vengeance of brothers and fathers. For example, good-hearted

Patroclus absconded from his homeland after he killed a man during a dispute over a game of knucklebones (a game similar to dice) (*Iliad* 23.84–88). On another occasion, Telemachus warns how quickly revelry among young men, especially when they are lubricated by wine, can turn hostile, escalating from exchange of words to exchange of slashing bronze (*Odyssey* 16.291–94). Even relationships between close comrades are tinged with the omnipresent possibility that some small dispute will rapidly become a large and dangerous one. When one of Odysseus' comrades – a kinsman – blames him for the Cyclops debacle, other shipmates must lay hold of Odysseus to keep him from killing the man (*Odyssey* 10.438–41).

These and other incidents justify van Wees' conclusion that "touchiness" is the most distinctive trait of the Homeric character.[1] Homeric men are socialized to strive hard for altitude in the dominance hierarchy; male behavior is governed by the dictum "always be the best and superior to others." As a result, the Homeric warrior evinces "a prickly sensitivity to what he regards as a lack of respect on the part of others, an irrepressible rage against any insult to his standing."[2]

According to van Wees, rivalry for social prestige is the main driving force of all Homeric conflict. Homeric men, in van Wees's view, have bottomless desires for social status and almost perfect intolerance for anything or anyone they perceive as diminishing that status. For van Wees, status rivalry is not only the root cause of interpersonal conflicts in the epics, like the fight over Briseis or the disputes over the chariot race; it is also the ultimate cause of conflicts between Homeric communities: "I would argue that violent competition for status within the community causes men to make private predatory expeditions abroad, and causes public wars."[3] Men who distinguish themselves in war, piracy, and raiding are the highest-status individuals in Homeric towns. Van Wees' conception of the root causes of Homeric conflict is clearly summed up in the title of his sterling book, *Status warriors* (1992). At the deepest level, Homeric men argue, strive, fight, and kill in order to gain favored access to the limited reservoir of community social prestige.

Van Wees is an esteemed Homerist, and the abundantly supported thesis of *Status Warriors* is widely considered credible and cogent. For my part, however, I find it difficult to define a single main cause of Homeric conflict – at least at the proximate level. At the ultimate

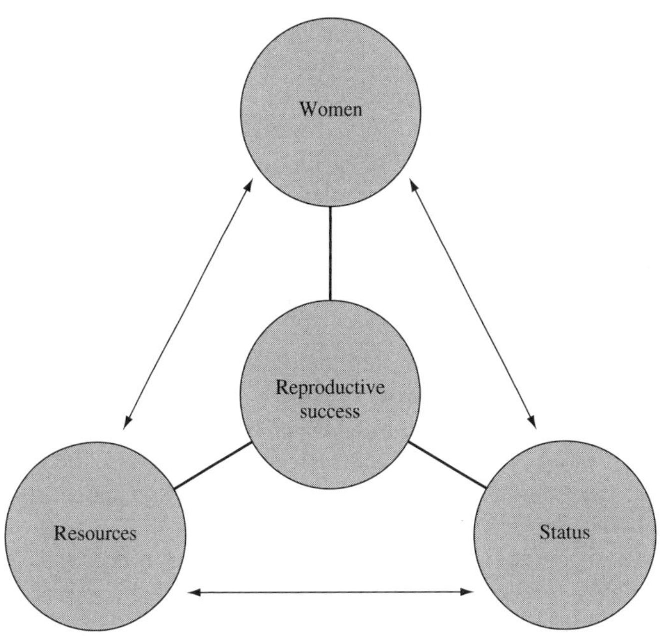

Figure 1. Non-hierarchical relationship among the three main, proximate categories of competition, all feeding into the ultimate goal of enhanced reproductive success.

level, I suggest that the motives of Homeric peoples – like all people everywhere – have been shaped by natural selection to promote relative reproductive success. From a biological perspective, the pursuit of high social status is a proximate means to the ultimate end of higher reproductive success. At the proximate level, subordinating Homeric competition for material resources and women to competition for social status seems to overlook the complex interrelationships among all three. Status is desired largely because it helps to determine one's share of communal resources; resources, in turn, are desired largely because wealth is a reliable route to high social status; social status and resources are desired, in part, because rich, high-status men enjoy privileged access to women, both slave concubines and legitimate wives; and the number and quality of women a man possesses is itself a road to higher status among men and greater prosperity due to the slaves' productivity (see Figure 1). Therefore, the *Iliad* and *Odyssey* demand that interpreters account for competition over resources, status, and women as major proximate motives for Homeric conflict, but they do not easily support the privileging of one motive over the others. This is illustrated in the variety of potential responses to the conflict over Briseis: is it a conflict over social status, over sex, or over a lifetime of productive labor? As discussed in the last chapter, scholars have tended to insist that it is one or the other, usually preferring the first explanation, whereas in reality it possesses elements of all three at once.

Van Wees exhaustively illustrates how competition for social status pervades all aspects of Homeric life, and plays a major instigating role in virtually all interpersonal and intergroup conflict. But, while this analysis provides satisfying explanations for many puzzles, it also leaves us with the jumbled pieces of a puzzle that is just as interesting and confusing: why would Homeric men compete so fiercely for status? How can acquiring something as intangible and fleeting as social status be worth the real risk of early death? Van Wees does not address this question. But one obvious possibility is that high-status men enjoy increased access to resources. Indeed, biologists *define* status (or rank) as "priority of access to resources in competitive situations."[4] But this only pushes the question back to another level: why should Homeric men be so willing to risk everything for resources – resources sought by Homeric men as much for showing off as for feeding their families?

The purpose of this chapter is to show that competition for status is, from an evolutionary perspective, a form of reproductive competition. Homeric men push seemingly trivial pursuits so far because what is really at stake is not, say, who has better eyesight or who cheated whom in a game of knucklebones, but who will be dominant and who subordinate – who will enjoy priority of access to *all* resources and who will not.

In 1989 the Dutch primatologist Frans de Waal published *Chimpanzee politics*, a groundbreaking book on the stunningly complex social lives of common chimpanzees. While de Waal was accused of anthropomorphizing his subjects, there can be little doubt that the word "politics" aptly describes the incessant, canny jockeying of chimpanzees for status within their social groups. De Waal's story, along with similar accounts by Jane Goodall and others, was replete with covert alliances and betrayals, estrangements and truces, social manipulations and machinations, and violent and bloodless coups. Fights were common, and to consolidate his position the alpha male Yeroen, along with an ally, once "murdered" an upstart rival. De Waal's explanation for the frenzied and unremitting struggle for social dominance is explicit in the subtitle of his book: *Power and sex among the apes.* Chimpanzees compete for dominance because it is a road to relative reproductive success while subdominance is a road to relative reproductive failure. While primatologists have done an increasingly thorough job of documenting this correlation in the female hierarchy,[5] these benefits are especially obvious in the male hierarchy. Not only do dominant males enjoy more total copulations, but they also monopolize an even higher proportion of copulations with estrous females of confirmed fertility. For instance, Yeroen was a partner in 75 percent of all copulations, and an even larger proportion of matings with the most desirable, mature females. Thanks to the relative simplicity of chimpanzee social life, it is easy for primatologists to see why males would compete so intensely over rank: the dominance hierarchy and the mating hierarchy are one and the same.

This relationship is not limited to chimpanzee groups, but is clearly evident across the primate order. And, far from being limited to primates, it is encountered across the animal kingdom. For those who study animal behavior there is simply no mystery as to why animals, especially the males, risk fierce competition for rank: higher-ranked individuals receive a larger share of precious, contested resources, including mating opportunities, than lower ranked individuals.

It would be stunning to find that the human situation was an exception, that social status was not reliably correlated with success in competition for resources, mates and, ultimately, higher reproductive success. And a great deal of evidence, gathered from diverse data streams shows that, indeed, we are not exceptional in this regard. As in other animal species the correlation clearly applies to human females,[6] but it applies with special force to males because of their greater variance in reproductive success.[7]

Human status rivalry received its classic exploration in Daly and Wilson's *Homicide* (1988), which sought to explain why the overwhelming majority of murderers and victims in the United States, Canada, and all around the world are male. Their analysis of homicides in American cities smacks familiarly of Homeric conflict. According to Daly and Wilson, most homicides in the urban regions they studied were the final results of "altercations of a relatively trivial origin." Like Homeric men fighting over knucklebones or acuity of eyesight, the participants in these "trivial altercations behave as though a great deal more is at issue than spare change or access to a pool table."[8] For Daly and Wilson, a large proportion of homicides are the "rare, fatal consequences of a ubiquitous competitive striving among men for status and respect. These social resources have come to be valued by the male psyche because of their positive fitness consequences."[9]

From this perspective the "touchiness" of Homeric men, their dangerous jostling for respect and prestige, seems less a puzzle that needs solving than another example of a well-established pattern in zoology and anthropology. As the anthropologist Azar Gat writes: "In traditional societies in particular, people were predisposed to go to great lengths in defense of their honor. The slightest offense could provoke violence . . . one's honor was a social commodity of vital significance, affecting both somatic and reproductive chances." He continues, "For this reason, humans were prepared to risk violence to gain and defend rank and esteem in the same way they were prepared to do so for subsistence goods, women, or kin. *In the final evolutionary analysis it all came to the same thing* [italics mine]."[10]

Homeric society seems to be one in which the correlation between status and mating hierarchies is particularly strong. This is most blatant in that high status men claim first access to the most and the best of the captured women. Thersites seethes at Agamemnon over the uneven allotment of all spoil, including captive women:

> Son of Atreus, what now do you find fault with and what do you need? Your huts are full of bronze, and many choice women are in your huts, which we Achaians give to you first of all, whenever we should take a city. Or do you still want gold which some man of the horse-taming Trojans shall bring from Troy as ransom for his son, which I or some other of the Achaians have led away and tied up? Or a young woman in order that you may mix with her in love and keep her apart for yourself? (*Iliad* 2.225–33)

While the poems are never again so explicit about the hierarchical distribution of women, we are certainly given the impression that all *basileis* leverage their positions to gain control of multiple women. For instance, Agamemnon was able to claim seven beautiful and skilled slave women just from conquered Lesbos and to promise Achilles the twenty most beautiful Trojan captives as a peace offering. Similarly Antilochus reminds Achilles of the many slave women gracing his compound, pointedly implying that he should not be chary about offering some of them up as consolation prizes in Patroclus' funeral games (*Iliad* 23.548–50). Even if exaggerated, the numbers of women involved in bearing Priam's sixty-two children, as well as the fifty slave women possessed by Odysseus and by Alcinous, also suggest a pattern whereby powerful men monopolize numbers of women.

But privileged access to women is only the most obvious sense in which the pursuit of high status is tantamount to the pursuit of high reproductive success. What of the pursuit of glory? Homeric warriors seek to accomplish deeds of military heroism partly to win immortal fame, and to assuage their terror of the oblivion of death. Consider Sarpedon's famous exhortation of Glaucus:

> O brother in arms, if escaping from this war we might always be ageless and immortal, I would not fight in the foremost nor send you into battle where men win glory. But now, since the countless fates of death are all around us, that mortals can neither escape nor avoid, let us go gain glory for ourselves or yield it to others. (*Iliad* 12.322–28)

However, in a less stirring preamble to these words, Sarpedon also suggests to Glaucus that heroic distinction has immense practical utility. In the war-torn Aegean, strong and valiant warriors are every society's most valuable resource, and they are handsomely rewarded for their risk-taking. Sarpedon says:

> Glaucus, why are we held in such honor in Lycia, with seats of honor, meats, and brimming cups, and all men look at us like we are gods? And why are we apportioned great lands along the banks of the Xanthus, rich in orchards and wheat-bearing fields? Therefore we must take our stand among the foremost Lycians and confront the raging battle, so that armored Lycians may say, "Not without fame are the leaders of Lycia, our chiefs who eat plump sheep and drink much-desired, honey-sweet wine. But their strength is good, since they battle alongside the foremost Lycians." (*Iliad* 12.310–21)

It may be argued that I am misreading this passage. After all, Sarpedon never directly answers the questions he poses, and Griffin is not alone in seeing here a primitive expression of *noblesse oblige*: the two chiefs must do something valiant in order to justify all that the community has *already* given them.[11] But I side with Donlan who sees "more than an implication in these words that should they fail in their duties they would no longer merit the honors they received."[12] In venturing out from the main throng of warriors, where all risk is evenly distributed, front-fighting chiefs take enormous risks. Only a small number of the leading warriors in the *Iliad* are *not* killed or wounded. It is difficult to imagine that they would continue to take such risks without strong, palpable incentives. This intuition would seem to be verified in Hector's stinging taunts of retreating Diomedes: "Diomedes, above all others the Danaans with swift horses paid honor to you with a seat of honor, meats and brimming cups. Now they will dishonor you, who are no better than a woman. Be gone cowardly puppet!" (*Iliad* 8.161–64). Hector's taunt announces what is only implicit in Sarpedon's exhortation: the behaviors of *basileis* justify their perquisites; if their behaviors change, so too can the perquisites. When Achilles withdraws from the fighting he does so partly in protest against the violation of this meritocratic principle: "A like portion has he who stays back, and he who wars his best, and in one honor are held the coward and the brave" (*Iliad* 9.318–19).

Readers have always had a tendency to emphasize the stirring part of Sarpedon's speech at the expense of the practical part. Considered as a whole, Sarpedon's words show that attaining copious glory has vast utility to men in their earthly lives. The warriors' insatiable need to hoard up more and more glory is at least as much about attaining the benefits of high status in earthly life as it is about being remembered by future generations.

Competing for vertical position in the status hierarchy is not the only way that Homeric men strive for limited resources. Homeric men also compete directly, consciously and intensely, over the resources themselves. As Moses Finley wrote, Homeric warriors are driven "by an almost overpowering accumulative instinct."[13] They are greedy for every type of material possession: precious metals, cattle, sheep, racing horses, carefully wrought jewelry, armor, spears and swords, pots, bronze tripods, rare fabric, and so forth. They will do almost anything to get more: enter competitions, solicit or steal it from hosts, and unashamedly kill for it in the course of raiding and brigandage. They love to brag of their wealth to friends and foes, to display it in their homes for all to marvel at, and to ostentatiously give it away, both to show that they can and to cement bonds of friendship and obligation.

Resource competition is sometimes cited as the root cause of war in Homeric society.[14] Many commentators have agreed with Finley's conclusion that "wars and raids for booty were indistinguishable in the world of Odysseus."[15] But, as with competition for social status, the next question often remains unaddressed: why should Homeric men so desire wealth that they are willing to kill, and risk being killed, to acquire it? This question gains special interest when it is considered that the treasures they seek often lack the practical value that might justify the risk.

THE RAVENING BELLY

> But no man can hide his ravening belly, a baneful curse that gives many evils to men. All for the sake of the belly we prepare well-benched ships for the barren sea, carrying evil to hostile men. (Odysseus, *Odyssey* 17.286–89)

Homeric-era Greeks would not have been strangers to hunger or even famine. The Spartan King Demaratus said that "Greece has always had poverty as her companion," and Thomas Gallant's ecological study describes the "highly precarious position of the Ancient Greek peasantry. With alarming regularity they would have found themselves running short of food in the face of climatically induced shortfalls in production."[16] Reflecting this precarious condition, Hesiod defines happiness in terms of fat crops and misery in terms of thin crops.[17] In times of grumbling bellies it is easy to see why men would take grave risks to procure the necessities to preserve their lives and those of their families. While this fact is virtually invisible in the *Iliad*, the *Odyssey* recurrently suggests that Homeric populations regularly knew hunger. Odysseus informs us of the unique misery of hunger, and of the desperate risks a man will take, the humiliation he will endure, just to silence the "accursed" (*oulomenos*), "hated" (*stugeros*) belly (e.g., *Odyssey* 7.215–21; 15.344–45; 17.473–74). While

Odysseus is in an especially vulnerable position – blown all around the world, dependent on the kindness of strangers – his words seem to convey deep, proverbial wisdom. Partly as a result of the ever-present threat of hunger, capturing the enemy's livestock is a prime goal of all Homeric raids. Other items of clear practical utility are also taken: foodstuffs, weapons, metals, cauldrons, fabrics, wines, hides, and other materials that can be used, directly or indirectly, to quiet hungry bellies. These facts have led some prominent commentators, like Finley, to argue that communities are finally battling for "essential supplies" like food and metals.[18] Finley's position receives eloquent support from the epigraph to this section, where Odysseus states that it is the most basic animal need, the need to silence the insatiable belly, which drives men to wage war. When resources are scarce, some must suffer and die so that others may survive and thrive.

There is at least as much emphasis, however, on the acquisition of prestige wealth as on the acquisition of practical wealth. Most of the loot the Greeks covet has both practical and prestige value: cooking tripods fashioned of pure bronze, armor inlaid with delicate gold and silver, splendidly embroidered fabrics, and horses that were expensive to maintain but provided limited practical labor. This booty is displayed in homes to advertise wealth and the warrior prowess that helped win it. Displays of bloodied spoils, stripped from the corpses of fallen enemies, are particularly valuable for advertising, in the most visceral way, a warrior's power and courage: every battered breastplate and helmet represent a man bested in mortal combat.* Finally, the displays are also useful for announcing that one has an extensive network of powerful friends; a significant portion of the displayed

* Successfully stripping armor may serve as something like a tangible count of "coup." Among Native American tribes coup was a display of conspicuous, reckless bravery in battle that brought the warrior great prestige. In Homer, stripping a foe's armor may serve a similar function: it can bring enormous glory largely *because* it is one of the most reckless feats a warrior can attempt. As numerous passages indicate, the most important defensive tactic on the battlefield is simple vigilance: warriors are always nervously scanning enemy ranks for charging foes and streaking missiles. When stripping armor a man must usually venture into the main killing zone separating the throngs of warriors; he must divert his eyes from the enemy, stoop over, and occupy his hands, all the while experiencing viciously concentrated attacks from the dead man's comrades. Many men lose their lives in the effort. Those who survive win great glory and a tangible proof of outstanding courage.

wealth is made up of gifts, given as symbols of friendship and mutual obligation.

In this light, even the capture of horses and herd animals is complicated, being as much about the conspicuous display of wealth as it is about the valuable fat, protein, labor, and hides that the animals will provide. Henry Fielding memorably called the *Odyssey* the "eatingest epic" in the world, for all the elaborate feasting that occurs as men barbecue on the seashore or entertain guests. The *Odyssey* sometimes feels like a long saga of men eating and drinking, occasionally enlivened with plot advances. In these episodes great heaps of precious meats are always consumed. *Basileis* hoard up stores of animal wealth far in excess of the physical needs of their households: even after adjusting for epic inflation, Odysseus' stock of 860 pigs, tended full-time by three servants, still suggests more pork than his family could consume in a lifetime, and this says nothing of his large herds of sheep and cattle. The animals are collected largely for the purpose of giving them away at lavish feasts and ceremonies, where valuable fatted hogs and cattle are slaughtered with abandon. Such feasts are reminiscent of the moka ceremonies of Highland New Guinea, or the potlatches of American Indians of the Northwest coast, where men hoarded up wealth for the express purpose of giving it away in exchange for social capital.

In this vein, some Homeric scholars have argued that gaining wealth is essential for acquiring and maintaining political power. In this model, Homeric chiefs wage aggressive war largely in hopes of acquiring loot, which can then be distributed to friends and retainers, thus enhancing power and prestige within the community.[19] The endlessly circular pattern of Homeric warfare is seen as a side effect of the fact that *basileis* maintain power through gift-giving; when stores are exhausted a chief must procure more loot or risk losing the allegiance of supporters.

In sum, intense Homeric competition for material goods is partly instigated by the pursuit of status and power. This is not to suggest that gaining resources is a proximate means to the ultimate goal of gaining social status. The relationship between resource and status competition is circular not linear: resources are sought in large part because they confer status, but status is sought in large part because it confers resources. Yet social and material resources are both pursued, in the final analysis, because they enhance reproductive success. An especially direct illustration of this principle is presented in the next section.

MARRIAGE

> In the course of every love affair the man has constantly to give small presents to the woman. To the natives the need of one-sided payments is self-evident. This custom implies that sexual intercourse, even where there is mutual attachment, is a service rendered by the female to the male . . . One would expect the sexual relation to be regarded as an exchange of services itself reciprocal. But custom . . . decrees that it is a service from women to men, and men have to pay. (Bronislaw Malinowski, *The Sexual Life of Savages in North-Western Melanesia*)[20]

When scholars tally the many challenges of constructing historically faithful portraits of Homeric society, they are sure to mention the confusion concerning marriage customs in the *Odyssey*. The poem contains unmistakable references to the institution of bride price (in which a man takes a bride only after a transfer of wealth to her family) as well as apparent references to the institution of dowry (in which the transfer of wealth flows in the opposite direction). Some societies do conditionally feature bride price and dowry at the same time. For instance, in India high-status families were forced to dower daughters while poor families could demand payment for theirs, and Moses Finley pointed out that similar customs existed in contemporary Greek villages.[21] However, bride price and dowry ostensibly coexist in the same social stratum of Homeric society. This has led some commentators to argue (1) that this coexistence is inconsistent with historical and anthropological precedents; (2) that this is some of the most powerful evidence of historically distinct layers in the poems; and (3) that the poems are therefore unhistorical conflations with little value for reconstructing any era of ancient history.[22] Ian Morris has, however, sharply challenged this argument, systematically examining every reference to dowry, and arguing that the case ". . . for the inconsistency of the marriage practices of the Homeric *aristoi* [elites] is very weak."[23] Morris shows that most of the references to dowry are based on debatable or misleading translations, and that the few unequivocal references are clearly exceptions to the general rule of bride price. Each of the three unequivocal references to dowry occurs when a *basileus* attempts to cement ties with a particularly strong, and therefore particularly desirable, son-in-law (*Iliad* 6.192–95, 9.146–48; *Odyssey* 7.134).

In actual fact, Homeric marriage customs are quite coherent. The *Iliad*, and especially the more romantic *Odyssey*, convey the message that men who would marry must first be able to afford a substantial transfer of resources to the potential bride and her family – the more desirable the bride, the more substantial the transfer. Unmarried young women are pragmatically described as "earners of oxen" (*Iliad* 18.593). In Homeric society, as with the Trobrianders, the "sexual relation" is regarded as something for which "men have to pay." For instance, Hephaestus earns the right to Aphrodite's hand by paying bride price to her father (Zeus), and Ares succeeds in seducing her partly by giving her "many gifts" (*Odyssey* 8.269) – at which point Hephaestus furiously demands that Zeus refund his bride price (*Odyssey* 8.317–20). Moreover, the detailed depiction of the wooing of Penelope drives home the message that competing for a wife and competing for resources often comes to *exactly the same thing*: the successful wooer is usually the man who is able to offer most. Of the wicked suitors' many affronts, one of the worst is their failure to abide by this custom. Penelope rails at them:

> Your way is not the customary way of suitors before now, suitors locked in strife over a goodly woman, a wealthy man's daughter. They bring cattle and plump sheep, a feast for the friends of the bride, and they give her splendid gifts, they do not devour another's goods without recompense. (*Odyssey* 18.274–80)

Later, Penelope frets about whether to continue her vigil for Odysseus or whether she should finally give in "to whoever is the best of the Achaians who woos me in the halls, he who offers countless gifts" (19.528–29). And, despite the suitors' bad behavior, they know that the man offering most will ultimately win Penelope's hand. Antinous tells his fellow suitors, "But let each man from his own home woo her and seek to win her with gifts. Then she can marry the one who gives most, the one fated to be her husband" (*Odyssey* 16.390–92; see also 15.16–18). These references are not anomalous; they are thickly strewn through the *Odyssey*. The competition for Penelope, as with competitions for other famous beauties mentioned in the poems (e.g., *Iliad* 9.553–64; *Odyssey* 11.288–97), symbolizes the fundamental dynamic of the Homeric reproductive economy: men compete for resources to trade for access to scarce and therefore precious female reproductive capacity.

The sense in which male competition for resources stands as an important means of competing for mates is not limited to Homeric society, but is the dominant pattern across cultures and, indeed, throughout the animal kingdom.[24] Writing in *Nature*, Kirkpatrick and Ryan report: "Abundant data shows that when males provide a nest site, food, or care for the young, females prefer mates who provide resources that enhance female fecundity."[25] Similarly, Homeric females are able to demand an infusion of resources in exchange for sexual access. This may initially outrage feminist sensibilities (although it comes close to the radical feminist axiom that all sex is prostitution). But this fact should neither surprise nor disturb us. For women, pregnancy and child rearing have always been terribly expensive: months of internal gestation, all the dangers of childbirth, months or years of lactation, and long years of intensive rearing effort. On the other hand, reproduction can be very cheap for men if they choose not to invest in their offspring. Demanding some form of up-front investment is a method that women and their families have developed to ensure that men bear a fairer share of the staggering costs of producing human life. Even in modern, western societies where the institution of bride price has died out, women still express clear preferences for wealthy, high-status men; across cultures women place a higher premium on the wealth and social status of potential mates than do males.[26] There is no great mystery as to why this should be. Resources are vital to women's reproductive success too.[27]

The mating preferences of Homeric women were *not* determined exclusively by practical, material considerations. As anyone who has read the epics can attest, there is much more to it than that. A more nuanced description of these matters will be presented in Chapter Six.

PRUDENT BOLDNESS

I have argued that Homeric conflict flows from three main, proximate sources – competition for women, social prestige, and wealth – all feeding into the ultimate goal of enhancing reproductive success. While Homeric men are fully conscious of their desires for women, status, and wealth, they have no consciousness of the ultimate, evolutionary reasons for these desires. Evolution does not "convince" organisms to pursue their reproductive interests by making them fully aware of genetic costs and benefits; rather it does so by designing organisms to pursue outcomes, such as high status, desirable mates, and healthy offspring, that amount to the same thing. While Odysseus, Hector, and all the rest know nothing about genes or evolutionary theory, they still compete for the best mates, hope for children to carry on their lines, tirelessly promote and defend the welfare of their families, and understand that attaining these goals depends in great part on the acquirement of riches, social and material; they are consumed by the basic challenges of survival and reproduction. But if this is true of humans generally, and if it is true of the world reflected in the epics, what do we make of the fact that so many Homeric warriors die young?

Consider the story of Iphidamas, reared lovingly to young manhood in the fertile land of Thrace:

> But when he reached the measure of splendid youth, his grandfather tried to hold him back, gave him a daughter to marry. But straight from the bridal chamber marched the groom when he heard report of the Achaian landing, and twelve beaked ships followed him ... And he came now face-to-face against Agamemnon, son of Atreus ... Iphidamas stabbed at the belt beneath the breastplate, he leaned into it, trusting his heavy hand. But he did not penetrate the shining belt. Long before that the point, smashing against the metal, bent back like lead. And then wide-ruling Agamemnon grabbed the spear in his hand and dragged it eagerly toward him like a lion and, pulling it from Iphidamas' hand, he struck his neck with a sword and loosed his limbs. And there he fell and slept the sleep of the bronze, pitiful man, far from his wedded wife, helping his people, far from his bride of whom he had known no joy, though he gave much to win her: first, he gave 100 cattle and then he promised 1,000 goats and sheep, which were herded for him in huge flocks. And now the son of Atreus stripped him and walked back to the thronging Achaians bearing the splendid gear. (*Iliad* 11.225–47)

This is one of several pathetic *Iliad* vignettes featuring the desperate attempts of young men, green at war, to win military distinction (see also *Iliad*, 11.328–35; 13.170–81; 17.33–60). These men are usually chopped down in the bloom of young life by adversaries who are, like Agamemnon, older, stronger, more careful, and more vicious. For men like Iphidamas, along with many hundreds of others who die in the epics, all competitive efforts seem to lead not to the evolutionary goal of genetic perpetuation but to genetic oblivion.

This is a critical problem. And it applies not only to my treatment of Homer, but to the larger claim of this book, that male conflict boils down to pitched reproductive striving. The problem is well illustrated by a Yanomamö shaman's description of the fate of brave warriors: "Most of the warriors ran when they saw how easily and quickly their best fighters were clubbed down. But brave warriors never run. That's why they don't live to be old men. All the brave warriors of Forgetful Village were clubbed until they staggered and fell to the ground."[28] How can it be claimed that male conflict is an end result of reproductive striving when such competition, especially in warlike societies, is so apt to result in early death? Is not the male tendency toward competitive striving more accurately viewed as biologically maladaptive (in the sense that it militates against passing on genes) rather than biologically adaptive (in the sense that it aids in passing on genes)?

One attempt to grapple with roughly this problem was provided in the attempt by the great biologist and statistician Ronald Fisher (1890–1962) to make evolutionary sense of the phenomenon of heroic risk-taking that went beyond "prudent boldness," and entailed the likelihood of the hero's death. According to Fisher, "forms of definite imprudence" were valorized in "all societies known to us . . . who have existed in the barbaric condition."[29] How, he wondered, could the evolutionary process result in propensities for this type of heroism when it puts the hero at a profound survival disadvantage? Fisher hypothesized that heroic imprudence could serve the fitness interests of the hero if the genetic costs of early death were offset by the benefits "conferred by the prestige of the hero upon his kinsmen."[30] Thus his formulation is an early version of William Hamilton's inclusive fitness theory, which would eventually revolutionize behavioral biology.[31] Fisher speculated that the families of killed heroes bask in reflected glory and prestige, and that the genetic losses warriors suffer through early death might therefore be outweighed by the enhanced fitness of relatives.

When Fisher was devising this idea he was thinking not only of primitive societies, but of the "barbaric" worlds reflected in the Old

English and Homeric epics. And, in his support, there is evidence that Homeric men consider the "good death" to be one that confers everlasting glory on their names and sheds honor on their descendants, especially their sons. For instance, early in the *Odyssey*, Mentes laments the fact that Odysseus did not die on the Trojan plain where he would have been glorified by his comrades, winning his son "great fame in days to come" (*Odyssey* 24.30–34). Similarly, when Odysseus' fragile raft is dashed by the furious storms of Poseidon, he bewails that he is about to go to a watery, anonymous grave – a "wretched death" (*Odyssey* 5.306–12), cheated of a hero's end, a hero's funeral, and a hero's glory (see also *Odyssey* 24.32–34; *Iliad* 21.278–84). Homer's is a world where social prestige and fame are heritable: warriors eke great social mileage from the grandest branches of their family trees and brag tirelessly about the great deeds of their ancestors. While gaining immortal glory is a desirable palliative to Homeric mortality fears,[32] it also carries more practical benefits, one of which is increased social capital for the hero's kin.

For all of these potential benefits, however, heroes are not, contrary to common assumptions, *in search of* "the good death." Fathers do their sons far more good alive than dead; even the sons of great heroes face potentially dire hardships when they lose their fathers. For instance, one potential fate of the soon to be fatherless son of Hector, Astyanax, is that men will steal his land, family allies will ostracize him, and he will be driven from feasts with fists and insults (*Iliad* 22.482–507). Another potential fate – the one that comes to fruition – is that he will be murdered by bloodlusting Greeks (*Iliad* 24.725–34). In Homer, no one wants to become a martyred hero. The desire for the good death is always conditional: *if* I must die (and *only* if), let me die gloriously. As an example, when faced with near-certain death at the hands of Achilles, Hector says, "Now my fate is upon me. Not without struggle let me die and not without glory, but let me first do a great act so that men still to come will hear of it" (*Iliad* 22.303–05; see also 12.321–28). Hector decides to seek a glorious death only after he has exhausted his other options – including the sheer ignominy of terrified flight in full view of his parents and the rest of the Trojan community.

Despite constantly courting death, both on the battlefield and in interpersonal brinkmanship, none of the warriors is planning to, or hoping to, die gloriously. Rather they are planning on performing brave feats in combat and earning the right to bask in the glory and the spoils. I would argue that, aside from a relatively few examples to the contrary, like the callow young men mentioned above, risk-taking rarely goes beyond the level of "prudent boldness." The best warriors occasionally fight in a reckless, headlong fashion, especially during the narratives of individual battle exploits known as *aristeiai*, but these are men who are aware of their martial superiority, and who usually have the explicit assurance of divine support. When the tide of the battle begins to turn against them, even great men consistently flee. As van Wees has argued – exhaustively, quantitatively, and I would almost say definitively – heroic norms actually make relatively modest demands on Homeric warriors.[33] For instance, heroic norms do not dictate that a man fight against superior numbers or stronger opponents and they do not forbid retreat. Van Wees concludes, "the hero, even at his wildest, is a sane and unadventurous sort of berserker."[34] In short, van Wees shows that Homer's warriors are generally not expected to be "Heroes"; they are expected to be prudently bold.

The internal monologues of several warriors show them performing a conscious calculus, weighing the costs and benefits of the safe path and the dangerous path. Typically the question is this: which alternative is more costly, shunning risk and therefore sacrificing reputation, or taking the risk to protect and enhance reputation? Homer shows us warriors weighing this question and coming to different conclusions based on their circumstances. For instance, the overmatched Hector initially decides to fight Achilles because the blow to his social prestige as the bulwark of Troy will be too high if he hides inside the walls like a coward (*Iliad* 22.99–110; see also 11.477–86; 21.544–70). On the other hand, earlier in the poem, Menelaus weighs the costs and benefits of fighting the inspired Hector and decides that the social costs of retreat are acceptable (*Iliad* 12.91–101).

In sum, *warriors take risks not only for positive rewards but also to avoid the social consequences of failing to take the risk.* Greek warriors hold one another to high standards and tirelessly strive to ensure that every man shares the grave risks of combat. They accomplish this by sharp and incessant goading, and by their acid contempt for the slightest whiff of cowardice. Every page of the *Iliad*'s "battle books" exhibits this continuous and crushing social pressure to fight bravely.

And the pressure is not only social, it is eminently physical. Sometimes men are forced to fight literally at spear point, with the known shirkers arrayed in front of stalwart warriors (4.299–300). On a handful of occasions Greek and Trojan chiefs go even further, darkly threatening to kill anyone who would hang back from the front (e.g., 2.391–93). Despite the constant flow of threats, insults, harangues, and pep talks, however, almost all of the great men in the *Iliad* are shown, often on more than one occasion, running from a fight at top speed, terrified.

Thus a Homeric man will generally not choose death over dishonor.[35] The massive apparatus of social pressure necessary to convince men to take risks suggests that battle shirking was a real problem, and that the natural tendency was not to throw oneself headlong into the melee but to hang back a little and take care.

But here is the vital point. Never taking risks, never demonstrating at least "prudent boldness," is not a path available to a Homeric man – not unless he can resign himself to occupying the bottom rung of the male social hierarchy, to experiencing the contempt of his peers, the disappointment of his kin network, and the diminishment of familial standing. The great chiefs – front-fighters all – owe their standing, and the privileges that come with it, largely to the fact that they shoulder great risks in combat. One wonders why Sarpedon or Iphidamas would risk all they have – young wives, children (in Sarpedon's case), prized land, wealth, and happiness – in military adventures. But, as argued above, this overlooks the point that *basileis* enjoy these benefits in large part *because* they bear the brunt of combat.

What is more, the battle shirker will also have to live with the disdain of women, who demand and respect courage in men (see next chapter). From an evolutionary perspective, this all describes a fate worse than death. A Homeric man who was not at least prudently bold would have little hope of success in intense reproductive competition in which social status is necessary for gaining mates and providing for children. Despite the risks of the different forms of reproductive competition – from status jockeying to war – Greek men accept these risks because they have to: in the Aegean warrior milieu, the greatest risk to a man's reputation, and thus to his fitness interests, was not taking a risk.

CHAPTER 6

Homeric women: re-imagining the fitness landscape

This book is about men – about their battles, real and ritualized, for dominance, wealth, women and, ultimately, for reproductive success. This emphasis is almost inevitable owing to the subject matter of Homeric poetry: men – men competing, venturing, arguing, killing, and being killed. The women in Homer's poetry, and this book, play mostly supporting roles or appear as mere extras; even Penelope is only the third most important character in the *Odyssey*, and no female character is so prominent in the *Iliad*. The women featured so far in this discussion have, with some exceptions, behaved passively. They have waited to be acted upon by men who hash out rights to them in exuberant competitions: men compete for women in contests, in combat, and by offering the biggest bride prices and the brightest wooing gifts. But were Homeric women really so passive, really so content to wait until "taken" by victorious men?

No. While women's strategies for surviving and reproducing are different from men's – most strikingly in that they are less likely to entail violent aggression – they are no less complex, effective, or potentially Machiavellian.[1] While mammalian biology dictates that women vary less in reproductive success than do men (see above, Chapter Three), there is still substantial variance. Thus women have much incentive to compete – for status, for the best mates, and for access to resources to provision their young. Women who were easy dupes for male exploitation could never pass on genes as successfully as women equipped to avoid exploitation, and even to act as exploiters themselves, in pursuit of their own goals. As Sarah Hrdy has written, the passive, compliant, apolitical, exclusively nurturing woman of the stereotypes surely never evolved.[2]

The Homeric epics, emerging from a muscular patriarchal culture, were composed by a man (or men, depending on how you answer the Homeric question), mainly about men, and largely for men.[3] Women are pushed to the poetic margins. For instance, since Homer rarely allows us to glimpse interactions among women, we have the vaguest sense of how and under what conditions they would have competed and cooperated with one another. However, women are not pushed entirely from his page. In Homer we see rich women and slaves, mothers and daughters, maidens and crones, portraits of female propriety and of wantonness; we see women in times of peace and peril, we see them bustle through their daily routines, and we see them confront extraordinary situations.

This chapter describes some of the ways Homeric women actively pursue their fitness interests. This may seem like a digression in a book on the competitive reproductive strategies of Homeric men but, for the following reason, it is not: to a marked degree, the dangerous competitiveness of Homeric men shapes the reproductive strategies of Homeric women, and the strategies of the women amply contribute, in turn, to the competitiveness of the men.

In order to assess female strategies as depicted in Homer, and how they influence male competitiveness, we must first accomplish a massive shift in perspective. We must break away from the position of predominant identification with men, which the poems force on most male and female readers alike, and try to re-imagine Homer's world from a female standpoint. Since this book analyzes the epics not only as works of literary art, but also as precious time-capsules reflecting Greek life sometime around the eighth century BC, we must also appreciate that Homer's women have passed through two distorting prisms: that of a vigorously male perspective and that of epic exaggeration and romanticization. However, the assumption of this chapter is congruent with those underlying the rest of the book: drawing on multiple streams of evidence we can "see through" the distortions to produce an anthropologically coherent reconstruction of some aspects of the lives of Homeric women.

The fitness landscape, as I am employing the term,* can be envisioned as a foreboding and inhospitable expanse, pocked with hazards, traced by deep canyons, fast rivers, and jagged mountains. On the horizon, for the person hearty enough to swim the rapids, scale the cliffs, and find and negotiate the snowy passes, one can just make out a land of gentle hills and fertile plains, representing the reward of reproductive success – the only thing that really matters in evolutionary terms. To understand the strategies of Homeric women we must first understand the fitness landscape they picked their way across. We must appreciate how different it was, how much more menacing, than those traversed by most women in modern societies. We must also appreciate how much different it was from those traversed by men. While Homeric women faced radically different challenges from those faced by men, the challenges were not less severe and the potential consequences for wrong turns were not less dire.

In short, the principal hazards facing Homeric women stemmed from the darker aspects of Homeric men: their propensities for violence, and for promiscuous and coercive sexual activity. Women sought to marry and raise families in a world where, virtually without warning, their husbands and kinsmen could be massacred, their children murdered or enslaved and raped, and they themselves could be raped and enslaved. Such scenarios were familiar enough to be the material of harrowing similes:

> As a woman weeps and flings herself down on her beloved husband, who has fallen fighting in front of his town and his people, trying to ward off the day of doom from his children and his town – seeing the man fall and convulse, she clings to him and pours out lamentations in a loud clear voice, while the enemy from behind prod her in the back and shoulders with their spears, leading her into bondage, to work and woe, while the most pitiful grief wastes her cheeks – so from under Odysseus' brows the pitiful tears fell. (*Odyssey* 8.523–31)

If they escaped the worst-case scenario – and probably most of them did[4] – Homeric women were obliged to pursue their goals within the tight and potentially dangerous strictures of intense male possessiveness

* Evolutionists will note that my usage of this term is non-standard.

and an exaggerated sexual double standard (for suggestions of this see *Odyssey* 5.118–29; 6.285–88). Running foul of male possessiveness or violating the strict sexual morality governing their behavior could bring severe consequences, ranging from reputational damage and abandonment, all the way up to physical abuse and even murder.[5] Finally, while strict sexual fidelity was demanded of Homeric wives, their husbands faced no social costs for open pursuits of promiscuous liaisons – if anything, promiscuity among the men was a mark of status and pride. While many Homeric women resisted, they were generally expected to endure the infidelities of their husbands, to face the real possibility of being supplanted by younger and/or more beautiful slaves, and to accept the likelihood that a significant proportion of family resources would be diverted away from their own children in support of their husbands' bastards.[6]

How did Homeric women negotiate these features of their fitness landscapes given that the only roles they were allowed to play were as wives, mothers, and household managers? Lacking political muscle in the community and physical muscle in the home, confronted with suspicious men who saw untrustworthiness as part of the essence of femaleness,[7] isolated by patrilocal marriage patterns from the protection of blood kin, confined by the nature of their work mainly to the household, and able to enhance their social and material capital *only* through marriage to the right type of man, how did Homeric women maneuver to give themselves the best opportunity to traverse their fitness landscapes: to survive, reproduce, and live to see their children reproduce?

BEAUTY IS POWER

When Odysseus takes leave of Nausicaa, finally going home to a reunion with his own wife, he says, "May the gods give you all your heart desires, a husband and a house, and may they also give you oneness of heart in all its excellence" (*Odyssey* 6.180–82). The words reflect something important about the limited scope available for female ambition in the Homeric world. Men are likewise strongly motivated by concerns of marriage and family. But they also strive intensely for social status, power, and riches. Odysseus' words suggest that women were content simply to make a good, stable marriage and raise a family. He would be wrong. Homeric women were also interested in status, power, and resources. However, women could gain these ends only by attaching themselves to a high-quality mate. Wives of high-status males gained privileged access to scarce resources and some degree of community standing. While women had little direct power, the wives (and lovers) of leading men were treated with great deference, and could enjoy considerable political influence.[8]

When it came to attracting desirable suitors, beauty was a woman's greatest asset. This is not to slight the role that social position played in marriage. Marriages in Homer serve as linkages for whole kin networks. Homeric men consider it useful and desirable to marry into rich and powerful families. Thus, when the son of Castor mentions his bride he brags that she was the daughter "of rich people" (*Odyssey* 14.211–13), not that she was beautiful. Furthermore, even the highest-status Homeric women, the wives of *basileis* and gods, do work that is utterly indispensable to the functioning and survival of the household. (These slaving "queens," "princesses," and goddesses are, for me, a particularly eloquent indicator of the simplicity of Homeric society. It is as though Homer is incapable of even imagining a social stratum where women's lives are *not* taken up with work.)[9]

However, while a woman's desirability is affected by her social rank, wealth, and skill at work, nothing about Homeric women is stressed as much as their beauty, and no female attribute is more important to men in choosing potential mates. The tremendous importance of beauty to female life outcomes is compellingly reflected in the famous story of the Judgment of Paris, which is identified in the *Iliad* (24.25–30) as the cause of the Trojan War. In this episode, which is described in detail in a preserved summary of a lost epic (the *Cypria*), Paris is chosen as judge of a beauty contest among Hera, Athena, and Aphrodite. To boost their chances, each goddess offers Paris a secret bribe. Paris' preference for Aphrodite's bribe of the love of the most beautiful woman in the world, over Athena and Hera's offers of power and glory, sets off a chain reaction that culminates in the Trojan holocaust and trails off in subsequent bloody years. The young Trojan's choice of Aphrodite inspires the unreasoning and everlasting hatred of Hera and Athena. Troy burns to satisfy their vain pique.

The myth symbolizes two interlocked truths about Homeric men and women. First, the goddesses' shameless maneuverings to be chosen by Paris, and their spiteful fury when passed over, indicate how important beauty was to Homeric women. It suggests that beauty formed a road to dominance of female status hierarchies[10] in much the same way that physical size and strength led to dominance of male hierarchies.* Beauty was the most potent weapon a woman wielded, not only for competing against other women, but also for competing on a more level footing with politically and muscularly powerful men. Second, the myth emphatically defines what is most important to men: finally every enticement pales before the allure of a desirable woman. Paris chooses Aphrodite to further his "grievous lustfulness" (24.30), a weakness consuming mortal men and immortals alike.

These truths feed on one another. Beauty is important to women because, as Paris' choice shows, beauty is so important to men. And this is not only because beautiful women marry better than the less beautiful. Rather, Paris' choice shows that desirable women possess something that men covet above all other things – and this is a source of endless power.

Hera fully deploys this power in her marriage to Zeus. In the *Iliad* we hear much of Zeus' overwhelming strength. He is "by far the strongest"; even a coalition of all of the other gods could not rival him in strength (*Iliad* 8.18–27; *Odyssey* 15.105–08). Zeus is the alpha male of all the Homeric alpha males that strut and preen and bellow their power – a portrait of puissance that effeminizes the most hirsute hero by contrast. Yet even Zeus is no match for a woman, provided she is not only beautiful but guileful (*Iliad* 19.95–99). Successfully competing against men requires equal measures of beauty and brains.

As Hephaestus says, "The Olympian [Zeus] is a hard foe to meet in strife" (*Iliad* 1.588–89), so most of the male gods do not even bother to try; and if they do, pain teaches them the error of their ways.

* Consider also Odysseus' warning to Melantho, the most beautiful of his female slaves. Still disguised as a beggar, he uses his own riches-to-rags story to illustrate how quickly Zeus can dash a person's fortunes. The moral of his tale: "Therefore, woman, beware that you too some day do not lose all the beauty wherein you now are preeminent among the handmaids" (*Odyssey* 19.81–82). Odysseus' analogy implies that loss of beauty is as devastating for a woman as a man's loss of wealth and status.

However, goddesses have more success because they harbor no illusions about their capacity to overcome Zeus through strength. Unlike male gods, goddesses can compete with Zeus by exploiting sexual vulnerabilities he shares with all men. Aphrodite, in her symbolic capacity of the sex drive, is the only force capable of defeating Zeus, an otherwise omnipotent being. While the other gods strain and cower under his sometimes capricious rule, Aphrodite always has her way with him. Zeus's sexual vulnerabilities are consistently depicted in the Homeric epics, Greek mythology, and the Homeric Hymn to Aphrodite:

> Muse, tell me the deeds of golden Aphrodite the Cyprian, who stirs up sweet passion in the gods and subdues the tribes of mortal men and birds that fly in the air and all the many creatures that the dry land rears, and all that the sea . . . There is nothing among the blessed gods or among mortal men that has escaped Aphrodite. Even the heart of Zeus, who delights in thunder, is led astray by her; though he is greatest of all and has the lot of highest majesty, she beguiles even his heart whenever she pleases and mates him with mortal women. (1–39)[11]

Hera exploits Zeus' sexual weakness with great skill, confidence, and intelligence. In a scene intriguingly reminiscent of the ritualistic arming scenes of the epics, where warriors carefully strap on all of their battle gear, Hera girds herself with female weapons and armor: she cleans herself with ambrosia, smears her gorgeous body with redolent olive oil and other perfumes, combs and primps her hair into sleek braids tousled about her shoulders, and decks herself in smooth robes, jewelry, and veil. Finally, between her breasts she tucks Aphrodite's embroidered breast band. Thus armed "with all this loveliness" (14.187) she sallies forth to meet Zeus and she quickly subdues him. At a glance he is seized with "sweet desire" (*Iliad* 14.328); "lust closely enwrapped his mind, just as when they had first mingled in love" (*Iliad* 14.294–95). She expertly seduces him, enervates him, and puts to sleep his "wise mind" (14.165) while she enacts her own agenda, turning the tide of battle against the Trojans she hates.

Other scenes suggest the ability of women to use their sexual appeal to manipulate powerful males and advance their own interests. For instance, Hera's stratagem succeeds only through the collusion of the god Sleep. Sleep's debilitating fear of crossing Zeus, and his steadfast refusal to entertain any of Hera's bribes, is instantly quashed by Hera's offer of a beautiful Grace, one of the younger ones, for a wife (*Iliad* 14.263–76). Similarly, Penelope cannily turns the lust of her suitors to her advantage. At one juncture in the poem, she arms herself as Hera does above, accentuating her beauty with oils, perfumes, and alluring dress and jewelry. She then displays herself to her suitors with the express purpose of wringing precious gifts out of them. Odysseus observes the whole performance, and rejoices "... because she drew gifts from them, bewitching their souls with winning words, but her mind was set on other things" (18.281–83).[12]

In short, Homeric women use the few tools their society cannot deny them – sharp intelligence, manipulative stratagems, and sexual allure – to ably defend and promote their interests in spite of their muscular and political disadvantages. Hera interferes with Zeus's plans at every turn: she hectors and badgers, flatters and wheedles, and she constantly maneuvers within her encumbrances to pursue her own agendas. Homer's portrait of Hera shows that a subtle and courageous woman could win substantial benefits in challenging her husband, but that she also faces dire risks. For her various transgressions, Zeus has physically tortured Hera in the past (*Iliad* 15.16–22), and when she pushes him too hard he warns her to yield lest he come for her with his "irresistible hands" (*Iliad* 1.565–67). But Hera has learned exactly how far she can push Zeus. In the *Iliad*, she plays him with ease, like a virtuoso playing children's music. She wins their wars by pretending to capitulate in their smaller battles, convincingly acknowledging Zeus's strength and authority, and making him feel that he has won the day. But when the battle of wills between Zeus and Hera winds to a close, Hera has successfully wrought her vengeance for the Judgment of Paris. Zeus's favorite city, Troy, is a smoldering ruin, his favorite people, the Trojans, are, depending on their sex, either dead or degraded, and his most beloved mortal son, Sarpedon, is dead.[13] Thus in sharp contrast to Homer's invocation to the muse (*Iliad* 1.5), it is *not* the will of Zeus that is accomplished in the Rape of Troy, it is the will of Hera.

In emphasizing the way that Homeric women exploit male sexual vulnerabilities, I do not mean to imply that all women in the epics are portrayed as calculating temptresses. Homeric women are not only the agents of Aphrodite, they are also, like Helen, her hapless victims; Aphrodite is, in fact, pointedly labeled as a "deceiver of women" (*Iliad* 5.349). Moreover, Homer celebrates romantic bonds as among the deepest and most rewarding in human experience (e.g., *Odyssey* 6.180–85). He shows that sex can be a political lever, but he also describes the desperation of Hector and Andromache on the wall, the tender pillow talk of Odysseus and Penelope, the sweet anticipation of young lovers, and interludes of comfortable warmth even in the long-fraying marriages of Zeus and Hera, Menelaus and Helen. But this chapter is less about describing the strategies of Homeric women and more about exploring how these strategies shape the qualities of Homeric men, especially their propensities for violence.

FEMALE CHOICE

Whoever her father commands; whoever pleases her. (*Odyssey* 2.113–14)

Making a good marriage was by far the most important challenge a Homeric woman faced in negotiating her fitness landscape. This may jar modern sensibilities, where we all grin a little at the feminist aphorism, "A woman needs a man like a fish needs a bicycle." While it may be more challenging, modern women can, and regularly do, negotiate their fitness landscapes without male protection, support, or provisioning of offspring. However, we too readily forget how unusual this situation is; in the tens of thousands of years of human history predating the novel conditions that engendered the feminist revolution, in order to survive, thrive, and see children reach maturity, a woman needed a man *like a fish needs water*. Lacking an investing mate, women had difficulty providing sufficient calories for their children, especially the vital fat and protein calories provided by male hunters; lacking protection, they faced the constant specter of sexual coercion and harassment.[14] Moreover, in preindustrial societies fatherless children had lower rates of survival due to deficient nutrition, smaller funds of kinship support and, in the worst case, the violence of potential stepfathers.[15] As Sarah Pomeroy writes, in the Homeric age and most of the rest of Ancient Greek history, "the lives of women lacking the protection of men were truly pitiful."[16]

But this dependence was mutual. In Homeric society, the ideal marriage was envisioned as an unshakeable partnership (*Odyssey* 6.180–85); men were also vitally dependent on their wives. Family survival in non-state societies could be a difficult and dangerous affair, and it required the participation of competent male and female investors. As in all preindustrial societies,[17] Homer's had a clear division of labor into male and female categories. While we often see the men engaged in sport, leisure, and idle debate, we almost never see women – whether free or slave, mortal or divine – doing anything but working. Young Nausicaa and her maids do play girlishly at ball, but only after they have spent the day scrubbing their knuckles and laundry in the river. Women weave and sew, prepare and cook meals, thresh and grind grain, pick grapes, haul heavy buckets of water, clean house, wash clothes, and raise children. The wives of important men have many maids, but they do not sit idly and watch them work. Rather they are more like forewomen of bustling production facilities, working alongside and supervising a female workforce as it churns out the broad variety of products needed to sustain a large household.

In short, Homeric men require mates who are much more than beautiful brood mares. In addition to beauty, men value loyalty, endurance, sense, decorum, and skill and industriousness in work. In short, they require – and therefore desire – extremely competent partners to help them negotiate the substantial challenges of subsistence in a world with ever-present dangers, small margins, and no social safety net beyond kinsmen and close friends.[18] Thus, while Homeric men place a high premium on physical attractiveness, the ideal mate is very far from an empty-headed beauty. This fact is embodied in Penelope – an ideal wife combining diverse and numerous virtues – and it is continually reinforced in female epithets that stress not only physical allure, but wisdom, good sense, and proficiency at work.

Of course, Homeric women were as constrained in their mate choice decisions as they were in making other important choices. In fact, while fathers, brothers, and potential husbands all had roles in arranging marriages, many references to marriage lack information about what role a girl played, if any, in choosing her own husband. But does this mean that Homeric women were at the mercy of their kinsmen when it came to mate choice?

A close look at the evidence strongly suggests that they were not. First, there is sustained attention to the details of only one potential marriage in all of Homer – the lead up to the (eventually averted) marriage of Penelope to one of her suitors. If Penelope's example is at all representative, marriageable women negotiated their mate preferences with those of their kinsmen, especially their fathers. The preferences of fathers and daughters appear to have been substantially aligned. For instance, Alcinous and Nausicaa both consider Odysseus to be an ideal mate/son-in-law, and suitors court potential brides and fathers-in-law in exactly the same way: by giving large bride prices to the father and expensive wooing gifts to the girl.

But their interests were not necessarily identical: a woman's family could realize great social and economic gains from her marriage. When brides "earn" oxen from the families of their grooms, it is the woman's family who principally benefits. In the *Odyssey*, for instance, all of Penelope's closest kinsmen – her father, her brothers, her son – pressure her to choose a new husband, in spite of her reluctance (*Odyssey* 15.16–18; 19.157–60; 19.530–34). We should assume that this pressure is not all self-interested: after twenty years, the men think it is time for Penelope to accept that Odysseus is obviously dead, for her to dry her tears and enjoy the pleasures of life and marriage while time remains. But they also stand to benefit economically. Penelope's family will receive a great infusion of wealth, and the suitors' steady consumption of Telemachus' patrimony will come to an end. Penelope's ability to resist this pressure for almost four years suggests that women, while not free agents in the marriage market, did wield significant influence. The tension between the preferences of a prospective bride and the wishes of her family is intimated in a suitor's comment that Penelope should marry "whoever her father commands; whoever pleases her" (*Odyssey* 2.113–14). And, while the risks were immense, women who were unhappy with their mates had infidelity as an option. Helen, Clytemnestra, and Aphrodite (not to mention Odysseus' slave women) all exercise this option, and Homer builds much tension around the possibility of Penelope straying. In short, the epics give the impression that women's mate preferences – hemmed in as they were by familial constraints – did have non-negligible scope for expression.

One could reasonably object that this picture, based as it is primarily on the example of Penelope, is merely a side effect of an unusual situation. Penelope is not a maiden; she is a grown woman, ostensibly widowed, and she is not surrounded by strong kinsmen. Was the situation markedly different for young women at the age of first marriage? Were they at the mercy of their kinsmen? For several reasons, I think not. First, the notion of powerless young women is manifestly at odds with the ubiquitous and clearly described Homeric custom of wooing gifts (e.g., *Odyssey* 6.158–59; 8.269; 11.116–17; 11.281–82; 15.16–18; 15.366–67; 19.528–29; 20.334–35). When a man seeks to win a bride he approaches *her* with gifts, not her father; negotiating a payment to the father appears to be a separate transaction. Such was the case, in fact, during Penelope's girlhood: Odysseus wooed her "with many gifts" (*Odyssey* 24.294). And Hector wooed Andromache in the same way (*Iliad* 6.394, 22.88), before paying her father a huge bride price and leading her to Troy (*Iliad* 22.471–72). If girls lack significant influence then why do suitors shower them with expensive gifts? Why if not to win favor? And why seek to win favor if girls lack influence?

Furthermore, while there are situations in Homer where girls are married off apparently without input (e.g., *Iliad* 9.141–48; 18.429–34; *Odyssey* 11.281–91), there are widely scattered indications that they usually had more freedom to follow their mating preferences. For instance, there are scattered allusions to tales of women as romantic agents, actively instigating illicit affairs (e.g., *Odyssey* 11.235–47; *Iliad* 6.160–62). And there are familiar images of youthful courtship – of young men and women displaying for each other at a dance (*Iliad* 18.593–606), privately trading soft words (*Iliad* 22.126–28), and sneaking off to consummate their love in secret from their parents (*Iliad* 14.295–96).

Finally, there is the evidence of comparative anthropology. Across cultures, even in those with arranged marriage, girls usually exert non-negligible influence over mate selection.[19] Thus the alternative to the hypothesis that women had a significant role in choosing their mates is to deny the generality of Penelope's example, to ignore the clear implications of wooing gifts and other aspects of youthful courtship, to downplay myriad instances of illicit affairs, and to posit that Homeric society was, in this respect, anthropologically unusual. As the examples of Aphrodite, Helen, Nausicaa, Circe, Calypso, Penelope, Anteia, Tyro, Melantho and others illustrate, Homeric women would have obviously had pronounced mate preferences. It is unlikely, based on the information in the poems and anthropological inference, that these preferences could have been entirely controlled and contravened by men.

On the contrary, Homeric marriage customs appear to be of the most common anthropological type: where the interests of daughters and their families are substantially, though not perfectly, aligned, and where the choice of groom is a negotiation between the young woman's preferences and those of her family.[20] I suggest that the Kipsigis, a pastoral group in Kenya, are one of many good models for the Homeric situation:

> Choice of marriage partners is technically made by the young woman's kin and is influenced, in part, by the man's bride-price, or bride wealth offer, in addition to his social reputation and his political influence. In some cases, the preferences of the woman and the best interest of her parents strongly conflict, and in these cases female choice is sometimes circumvented by the woman's kin . . . In most cases, however, the parents' decision is influenced by their daughter's preference . . . With the Kipsigis, female choice is . . . intertwined with the material and political interests of the woman's kin, but in most cases these interests largely coincide with her preferences.[21]

SIZE MATTERS

> To an extraordinary degree, the predilections of the investing sex – females – potentially determine the direction in which the species will evolve. For it is the female who is the ultimate arbiter of when she mates and how often and with whom. (Sarah Hrdy, *The woman that never evolved*).[22]

The fact that, in most species, females choose and males compete to be chosen means that the female's preferences go a long way toward determining the traits and qualities of the male. Female preferences and male characteristics co-evolve, the one always shaping the other. If men, for instance, tend to love and invest in their children, it is partly because ancestral women rewarded fatherly men with sexual access while denying it to those who lacked paternal feelings and a corresponding predisposition to invest in children. Likewise, if men compete for status and dominance, it is partly because ancestral women rewarded high-status, dominant men with reproductive opportunities. John Hartung was not being frivolous when he said, "males are a breeding experiment run by females."[23] Rather, he was colorfully expressing the core of Darwin's theory of sexual selection: the choices of females significantly shape many, though by no means all, male traits.[24]

What qualities do Homeric women seek in their mates, and why? First, as suggested in the last chapter, it is clear that they look for a man capable of gaining and controlling resources. At a minimum a suitor (and/or his family) must be able to afford a substantial transfer of resources to the bride and her family. As discussed above, the epics recurrently suggest that the best way for a man to woo a woman is to shower her with gifts. The payment of bride price, along with the less formal wooing gifts, indicates a suitor's ability to provide material care for a woman and her children.

While possession of a minimum level of wealth seems an absolute prerequisite for any suit, Homeric women also care about the physical appearance of potential mates.[25] In this, the pragmatism of Homeric women only apparently gives way. As we shall see, their attraction to men with certain physical characteristics is as practical as their attraction to men with appealing socio-economic profiles.

While Homeric women gravitate toward handsome men – men with glossy hair and beards, taut skin, and handsome faces – they seem particularly attracted to men who are large and strong. Odysseus is as devastating a romantic hero as he is a martial hero; while not as tall as Agamemnon or Menelaus (*Iliad* 3.193–94, 3.210) he is never described as short and he is once described as tall (*Odyssey* 21.334). Moreover, he is so powerfully built that, even amid a swarm of strong warriors, he stands out like a great strapping ram among ewes (*Iliad* 3.197–98). Women move to him as though magnetically compelled. Such is the case, for instance, when Odysseus' charms sweep Circe, Calypso, and Nausicaa, not to mention Penelope, off their sandal-clad feet. Odysseus is a composite representation of all the things, according to folk wisdom and science,[26] women crave in their mates: he is unfeasibly handsome, dominant, intelligent, rich, and vigorous. Odysseus would be as comfortable in the world of the modern-day Harlequin Romance as in the world of the *Odyssey*.

Homer stresses all of these qualities, not least of all his masculine size, strength, and vigor. Homer and his characters unabashedly marvel at Odysseus' massive arms, his broadly muscled shoulders, and his rippling hero thighs (e.g., *Odyssey* 8.457–59; 11.11–21; 11.336–37; 18.66–72). While men take note of Odysseus' appearance – carefully marking him as a formidable potential foe or ally – so too do women. For instance, after Odysseus has washed away the muck and brine of his ordeal at sea, young Nausicaa sees how handsome he is, how strong and impressive. She gazes on him "in wonder" and sighs to her maids, "If only such a man were called my husband, living here, and it pleased him to stay here forever" (*Odyssey* 6.244–45). Similarly, the scenes with Circe and Calypso, breathtaking goddesses who lust after Odysseus and hope to marry him, confirm Odysseus' status as a masculine ideal.

Moreover, there is some evidence that Penelope does not remarry partly because no man measures up to Odysseus in physical power and fighting spirit. By personally organizing the archery competition to choose a new husband, Penelope forsakes the usual custom of favoring the suitor who offers most. The contest is designed to identify the man with most strength and skill – the man who can, figuratively and literally, wield Odysseus' massive bow. Penelope usually huddles in the women's quarters and wails her fate while the suitors enjoy their drunken sports. But during the contest Penelope joins them, carefully observing as each suitor pitifully fails to string Odysseus' bow. The scene is a mating ritual, reminiscent of bird leks, in which a receptive female sits and observes while flocks of males dance, ruffle, preen, and swell their chests in hopes of being chosen. When Odysseus easily bends and strings the bow, and coolly makes a shot that is virtually impossible, we can see that *here* is a man worthy of the choosiest woman in the world, for not even Helen had more than 100 suitors to choose among.

The preference of Homeric women for large and strong men is not arbitrary. As described in Chapter Two, with only a couple of exceptions, the leaders of Homeric groups – whether of war parties or towns – are described as their largest, most powerful, and most formidable members. In Homer, as in many ethnographical societies, the "big men" *are* big men, and they enjoy clear advantages in competition for wealth and prestige.[27]

DEMONIC MALES

As the Rape of Troy demonstrates, women obviously have much to lose from male competitiveness, perhaps especially when it moves beyond the individual level to competition between groups. Among groups of humans, as among some other social animals, including lions and gorillas, male competitiveness can have disastrous consequences for females. When one group of males vanquishes another, it can mean death for young children.[28] Moreover, it can mean rape – the loss of the precious prerogative of joining reproductive fortunes with the best man available. Obviously, these outcomes run counter to female fitness goals. How did ancestral women respond to these selection pressures? Paradoxically, it was probably by choosing men who were more, not less, competitive.

Homeric women played a role in perpetuating male competitiveness and violence by rewarding brave warriors with favor and denying it to the weak and uncourageous. These dynamics are reflected in Helen's disgust at Paris' performance in his fight against Menelaus. Paris is soundly thrashed by Menelaus, who drives him to the ground and is dragging him off the field to execute him. However, Aphrodite intervenes and spirits Paris off the field in a mist, depositing him in Helen's boudoir. When Helen finds him she is not elated that her lover has survived; she is appalled and ashamed. Instead of tending his wounds, and soothing his injured pride, she conducts an emotional assault on the beaten man that is as furious as Menelaus' physical assault. She is so disgusted by his weakness that she cannot look at him; with eyes averted, she taunts him with reminders of his boasts of strength, and coldly expresses her regret that he survived the encounter (*Iliad* 3.428–36).

Crucially, at this moment, Helen is filled with revulsion for Paris, the paragon of male sexual attractiveness. She tells Aphrodite, "To that place [Paris' bed] I will not go. It would be disgraceful to share his bed. All of the women of Troy would heap blame on me" (*Iliad* 3.410–12; see also 6.349–53). Despite her contempt for him, Paris finds her more attractive than ever and wants ardently to take her to bed. Helen has no interest, but consents when Aphrodite threatens her with dire consequences. The whole scene carries the message that Homeric women respect bravery and strength in their men, and are loath to reward the weak and cowardly with favor. These tendencies are reinforced by social pressure from the female community as a whole ("the women of Troy would heap blame on me"). The scene also communicates the strong effect this fact has on the men, since Helen's tirade shames Paris back to the battlefield. After taking leave of Helen, Paris runs into Hector, and tells him: "I only wanted to give myself over to anguish. But my wife convinced me with winning words, urged me back to the fighting" (*Iliad* 6.335–36).

The respect of the Trojan women for men of valor is similarly communicated in Hector's fond – and sadly chimerical – daydream that his doomed son will one day be a fierce and mighty warrior. He envisions his baby as a grown man, returning from battle, laden with bloody trophies stripped from dead foes. Part of the savor of the vision is his anticipation of Andromache's own satisfaction, as an aging mother, in claiming such a brave, capable son (*Iliad* 6.476–81). That warriors may have regularly presented battlefield spoils to women is also suggested by Zeus' statement that he will not allow Hector to survive to present Achilles' armor, stripped from Patroclus, to Andromache (*Iliad* 17.201–08).

These scenes suggest that Trojan women respect and expect valor in their men. This is despite the fact that Andromache futilely begs Hector not to go back to the plain, but to defend Troy from behind the walls. Of course, as a loving wife, Andromache fears for Hector's safety and has strong misgivings about his return to a pitched battle. But, despite her restraining words, Hector insists on venturing back to the field. And his reasons for doing so are instructive. He says that, as much as he would like to remain with his family, he must rejoin the fight or "feel great shame before the Trojans, and the Trojan women with the trailing robes" (6.441–42). This is not the first or last time that a warrior goads himself to fight, at least in part, by considering his reputation among women. Paradoxically Hector's decision to resist his wife's pleas seems based in the fact that, were he to submit, he would not be the great warrior that she loves and respects.

The evidence suggests that Homeric women find those men most attractive whose bodies signal formidable warrior potential. The ugliest man in Homer is Thersites, whose body – scrawny, stooped, lopsided – highlights his weakness. There is something important behind the fact that the most physically desirable men are usually the greatest warriors. The greatest mortal warrior, Achilles, is also the most beautiful Greek on the field (*Iliad* 2.673–74); the second best warrior, Ajax, is also second in physical beauty (17.277–80). Perhaps importantly, Achilles and Ajax are also defined as the largest Greek warriors by far – the only ones who could wear each other's armor (*Iliad* 18.188–93). Eurypylus and Memnon – preeminent warriors among the Trojan allies and leading heroes elsewhere in the Trojan Cycle – are identified by Odysseus as the handsomest men he has ever seen (*Odyssey* 11.519–22). And the war god, Ares, is gorgeous, the natural mate for the most desirable goddess, Aphrodite (*Odyssey* 8.309–10).

Thus in Homer, as with much of Greek myth and literature, the war hero is virtually synonymous with the erotic hero. This is true of Odysseus, of the Athenian hero Theseus, and of the greatest Greek hero of all, of whom Plutarch wrote, "It would be a labor of Heracles to enumerate all his [Heracles'] love affairs, so many were they."[29] The one prominent exception to this pattern is Paris, who is breathtakingly handsome but uncourageous.[30] Paris is so weak that Menelaus – far from the strongest Greek – overcomes him barehanded, after his sword has shattered and his spear has been thrown in vain. But Paris actually represents the exception to prove the rule. Because Paris does not *look* like a wimp; he has all the physical appeal of a formidable warrior. When Hector harangues Paris for attempting to shirk the fight with Menelaus, we learn of a powerful correlation between male physical attractiveness and fighting strength: "I think the long-haired Achaians will scoff, saying you are our best champion on account of your fine looks, but there is no might in your heart, no courage" (*Iliad* 3.43–45).

In summary, the epics suggest that women's mating preferences are partially responsible for the violence of individual men and of the culture as a whole. Women in Homer are not only the victims and objects of male violence, though they certainly endure great traumas at the hands of men. Rather, through an active system of sexual and reputational rewards to men with powerful bodies, combative dispositions, and courageous spirits, they reinforce, encourage, and perpetuate male competitiveness. This is in no sense to "blame the victim," because Homeric women have little choice in the matter.

They are forced down this path less by the meddling of their kinsmen in their romantic choices than by the behaviors of males in their world. As the primatologists Wrangham and Peterson argue, in their book on the evolution of aggression in humans and other apes, once males develop what they call "demonic" reproductive strategies – characterized by intense, frequently violent competitiveness – females have little choice but to reward them with sexual access. In the course of human evolutionary history, women have consistently chosen mates with the capacity for aggressive behavior for an utterly compelling reason: there are dangerous and aggressive men in the world.[31] This is part of Andromache's attraction to Hector: he stands between her and the aggression of other men, protecting their child, and warding off her "day of bondage" (*Iliad* 6.462–63). A viciously cyclical feedback loop takes hold: men can be dangerous so women reward the strong and potentially aggressive with sexual access; as a result males grow, generation by generation, more "demonic," both by genetic predisposition and by socio-cultural pressure; this, in turn, places women in the position of having to select for progressively more demonic mates. Demonism breeds demonism, and neither men nor women have much choice in the matter.

Homeric violence feeds, in part, on this vicious cycle of female preferences for males with demonic potential and male attempts to behave with measured demonism so as to win and maintain favor. As with all vicious cycles this one is difficult to disrupt: men cannot be "angels" and win a wife; women cannot choose a man without a demonic streak because pure angels are highly disadvantaged in a world of potential demons. In the next chapter I describe another vicious cycle that feeds Homeric violence. Together, these cycles of violence, and the inability of the people to break out of them, helped to shape Homeric philosophy and theology.

CHAPTER 7

Homer's missing daughters

As discussed in Chapter Three, the anthropological myth of a golden age of primitive harmony has been laid to rest by recent analyses; the vast majority of band and tribal societies on the ethnographic record experienced regular or periodic warfare, and homicide rates in prestate societies typically outpaced those of state societies by a decisive margin. In all societies, and in most animal species, males are responsible for most violent behavior. This pattern has a single primary cause: a fundamental shortage of female reproductive capacity relative to male demand. Human tendencies toward mild polygyny (even in *de jure* monogamous societies), short female reproductive life spans, male preferences for relatively more promiscuous mating, and female preferences for relatively less promiscuous mating, give men strong incentives to compete for access to scarce female reproductive capacity. This imbalance of female supply and male demand is universally encountered and determined by our mammalian biology.

However, just as clearly there is large variation from society to society in the level, type, and intensity of male violence. Hobbes was wrong when he argued that primitive people were locked into a state of constant and brutal warfare, *omnium contra omnes*. The rates of intergroup warfare characteristic, for instance, of Amazonian and Highland New Guinean populations were far in excess of those of the Inuit or the !Kung San Bushmen. The latter groups had high homicide rates – staggeringly high in the case of the Inuit – but low frequency of warfare. These variations resulted from environmental, not genetic, differences. For instance, it has been suggested that the Inuit and !Kung rarely fought wars simply because they inhabited harsh lands that others did not consider worth fighting over.[1]

In short, it is clear that levels of human violence are not biologically determined; they are very strongly influenced by variations in social and physical environments. Much the same gene pool that gave us the bellicose warlords of Mycenaean and Late Dark Age Greece, and the military genius of Classical and Hellenistic Greece, gave us the relatively meek peoples of later centuries; warmongering Vikings and peace-mongering modern Scandinavians emerged from similar genetic stock. The question posed in this chapter is, which environmental factors were responsible for high levels of violence in Homeric society? Contributing factors in the physical environment that sliced the Greek world into many small polities were discussed in Chapter Two. The present chapter considers aspects of the sociocultural environment that helped produce bellicose men and communities.

My hypothesis, based on models developed in comparative anthropology, is that intense competition in Homeric society was a result of a persistent and pervasive shortage of available young women relative to young men. Two factors conspired to sharply exacerbate the default shortage of female reproductive capacity that characterizes the human condition. First, the polygynous institution of slave-concubinage allowed high-status men to monopolize numbers of women. Therefore, even if actual sex ratios were equal, the *operational* sex ratio (the number of available men to available women) would not have been. Since Homeric-era Greeks mainly raided one another or neighboring non-Greeks, the circum-Aegean population of reproductive age women would have been unevenly distributed across communities. Second, operational sex ratios may have been further skewed through excess mortality of juvenile females brought about by preferential female infanticide, probably via exposure, and/or differential parental care (e.g., weaning girls at an earlier age or providing insufficient nutrition in times of hardship).

As with most attempts to reconstruct prehistoric societies, these claims, beset by problems of scarce and inconclusive evidence, must be considered preliminary and provisional. My case for excess female mortality (EFM) will provoke the greatest skepticism, and rightly so given the paucity of the evidence. So I will spend the bulk of my time with these arguments. But first I must introduce the anthropological research on which these ideas are based.

MALE-BIASED SEX RATIOS AND VIOLENCE

When, owing to female infanticide, the women of a tribe were few, the habit of capturing wives from neighboring peoples would naturally arise. (Darwin, *The descent of man*)[2]

Perhaps the strongest predictor of violence in a society is its operational sex ratio, especially the ratio of available *young* men to *young* women.[3] Over the last thirty years researchers have shown that the more the sex ratio favors males in a society, the more violent will they be. The political scientists Hudson and Den Boer's literature review concludes:

> Theory suggests that compared with other males in society . . . [men left without mates owing to skewed sex ratios] will be prone to seek satisfaction through vice and violence, and will seek to capture resources that will allow them to compete on a more equal footing with these others. *These theoretical predictions are substantiated by empirical evidence so vast and so compelling as to approach the status of social science verity* [italics mine].[4]

Hudson and Den Boer focus on East Asia, especially China and India. Because of sex-selective abortion, preferential female infanticide, and neglect of young girls, there are now tens of millions of surplus young males in East Asian populations. Since unmarried men have, on average, significantly higher levels of circulating testosterone than married men of the same age, Den Boer and Hudson describe societies that are dangerously saturated with testosterone. The Chinese call these surplus males, who are usually "losers" in societal competitions for wealth and social status, "bare branches" owing to their lack of fertility and the forlornness of the image. While Hudson and Den Boer show that proliferating bare branches have contributed to increased rates of violent crime and other forms of socially disruptive behavior within Asian societies (especially China and India), their main warning is of a potential spill over into aggressive war.[5]

The problems of high operational sex ratios are not limited to East Asia. For instance, the behavioral ecologists Mesquida and Wiener demonstrate a strong statistical correlation between the proportion of young males in a nation's population and its frequency of warfare.[6] Likewise, Courtwright's survey of homicide in American history shows that murder rates were highest where the local population had the most unmarried young men and the fewest unmarried young women.[7] Critically, these studies suggest links between male propensities for violence and mate competition. The problem is not with the absolute numbers of men in a society. The problem is not with young men who are "fruitful branches." The problem is with "bare branches" competing for the opportunity to bear fruit.

As compelling as the historical and sociological studies are, the anthropological data are more so. For instance, high rates of female infanticide among the Inuit meant that females of marriageable age were scarce, which resulted in pitched mate competition and tragically high rates of male mortality.[8] The Inuit themselves were aware of this imbalance, saying "boys will have to kill each other" in order to win wives.[9] Likewise, among the Yanomamö, where there were once forty excess young men for every 100 young women, violence over women was notoriously nasty and devastating.[10] Similar correlations between masculinized juvenile sex ratios and high rates of violence have been identified in case studies of indigenous New Guineans, Tahitians, and Maori, as well as among the Sharanahua, Xavante, and Cahinahua of South America.[11]

While these case study data are suggestive, the large-scale statistical studies best reveal relationships between available females and intensity of violence. The largest study was conducted by Divale and Harris who gathered data from 561 band and tribal populations drawn from 112 societies that were, as a group, "generally representative of the universe of preindustrial societies."[12] Across cultures, Divale and Harris found the familiar relationship whereby a paucity of marriageable females reliably led to high rates of violence (specifically, warfare) and high levels of adult male mortality.

Divale and Harris' survey is especially valuable because they scoured for variables to explain *why* sex ratios came to favor males in the first place. Since the sex ratio at birth in all human societies hovers around 105:100,* and since juvenile mortality from natural and external causes is almost invariably higher for males than females,[13] strongly male-biased juvenile sex ratios are almost invariably the result of EFM due to infanticide, sex-selective abortion, and/or neglect.

* The sex ratio is conventionally given as the number of males to females. A *high* sex ratio is heavy on males, a *low* sex ratio is heavy on females.

Divale and Harris discovered that a single variable predicted male-biased juvenile sex ratios: warfare. In societies that had gone at least twenty-five years without war the juvenile sex ratio averaged 104:100 while the adult ratio averaged 92:100. These figures are consistent with naturally occurring sex ratios the world over: the sex ratio at birth slightly favors males while adult sex ratios favor females as a result of their superior life expectancies. However, of the 160 populations that had recently experienced war, the juvenile ratio averaged 128:100 while the adult ratio dropped to 101:100. In societies known to practice *both* warfare *and* preferential female infanticide the juvenile and adult ratios were, respectively, 133:100 and 92:100. This describes staggering rates of EFM and of adult male mortality.

In previously war-torn societies sex ratios returned to normal levels precisely when those societies became pacified by nation states. From this result, Divale and Harris concluded, "The change in the sex ratios with the cessation of warfare is strong evidence that warfare and not some other variable is responsible for these demographic effects."[14] In other words, war-waging societies tended to manipulate sex ratios in order to maximize the number of fighting males.

Divale and Harris phrased their explanation for these trends in the form of a prediction: "Wherever preindustrial warfare occurs, we suggest that a premium survival advantage is conferred upon the group that rears the largest number of fierce and aggressive warriors."[15] Phrased differently, in war-prone preindustrial societies, failing to skew sex ratios in favor of males, and thus failing to maintain a balance of power with enemies, was a recipe for disaster. Divale and Harris' discussion of warrior motives is consistent with those Hudson and Den Boer ascribe to "bare branches":

> Sex can be used as the principal reinforcement for fierce and aggressive performances involving risk of life ... women are the reward for military bravery ... Polygyny is the objectification of much of this system of rewards. At the same time, polygyny intensifies the shortage of females created by the postpartum manipulation of the sex ratio, producing positive feedback with respect to male aggressiveness and fierceness, and encouraging combat for the sake of wife capture.[16]

Thus high sex ratios are both a primary cause *and* a primary effect of male violence, producing a vicious cycle from which it is difficult to escape. In such societies, men vie intensely to avoid becoming bare branches, but men face this risk precisely because they live in an environment rent by chronic conflict.

Divale and Harris' study does not stand alone. For instance, the anthropologist Barry Hewlett found that fifty-seven non-state populations with male-biased juvenile sex ratios all had one thing in common: "They regularly engage in warfare and, as a result, experience relatively high male mortality."[17] Hewlett's study also added a new wrinkle by demonstrating that the relationship between high sex ratios and violence applied to violence *within the group* as well as to war: in general, the more the juvenile sex ratio favored males the higher were the rates of homicide.

In summary, the studies reviewed in this section lead to the specific expectation that prestate societies experiencing frequent war and high male mortality – like the society reflected in Homer – will likely have markedly male-skewed juvenile sex ratios. Moreover, as we will soon see, Homeric society shares many features with societies known to have high sex ratios. This could be solely the result of Homeric polygyny: high-status males monopolize the reproductive capacities of multiple females, necessarily making bare branches of other men. As Hudson and den Boer stress, a significant rate of polygyny is "functionally equivalent" to a masculinized sex ratio.[18] However, there are also intriguing, albeit indirect, suggestions that Homeric-era Greeks may have actively manipulated sex ratios in favor of male offspring. But before attempting to support this more speculative argument, let me briefly review the evidence for the less controversial case: with or without sex ratio manipulation, de facto polygyny would have tilted operational sex ratios markedly in favor of males.

HOMERIC POLYGYNY

If we believe that the social picture of the Homeric epics is at all reflective of historical realities, we must conclude that the institution of slave-concubinage would have led to significantly imbalanced distributions of women across Aegean communities. While Homeric men could not normally have multiple wives, most high-status men are in fact polygynists; they hoard multiple slave-concubines in addition to their wives (see above, Chapter Four). The erotic element of these relationships is often explicitly portrayed, and is clearly reinforced in an abundance of concubinal bastards. Slave women are never taken from within the slaveholder's group; they are invariably women who have been captured in war, opportunistically kidnapped by traders or pirates, or purchased (usually after being kidnapped or captured). Homeric raids did not target far-flung foreigners; they targeted peoples in or abutting the Greek homelands. Thus slave women would not have been imported from the non-Greek world so much as from non-allied circum-Aegean communities. Therefore, even if the actual sex ratios of Greek populations were roughly equal, operational sex ratios would have tilted significantly in favor of males: for every extra woman possessed by a high-status man, some less fortunate or less formidable Greek lacks a wife.* Women would therefore have been concentrated in certain communities and, within those communities, in the households of powerful men.

As we have seen, the practice of polygyny, by unbalancing the distribution of women, would be predicted to lead to higher rates of intergroup and intragroup violence. Divale and Harris' assessment of the motives of prestate warriors applies quite nicely to Homeric warriors as well (see Chapter Four): "Sex can be used as the principal reinforcement for fierce and aggressive performances involving risk of life . . . women are the reward for military bravery . . . Polygyny is the objectification of much of this system of rewards."

But what of imbalances in actual sex ratios? Homeric society fits the "profile" of a sex-ratio-manipulating society. Given the anthropological, sociological, and historical evidence that violent, polygynous societies are likely to manipulate sex ratios in favor of males, one might suspect its occurrence in Homer. Indeed, I am not the first to raise this possibility. For instance, Guttentag and Secord argue that many aspects of Homeric society – women treated as chattels, intense war, marriage by capture or contest, and a sharp sexual double standard – are consistent with the possibility of EFM. On the basis of similar observations, as well as skeletal information

* Possible hints of this can be found in the *Odyssey*, where the faithful herdsmen, Eumaeus and Philoetius, lack wives. Eumaeus suggests that masters had the ability to distribute wives to male slaves in return for long, loyal service (14.61–66). And Odysseus himself promises to arrange marriages for the herdsmen in exchange for help in fighting the suitors. These dynamics may suggest an effect where celibacy trickles down to the lowest levels of the male status hierarchy.

from cemetery excavations, Pomeroy also suggests that EFM may have characterized Homeric society.[19] The remainder of this chapter describes the sparse, indirect, yet still credible evidence that Homeric era Greeks may have biased sex ratios in favor of males, starting with a short review of what is known about EFM in ancient Greek history.

SEX-RATIO MANIPULATION IN GREEK HISTORY

If you have a son, you bring him up, even in you're poor, but if you have a daughter you expose her even if you're rich. (Poseidippus)[20]

One of the most interesting and fiercely contested questions in ancient history is the extent to which Greeks of different times and places may have abandoned (exposed) unwanted infants and, more specifically, the extent to which this practice would have disproportionately affected females.[21] That the Greeks exposed infants they were unwilling or unable to care for, and that they exposed more females than males, is supported by many lines of evidence: cemetery excavations revealing a consistent over-representation of male remains (exposed females would not have received proper cemetery burial); information on public monuments and family records, which frequently list many fewer female children; literary sources that explicitly refer to the practice of abandonment generally and preferential female abandonment specifically (like the fragment from Poseidippus above);[22] and inferences based on practice in other cultures where the evidence is more complete. Finally, many scholars believe that the Greeks also biased sex ratios more passively, by weaning daughters earlier and investing the bulk of familial resources in males.[23]

However, the evidence is frustratingly amenable to contrary interpretations. Fewer female names in public records may reflect simple sexist bias rather than a real shortage of females. The same goes for the shortage of female cemetery remains, which may also result from relatively small and gracile female bones decomposing more quickly than male bones. And the literary references can be undermined on a variety of different grounds. In short, it has been possible for scholars to develop plausible historical scenarios where rates of abandonment, disproportionately affecting females, were demographically significant;

it has also been possible for skeptics to reject these scenarios by systematically undermining the evidence. As with many important controversies in ancient history, the currently available evidence is simply incapable of resolving the dispute.

My goal is not to attempt an exhaustive analysis of arguments favoring and disfavoring the hypothesis of EFM in Greek history.[24] It is only within my scope to characterize the preponderance of scholarly opinion: in some times and places in Greek history abandonment of infants was common; this practice frequently resulted in death; these deaths disproportionately befell females; and these demographic effects were exacerbated by the neglect of female relative to male offspring, especially as regards nutrition. Considered in isolation, none of the evidence in favor of juvenile EFM in Ancient Greece compels belief. However, most scholars who have weighed the total evidence have judged – cautiously, tentatively – that EFM through exposure and/or neglect was a significant phenomenon during much of ancient Greek history.

In fact, for all the fierce controversy, *almost every main participant in these debates*, even the most rigorously skeptical, has agreed that female infants and juveniles in ancient Greece tended to die – of whatever causes – at higher rates and that, as a result, juvenile sex ratios were often skewed toward males. Even those who are most dubious of the widespread exposure of baby girls tend to credit the evidence that girls suffered higher mortality owing to poor nutrition and other factors.[25] Even those scholars most closely identified with arguments against preferential female exposure in classical Athens (the most heated debates have focused on classical Athens), accept its probability in other times and places.[26]

The point of this discussion is not that evidence favors the hypothesis that sex-ratio manipulation was common in Homeric society. While available evidence is consistent with this hypothesis, evidence from the Late Dark Age is, unfortunately, particularly shaky relative to other eras.[27] The point is that Homeric society is part of a cultural tradition in which, most scholars believe, juvenile sex ratios tended to favor males. While we can hope that hard evidence will eventually settle this question, the best evidence for EFM in Homer comes not from archaeology but from information in the poems themselves and inferences based on cross-cultural studies.

HOMER'S MISSING DAUGHTERS

Let me be clear: there is no direct evidence for EFM in Homeric society; in all of Homer there is not a single suggestive reference to preferential female infanticide and/or neglect. In fact, the one Homeric reference to infant exposure features Zeus and Hera's abandonment of their crippled infant *son*, Hephaestus (*Iliad* 18.394–405); even the non-infanticidal sacrifice of Agamemnon's daughter Iphigenia, which is described in other sources, is not mentioned in Homer. A good deal of anecdotal evidence is consistent with the possibility, but also with other explanations. For instance, potentially relevant information is conveyed in the genealogies that are liberally wedged between events in the poems (genealogical data have frequently been used to explore the possibility of EFM in other historical eras).[28] Priam's sons outnumber his daughters four to one; Zeus mentions many illegitimate sons and no illegitimate daughters (*Iliad* 14.312–28); among the dead "wives of the mighty" (11.227) that parade by Odysseus in the underworld we hear of seventeen sons and only one daughter (*Odyssey* 11.23–332); Nausicaa is apparently an only daughter among five brothers (*Odyssey* 6.57–65); Briseis mentions three brothers and no sisters (*Iliad* 19.291–300); Andromache mentions seven brothers and no sisters (*Iliad* 6.414–30); Hector, Sarpedon, Achilles, and other young warriors have sons and no daughters; and, while we never hear of Nestor's sisters, we know he has eleven brothers along with seven sons (11.692–93). Although there are a couple of instances in Homer where daughters outnumber sons,[29] a dearth of daughters is obviously the rule. However, while this information is consistent with the possibility of EFM, it is just as likely that the dearth of *references* to daughters is a simple artifact of male biases in the culture and the epics.

More telling than the genealogical information is the apparently robust cultural preference for sons over daughters, because EFM is cross-culturally linked with acute son preference and strongly patriarchal ideologies.[30] For instance, on the Trojan battlefield the homesick Greek warriors frequently refer to their families across the sea. However, when they specifically mention sorely missed family members they refer to wives, sons, and children, but not specifically to daughters. In fact, warriors' references to sons back on the home front – and mirror-image descriptions of home-front fathers fretting over their warrior sons – are common and comprise some of Homer's most touching passages. This is in keeping with the common sentiment among classicists that the strongest affection in the Homeric poems passes between fathers and sons.[31] When Homer wants to evoke pathos in his audience, he often does so by recounting stories, sometimes in the form of similes (e.g., *Iliad* 24.222–25), that evoke the grief of parents who lose a son or the joy of a long-delayed reunion between a father and his son. The worst losses a man can suffer are of full brothers ("born in the same womb") or of sons (*Iliad* 24.46–47). And perhaps the most crushing tragedy that can befall a family is the death of an only son (e.g., *Iliad* 19.334–37; 14.488–505; 24.538–40). Agamemnon dies lamenting the fact that he was not able to see his son once more, and in death his shade asks Odysseus whether his son still lives. But he does not mention his three daughters (*Odyssey* 11.452–61). Odysseus says of Ithaca that "it is a rugged land but good for raising boys" (*Odyssey* 9.27). And the great tragedy of Phoenix's long life is the curse of never bouncing a son on his knee (*Iliad* 9.453–95). In short, almost 28,000 lines of poetry consistently convey the impression of cultural preference for sons over daughters. References to parental affection for daughters (e.g., Chryses for Chryseis, Alcinous for Nausicaa, and Zeus for Athena and Artemis) unequivocally demonstrate that Homeric men were capable of deeply loving their daughters, but these references are relatively few.

However, textual evidence for son preference, like the evidence for daughter shortage, is insufficient to compel belief in EFM – both phenomena may be artifacts of Homer's relentless focus on males. The best suggestions of EFM in Homeric society are indirect. The evidence *does not* allow us to conclude that EFM characterized Homeric society. It allows us to conclude this: based on what we know about Homeric society on firm ground, and on what we know about EFM in other societies, conditions were very ripe for it.

DIFFERENTIAL PAYBACKS

To this point I have suggested that much of the conflict between and among Homeric males is directly or indirectly over possession of women. Further, I have suggested that the intensity of this conflict can be traced, at least in part, to acute shortages of young women relative to young men. Finally, I have argued that the shortages might have originated in two practices. First, polygyny: the monopolization of multiple women by single men initiates a celibacy "trickle-down effect" – an explosive surplus of young men with little to lose through intense competition for scarce women and for the social and/or material resources these women demand in a "seller's market." Second, parental manipulation of juvenile sex ratios in favor of male offspring, either through active infanticide by exposure or more "passive" means. However, this leaves an important question unanswered. Why would Homeric parents bias investment in favor of sons?

This section addresses the potential motives of Homeric families for preferring sons over daughters, arguing that it would not have been a strategy for overall population control or a misogynous reflex but a matter of family survival. In Homeric society sons were, quite literally, more valuable to their parents than were daughters – socially, economically, and politically.[32] Comparative anthropology suggests that in societies where one sex or the other reliably "pays back" more on parental investment, manipulation of juvenile sex ratios is common.[33]

In large part, the answer to the question of why Homeric families might have invested preferentially in male offspring is the obvious one offered by Divale and Harris: "Wherever preindustrial warfare occurs, we suggest that a premium survival advantage is conferred upon the group that rears the largest number of fierce and aggressive warriors." While this would likely have been true at the group level Divale and Harris were thinking of, the poems contain strong evidence that it was also true at the level of individual families. In fact, the poems convey an overwhelming sense of the priceless value of sons to their families, something that is not even suggested for daughters.

As in most prestate worlds, "kinship thinking permeated" Homeric society.[34] *Basileis* with close male kin, many and strong, would have typically enjoyed great influence.[35] While there happen to be important exceptions to this pattern, represented especially in the small numbers of male kin supporting Achilles, Odysseus, and Agamemnon, these represent exceptions that emphasize the rule. First, we learn that Achilles' and Odysseus' small numbers of male kin are both anomalous and a potentially devastating problem for both men and their families. As we will see below, the fact that Odysseus and Telemachus come from a line of only sons is singled out for its rarity and its precariousness. Likewise, the fact that Achilles' father, Peleus, has only one son is presented as unusual in powerful families: "But even for him [Peleus] a god devised evil, there was no generation of strong sons born in his home, he brought into the world just one son, doomed to an untimely death" (*Iliad* 24.538–40). As a result, Achilles frets about his father, ever exposed to the depredations of greedy and ambitious men, lacking the protection of sons (*Odyssey* 11.492–503; see also *Iliad* 24.486–89).

Aging *basileis*, like Peleus and Odysseus' father, Laertes, face danger and hardship without the protection of vigorous sons. This contrasts with the depiction of ancient *basileis* like Nestor and Priam who maintain great power, privilege, and standing largely because both are blessed with numbers of extremely formidable sons (Priam holds great power because of his "wealth and sons" (*Iliad* 24.543–46), but he also has direct support from more distant kinsmen, like his nephews and sons-in-law). And, as fathers face dangers without strong sons, so too do sons when deprived of fatherly protection. For instance, Hector's son Astyanax faces three possible fates upon the death of his father: infanticide at the hands of blood-lusting Greeks, slavery, or ostracism in Troy. As Pisistratus says in the *Odyssey*, "A son suffers many sorrows in his home when his father is gone, when there are no others to lend aid. So it is now with Telemachus. His father is gone and there is no one among the people who will defend him from evil" (4.165–67).

In fact, all of the problems Telemachus faces in the *Odyssey* – constant humiliation, the depletion of his wealth, the mistreatment of his mother, sexual trespasses on the family slave women, and a close brush with death – are results of his weakness: his personal inexperience as a fighter and his inability to call on a network of support, especially kin support. For instance, in book 16 of the *Odyssey*, Odysseus, still disguised as a beggar, asks his son why he puts up with the suitors' abuses:

> Tell me, though, are you willingly subjected or do people throughout the land hate you, listening to the voice of a god? Or are your brothers to blame, in whose fighting a man trusts even when a great quarrel arises? (*Odyssey* 16.95–98)

Telemachus' answer communicates the vital importance of strong sons to a family's prosperity and their very survival:

> Neither do the people at large bear me any grudge or hatred, nor can I blame brothers, in whose fighting a man trusts even when a great quarrel arises. For the son of Cronos made our line single. Arcesius begat Laertes as his only son, and he as a father in turn begat Odysseus, and Odysseus begat only me and left me in his house, and had no joy of me. That is why numberless enemies are now in the house. (*Odyssey* 16.114–21)

Telemachus is gravely imperiled by a lack of male relatives, especially brothers, who can fight by his side. The poems convey the sense that Achilles and Odysseus rise to prominence *despite* their weak kin networks, and because they are the two most formidable men in the entire world.[36]

As in other preindustrial societies, prior to the advent of formal law codes or official bodies for enforcing them, Homeric families were responsible for deterring violations of their interests and exacting justice – usually in the form of vengeance, sometimes in the form of compensation payments – when deterrence failed. While it appears that some high-status Homeric families were able to import young men into their households as mates for their daughters (e.g., Priam, Nestor), patrilocality, with young women leaving paternal households to join those of their husbands, was the rule. This is exemplified in the marriages of Menelaus' son and daughter:

> His daughter he was sending on to the son of Achilles [Neoptolemus], breaker of ranks, for in Troy he agreed to give her to him . . . So he was sending her with horses and chariot, to the famous city of the Myrmidons, ruled by Neoptolemus. But for his son, stout Megapenthes born of a slave woman, he brought forth from Sparta the daughter of Alector. (*Odyssey* 4.5–12)

Patrilocality, along with partible inheritance of paternal estates among sons, were adaptations designed to ensure that brothers and sons stuck together, maximizing the fighting and working force of the family.[37] Thus Homeric villages can be viewed as conglomerations of "fraternal interest groups," an anthropological term for

> . . . power group[s] of related males that resort to aggression when there is a threat to the interests of one of its members. In a society with these groups any act of violence will be followed by another, thereby eliciting a chain

reaction. Members of the group act with the assurance that his group will support him through thick and thin. Thus any individual act of violence can lead to conflict between fraternal interest groups, and much intrasocietal aggression can be attributed to the power groups and their struggles for power.[38]

Fraternal interest groups are important not so much for exacting vengeance once one has been trespassed upon, though Homeric men take great consolation in revenging and being revenged, but for deterring trespass in the first place (e.g., *Iliad* 14.479–85). In Homer, men are relentless in pursuing vengeance for wrongs perpetrated against their kin. The fugitive Theoclymenus demonstrates this point, while providing further support for a correlation between large male kin networks and political power:

> I have left my fatherland because I killed a man of my own tribe who had many brothers and kinsmen in horse-pasturing Argos, and mightily they hold power over the Achaians. I flee to escape death at their hands, a black fate. It is now my lot to wander among men. So take me aboard your ship, since in my flight I come to beg of you: don't let them kill me; I think they are in pursuit. (*Odyssey* 15.272–78)[39]

On the other hand, the epics frequently and explicitly convey the message that families lacking muscle, and thus a credible threat of relentless vengeance, were seriously disadvantaged. For instance, when Telemachus seeks information from Nestor on the murder of Agamemnon, the first question that enters his head is, "Where was Menelaus? . . . Was Menelaus not in Achaian Argos, but roaming somewhere among men, so Aegisthus found the courage to kill him?" (*Odyssey* 3.249–52). And when Menelaus himself, still struggling to return home from Troy, learns from Proteus of the murder of his brother, Agamemnon, he is advised: "Strive to return to your fatherland for you will either find him still alive or Orestes will have already killed him, and you will arrive in time for the funeral feast" (*Odyssey* 4.545–47). Indeed, Orestes does beat Menelaus to the kill, justifying the fragment from the lost epic the *Cypria*: "Foolish the man who, while he kills the father, leaves the son behind."[40] Moreover, it must be stressed that Agamemnon's murderer felt he could act with impunity *because* his deterring brother was abroad and because he had only one young son among several daughters.

The *Iliad* further emphasizes the importance of male kin through multiple examples of brothers leading expeditions together (see *Iliad* 2.484–877), and at least a dozen examples of brothers who fight side by side, fiercely defending one another in life and seeking immediate revenge if one of them is killed. For instance, in one scene Acamus avenges his slain brother and vaunts to the Greeks: "Think how Promachus sleeps overpowered by my spear, so that the blood price does not go long unpaid. And this is why a man prays for kinsmen to be left in his halls, to ward off harm" (*Iliad* 14.479–85; see also 11.328–34; 11.426–33; 12.370–71; 13.533–39; 17.377–83, etc.). As with Telemachus' words above, the numerous scenes depicting brothers fighting shoulder to shoulder, protecting and avenging one another, show that men can and must rely most completely on their brothers. Hector, for example, fleeing ignominiously from Achilles, is buoyed with hope and decides to stand and fight only after Athena cruelly tricks him into believing that a favorite brother, Deiphobus, has come to fight at his side (*Iliad* 22.226–59).

The dictates of the feud system are clear throughout both poems, but they are made particularly explicit at the end of the *Odyssey*, after the massacre of Penelope's suitors. Their kinsmen burn with the need for vengeance and fear the everlasting disgrace of failing to act before Odysseus and Telemachus flee (*Odyssey* 24.426–37). The rigidity of the revenge imperative is clearly communicated at the end of the poem, when Athena ends the blood feud before it can properly start by purging the memories of the suitors' kin of "the killings of their sons and brothers" (*Odyssey* 24.484–85). Homer's invocation of this precursor *deus ex machina* suggests that the only sure way to avert the reciprocal killings of a blood feud is through miraculous supernatural intervention.

Finally, as important as kin networks are for defending familial interests, ensuring just treatment, and deterring mistreatment, there is another side to the coin. In Homer, it is said repeatedly that top *basileis* "rule by might," and might is determined not only by one's personal prowess, but by the number, age range, and sex ratio of the kin network. Muscular kin networks could assert their interests over weaker networks. Large kin networks achieve positions of eminence in their communities, and thus the capacity to resolve conflicts in their favor. Contrary to the suggestions of some commentators,[41] the

Homeric world was not a lawless, Hobbesian milieu where strong men could throw their weight around with impunity. Rudimentary systems of justice were sometimes set into motion (e.g., *Iliad* 18.497–508), and we can assume that, as in band and tribal societies, coalitions of the weak would have formed to check and/or punish the excesses of the strong.[42] However, just as clearly, men with large funds of kinship power could turn this to their advantage. Consider Odysseus' words, spoken while he is masquerading as the son of Castor: "For I was fated to prosper among men, I did many reckless things, giving way to my might and courage, depending on my father and my brothers" (*Odyssey* 18.139–40).

There are some other cases where prominent men have only one son. These include Achilles, Hector, and Sarpedon. But, while the ages of most Homeric men are ambiguous, we certainly have the sense that these are young warriors with most of their reproductive lives in front of them. Hector and Sarpedon both have young wives and single infant sons, and Achilles has not yet married (one summary of the *Cypria* says that Neoptolemus was given his name because his father was young, *neos*, when his father went to war, *ptolemein*).[43] Homer mentions only one son of Menelaus – the bastard Megapenthes – but this provides no basis for assuming that he does not have other illegitimate sons (Helen has no children with Menelaus after the birth of their daughter, Hermione).

Nonetheless, Bryant has argued, not without warrant, that the instances of Homeric families with single sons are consistent with Hesiod's advice that men should avoid problems of inheritance by limiting themselves to one son.[44] However, Hesiod displays a "confused attitude" toward family planning:[45] he immediately contradicts himself by acknowledging that more sons can pay off through their greater productivity. In my judgment, the preponderance of evidence supports a general correlation between large kinship groups and political power in Homeric society. While there are exceptions to this rule, most of the cases are portrayed as exactly that: exceptions. The general picture of the epics indicates that there were great incentives favoring the formation of large fraternal interest groups. Based on what we know about kinship and political power in prestate societies, it would be a significant ethnographic anomaly to encounter a prestate society where levels of political influence were not in some degree proportionate to the size of the kin group.[46] We would expect this proportionality to be especially pronounced in the Homeric world, where strength was vital not only to a family's prosperity, but to their very survival.

In summary, Homeric society possessed conditions that would have favored the active or passive manipulation of sex ratios in favor of male offspring. This would not have been a means of overall population control; counter-intuitively, neither demographic theory nor empirical studies suggest that widespread juvenile EFM necessarily leads to population decline.[47] Indeed perhaps most biologists and anthropologists now argue that sex selective infanticide – far from being a means of limiting overall population – functions as a means of maximizing parental reproductive success. Individuals trade short-term genetic losses for long-term genetic gains.[48] Further, the hypothesis that Homeric era parents were manipulating sex ratios in favor of male offspring does not imply that women were despised. As a host of commentators have emphasized, there is more evidence of philogyny in Homer than misogyny.

Rather, in a conflict-torn world lacking formal justice, networks of male kin were critical for asserting and defending family interests; families with insufficient physical and political muscle risked being taken advantage of or being driven extinct, while families with strong kin networks could throw their weight around, ensuring that disputes were settled in their favor. While this discussion has not emphasized group-level dynamics, it is obvious that these same incentives would have applied at the community level. In a world where large networks of male kin were richly favored and small networks were significantly disadvantaged, families (and communities) would have felt pressure to reduce investment in daughters in order to produce more sons.

Furthermore, the ability of sons to directly assert and defend family interests would not have been the only pressure to produce sons at the expense of daughters. Sons in Homer also appear to offer their families more in the way of productive value, partly because sons who grow up to become capable warriors seize rich social and material spoil for their families. Moreover, even in times of relative peace, sons may contribute more. For one thing, males (slave and free) are responsible for the production of virtually all food, vegetable and animal, and for bringing home all of the raw materials required for a functioning household. Women (slave and free) mainly confine their labor to processing the raw materials that men bring home. The primarily indoor nature of female work is, perhaps, the source of Homer's recurrent female epithet, "white-armed." Moreover, the economic value of Homeric daughters, while significantly enhanced by bride-price payments, is severely diminished by the fact of patrilocality: sons stay with the paternal household to contribute a lifetime's effort whereas daughters leave to expend their labors on behalf of another household.

Comparative anthropology shows that in milieus where the productive value of sons and daughters is unbalanced, manipulation of sex ratios is relatively common. For instance, Hewlett's study of EFM in prestate populations concludes: "Male-biased juvenile sex ratios will exist in societies where . . . *males contribute more calories to the diet than females*, or where male mortality is high due to frequent warfare or risky subsistence tasks [italics mine]."[49] The Inuit exemplified this dynamic. Inuit women provided indispensable labor by processing food brought home by male hunters, but they were considered less valuable than males because they did not directly procure food themselves.[50] The result of this was noted by an early explorer: "The most glaring consequence of the struggle for existence is manifested in the way which they try to breed the greatest possible number of boys and the fewest possible girls."[51] Later censuses revealed strikingly high rates of female infanticide averaging 21 percent of all female births across ten communities.[52] This same relationship has been demonstrated in many other societies, perhaps most prominently in India and China.[53]

Finally, we should not overlook Hewlett's other predictor of male-biased juvenile sex ratios – high male mortality. It is obvious that adult male mortality is high in the Homeric world due not only to violence inside and outside the group, but also to the risks men faced in peacetime activities like hunting large game, fending hungry predators away from flocks, and plying the seas.

In short, intriguing evidence, albeit wholly circumstantial, supports the hypothesis that operational sex ratios in Homeric society, already skewed toward males through de facto polygyny, might have been further exaggerated by some degree of EFM. The support for this claim is given

- by comparison with sex-ratio-manipulating societies from history and ethnography;
- by evidence from different eras of Greek history for EFM due to abandonment or inferior nutrition;
- by an apparent scarcity of daughters;
- by an apparent cultural preference for sons;
- by the competitiveness and violence of the men (especially the young, mainly unmarried ones who are said to stir up trouble, e.g., *Odyssey* 12.440);
- by the centrality of intense competition and combat over women;
- by the high rates of adult male mortality;
- by the greater productive value of sons;
- by the great advantages of large fraternal interest groups, and by the perils of small ones.*

In making this argument I am playing an educated hunch. Sex-ratio manipulation occurs under specific and fairly predictable conditions, many of which were present in Homeric society. My argument is that features of Homeric society and conflict are tantalizingly consistent with the possibility of acute shortages of young women due to the

* Of course, many of the pressures described in this chapter applied throughout Greek history. Can this theory of Homeric conflict be applied to other epochs of Greek history? Addressing this question is beyond my scope and expertise. However, I will briefly say that the Mycenaeans were also warriors and raiders, and extant Linear B tablets suggest extreme imbalances in their holdings of female and male slaves. Tablets from Pylos "name 700 female slaves, with their 400 girls and 300 boys who 'belong to them'" (Fields 2004, 46). These women are often described as "captives" and "the fact that they are usually mentioned with their children but not with men implies the familiar raiding pattern of predatory war bands, where the men are killed and the women carried off" (Fields 2004, 46–47). Thus I can imagine that similar patterns to those I have proposed could have extended back through the tribal Dark Age to the era of the great Mycenaean palaces. Greeks in subsequent eras continued to experience frequent conflicts. In these conflicts, slaves were taken, more females than males, and sexual exploitation was common (see Rihill 1993; Finkelman and Miller 1998; Lerner 1986; Wiedemann 1981). Moreover, as previously discussed, there is widespread scholarly support for juvenile EFM in these periods. And EFM has been connected to practices that were famously characteristic of Greece, including higher rates of prostitution and homosexual behavior, and lower marriage ages for girls (Hudson and Den Boer 2005, 203). Thus it seems at least plausible that these demographic factors may have played *some* role in Greek fractiousness in post-Homeric periods. However, this is obviously an idea with expansive implications, and I would not wish to see it promoted without much deeper analysis of the evidence.

practices of polygyny and/or EFM. I believe that the evidence in favor of the first claim is quite strong, and that the likelihood of high *operational* sex ratios should be conceded regardless of what one thinks about the hypothesis of high *actual* sex ratios.

If either or both of these hypotheses are correct they have the potential to explain a lot about Homeric society. In the next chapter, I suggest that a shortage of women may help to illuminate the well-springs of Homeric tragedy and the frequently cruel and capricious natures of the gods and fate.

CHAPTER 8

The Prisoner's Dilemma and the mystery of tragedy

Aristotle's *Poetics* seeks to categorize the main features of tragedy. It argues that the most representative and successful tragedies describe the misfortunes of good, not wicked, men. The tragic outcome flows not from the hero's viciousness or depravity, but from cosmically unfortunate tricks of circumstance, simple error, or some blemish in the hero's character.[1] And, for Aristotle, tragedy's sine qua non is that it first arouses, and then cathartically purges, the emotions of pity and fear: "[tragedies are] imitations not only of actions which are complete but of such that inspire pity and fear . . . . pity is aroused by the plight of the man who does not deserve his misfortune, and fear by the predicament of men like ourselves."[2]

The *Poetics* draws sharp distinctions between the genres of tragedy and epic. But nowhere does Aristotle contend that epics cannot be tragic. After all, he reminds us that many tragedies – those once and still considered exemplars of the genre – are based on episodes culled from epic poems. Thus it is consistent with Aristotle, and with broader ancient and modern tradition,[3] to say that Homer, especially in the *Iliad*, evokes deeply tragic effects. The *Iliad* teems with tragic heroes and heroines: Hector, Andromache, Priam, Hecuba, Achilles, Patroclus, and on down the line to the unnumbered bit players who suffer and die in the poem. And Homer draws them sympathetically, as good men and women who do not deserve their agonies. They are trapped not by personal depravity or viciousness, but by the malevolence of fate and circumstance, and by weaknesses – greed, ambition, lust – shared by all. And their plights are hopeless: struggle as they may, Achilles will die and Troy will be raped.[4] The *Iliad* describes the sad and wretched aspects of the human condition with infinite tenderness, and it has never failed, in the course of almost three millennia, to arouse pity and fear.[5] While the *Odyssey*, with its happy ending, is rarely felt to be a tragedy today, it actually fits quite snugly into Aristotle's tragic template and shares elements of the *Iliad*'s pessimism and fatalism.[6]

Aristotle argues that the best tragic plots provoke wonder and surprise. But he discourages tragic plots that provoke these effects through recourse to the *alogon*. *Alogon* is a difficult word to translate, but it conveys a sense of negation (*a-logon*, without *logos*) – of law, reason, rationality, cause and effect. The word describes things that are irrational, absurd, unaccountable, inexplicable. Sections of the *Poetics* are so opaque that some scholars have wondered whether the volume may be a student's lecture notes rather than the great thinker's painstakingly crafted case. Is or is not, in Aristotle's view, the *alogon* strictly absent from the best tragedies? My own feeling is that Aristotle was using the word *alogon* in a narrow sense. He was talking about the basics of staging a play, where some of the irrational elements of epic – giant monsters, talking horses, gods fighting in the battles of men – would look ridiculous and annihilate verisimilitude.[7] But the *alogon* in a different, deeper sense – in the sense of the strangeness and mysteriousness of human experience – is certainly not alien to the best tragic dramas and it is not alien to Homer.[8] On the contrary, *alogon* is a profoundly appropriate descriptor of the tragic dimensions of the Homeric universe. People are generally good, yet they are the helpless prey of forces they cannot comprehend, explain, or confront. At the core of tragedy generally, and the Homeric worldview particularly, is an insoluble mystery that is fundamentally *alogon* – incomprehensible, absurd, mysterious.

In Homer, tragic phenomena can only be explained through recourse to the supernatural. People suffer helplessly owing to the nature of the universe: the gods are maniacs, and fate is often as pernicious as it is immutable. In this chapter I suggest that the *alogon* core of Homeric tragedy can be explained without invoking the supernatural. Theory and data from anthropology and evolutionary biology – combined with the game theory scenario of the Prisoner's Dilemma[9] – provide valuable clues to the mystery of Homeric tragedy. But I must first describe the features of Homeric tragedy that I seek to illuminate.

HOMERIC TRAGEDY

And yet I am told these very Greeks are wont to wage war against one another in the most foolish way, through sheer perversity and doltishness. (Herodotus, *The Histories*, 7.9, Trans. George Rawlinson)

Contrary to the claims of some commentators, most famously Simone Weil,[10] the *Iliad* is not an anti-war poem. Homer displays war's terrible, noble beauty along with its horror. His descriptions of men fighting and dying can be frenetic or languid, but they all reveal something wonderful about men competing at fullest capacity for the highest stakes. Homer's treatment of war is, in this sense, thoroughly unmodern. Ares, "insatiate of war" (*Iliad* 5.863), represents a real side of Homeric males, and when they feel the war lust, battle becomes "sweeter to them than to return in their hollow ships to their dear native land" (*Iliad* 2.453–54; 11.13–14). At times Achilles hates war, but on other occasions we see him "always yearning for war cries and battle" (*Iliad* 1.492), and we are told that "strife and war and battles are dear to [him]" (*Iliad* 1.177). Similarly, Odysseus reveals an authentic aspect of his personality when, as the son of Castor, he first brags of his prowess in war and then of his love for it:

Such a man was I in war. But I never loved working the land nor managing a household, work that provides for splendid children. But I always loved oared ships and war and polished spears and arrows, baneful things at which others shudder. But I loved those things which a god placed in my heart, for different men rejoice in different work. (*Odyssey* 14.222–28)

This frank depiction of the allure of war is part of the verisimilitude of the *Iliad* and, to a lesser but still marked extent, the *Odyssey* – it reflects something that has been reported by warriors throughout history, but which is often suppressed in our age: for all of its terrors, war can be attractive and invigorating. As General Lee reputedly said at the battle of Fredericksburg, "It is well war is so terrible, else we should grow too fond of it."

Yet the *Iliad* is even less a glorification of war than a condemnation of it. War can bring glory, but it is also characterized in a series of formulas as wretched (*oïzuros*), evil (*kakos*), painful (*argaleos*), full of tears (*poludakrus*), bitter (*drimus*), tearful (*dakruoeis*), and grievous (*algeinos*). The poems revel in pagan guiltlessness over the beauty, grace, and delectability of the hero's form. With the definition in his huge muscles heightened by sweat or a sheen of good olive oil, he looks just like a handsome young god. But when wild Ares runs loose among warriors, he hacks and saws and pokes at them until they spill out of their skins and flop and splash in the dust, no longer strong, vigorous or beautiful.

And Homer never looks away. With the anatomist's cold fascination, he stoops down to muck in the corpses, tracing the course of tendons, the mechanics of joints, the logic of organ position. The *Iliad* has been called "a poem of death," in part because of its limitless repertoire of slayings. Homer devotes thousands of lines to describing the killings of almost 250 named warriors and those of hundreds more who die anonymously.[11] The poem is full of formula and repetition, but his descriptions of death bubble up from a deep creative well.[12] Breached with surprising ease by the cold bronze, the body's contents pour forth in viscous torrents: portions of brains emerge at the ends of quivering spears, young men hold back their viscera with desperate hands, eyes are knocked or cut from skulls and glimmer sightlessly in the dust. Sharp points forge new entrances and exits in young bodies: in the center of foreheads, in temples, between the eyes, at the base of the neck, clean through the mouth or cheek and out the other side, through flanks, crotches, buttocks, hands, navels, backs, stomachs, nipples, chests, noses, ears, and chins; through hip, shoulder, elbow, jaw, and knee joints. Arms, legs and heads are severed from bodies; joints and bones are crushed by flung rocks; tendons, muscles, jugulars, windpipes, and spinal columns are sliced, ruptured, and crushed; tongues are cut away and teeth blasted from gaping mouths; kidneys, bladders, hearts and livers are skewered as they pulse and filter; jagged rocks pound through casings of bronze and skull to pulverize and spatter brains. Spears, pikes, arrows, swords, daggers and rocks lust for the savor of flesh and blood. Blood sprays forth and mists the air. Bone fragments fly. Marrow boils from fresh stumps.

Their limbs go slack and the men crash down like poplars, like young striplings, like great mature oaks; they stagger and fall like animals stunned for butchering; they sprawl face first; dust billows and armor booms; writhing like earthworms in pooled blood, they bellow and roar out their lives; the hateful darkness takes them.

In the aftermath of battle, blood flows from a thousand mortal or maiming wounds, turns dust to mud, and fattens the grasses of the plain. Men plowed into the soil by heavy chariots, sharp-hoofed stallions, and the sandals of men are past recognition. Armor and weaponry litter the field. Bodies are everywhere, decomposing, deliquescing, feasting dogs, worms, flies, and birds. Once handsome as young gods, the men "lay sprawled on the field, craved far more by the vultures than by wives" (*Iliad* 11.161–62). The survivors stagger back to the citadel or wade out into the sea to lave their wounds and scrub away clotted gore.

In short, it is hard to read the *Iliad* without gaining new respect for the unfathomable waste and stupidity of war. Homeric men have some positive feelings toward war because it can bring them good things: slave and wives, livestock and other possessions, lasting social prestige, camaraderie, adventure, and the knowledge of courage. But the evils of war are larger and crueler: the menacing wink of edged bronze; the deaths of kinsmen and comrades; and the constant knowledge that what goes around comes around. Today Trojans are robbed, massacred, and raped. Tomorrow it could be Ithacans, or Mycenaeans, or Pylians because the war god "rages randomly" (*Odyssey* 11.537) and all men are alike to him – "he who kills, he kills" (*Iliad* 18.309).

By providing short, tender, achingly particular biographies of men killed in battle, Homer reminds us that every glorious victory forces inestimable sorrow on a man and his entire family. In these so-called *necrologues* Homer paints sad contrasts between the terrible and terrifying deaths of young men and the daily satisfactions of peacetime life: the security of loving parents, the embraces of a young wife and small children, and the simple toil of peacetime. Through his constant references to bereaved relatives, through his anticipation of their wracking griefs, he reveals a sad ripple effect that crosses the sea to lick Greek shores. We are left with the vision of an Aegean world quaking with grief, all radiating from the Trojan epicenter.

Paradoxically, however, the *Iliad* is nothing if not a celebration of life's beauties. It accomplishes this not in spite of the poem's savagery but through it. Homer shows us that there is nothing like death to accentuate life's preciousness, nothing like mangling bronze to remind us of the body's beauty, nothing like a child's or brother's untimely demise to remind us of the power and significance of our kinship bonds. And the *Iliad* multiplies the deaths incessantly, increasing the significance of human life exponentially, death by death. The *Iliad* is a celebration of life in the context of painful, untimely, and mass death, and it draws its power from this source.[13] Through its close depiction of all the ways that men can kill and die, the poem shocks us into feeling how short life is and how precious.

And what was it all for? At the end of the *Iliad*, Hector has been killed and mutilated, and we know with the certainty of divine edict that Troy will be robbed, raped and immolated. Cruelly, Priam is able to foresee the calamity in vivid detail:

> Have pity on me while I still live, ill-fated as I am. On the threshold of old age, father Zeus will lay a grievous fate on me after I have seen many evils, my sons destroyed and my daughters dragged about, and the chambers of my home ravaged, and the infant children dashed on the ground in the direness of battle, and my daughters-in-law dragged off in the murderous hands of the Achaians. And myself last of all, at my front gate my dogs will tear my flesh apart, after some man has seized the life from my limbs by throw or thrust of sharp bronze – the dogs I raised in my halls to be at my table and guard my door will drink my blood in their madness and lie down in the gateway . . . [It is well and good for a young man to die in battle] but when an old man is slain, and the dogs disfigure his grey head and grizzled beard and the parts that are private, this is the most lamentable thing to befall wretched mortals. (*Iliad* 22.59–76)

While a Trojan remnant led by Aeneas is destined to survive, and while the lives of Trojan women will also be spared, the Rape of Troy is genocidal: the destruction of Priam's fertile genitals symbolizes the destruction of Troy's cultural and biological essences.

Thus the fact that the Trojans lose the war is clear. But the Greeks win only in a technical sense. In Troy, the best of the Achaians were slain (*Odyssey* 3.108). Other Greeks survive the conflict, but their triumphs are mainly pyrrhic; not one of the survivors – Nestor, Odysseus, Menelaus – is able to recall the war except in a spirit of tearful regret. Each man spent a full decade of his life sleeping in makeshift structures, far distant from wives and children; all suffered terrible losses and combat traumas, both physical and psychological.[14] When the war finally ends they do not, for the most part, go home to revel in their spoils and languish in the esteem of retired war heroes. Rather the men face awful calamities on their voyage home, and the murderous ambitions of upstarts upon their return. Homer's vision of the Trojan War and its aftermath is not, then, a vision of winners besting losers, but of losers besting losers. Everyone loses.

Yet for all the miseries of war, for all the protestations of a preference for peace and its pleasures ("sleep and lovemaking, the sweetness of song and stately dancing," *Iliad* 13.620–39), and for all the vitriolic and universal hatred of war as personified in Ares, the possibility of actually renouncing fighting rarely occurs to the men. Rather, war is presented as a simple fact of life. It is not an optional activity; it is thrust irresistibly onto men, like the weather or the "hatefulness" of old age. As Simone Weil wrote, war is presented as a *force* that men are subject to – a force to be endured without hope of influencing.[15]

This sense of inevitability is most prominently displayed in Achilles' recognition that the benefits of war are outweighed by its dire costs. He claims that his life of "fighting men for their wives" (9.327) has been essentially pointless, gaining him nothing. He vows to go home at once, choose a bride, and enjoy his wealth in peace (9.355–429). But almost immediately after reaching this conclusion, and *prior* to the death of Patroclus, his resolve falters and he says that he will stay with the army after all (9.649–55); and this is exactly what he does. By the *Iliad*'s end he is again full of battle boasts as he fights for revenge and glory: "But now let me seize great glory and drive some deep-bosomed Trojan or Dardanian woman to moan while wiping the flood of tears from her tender cheeks with both hands!" (*Iliad* 18.121–124; see also *Iliad* 22.393–94).

There is a sense in the *Iliad*, conveyed in the drama of Achilles, that the unceasing scramble for military spoil and glory is stupid and painful, but there is finally no escape from it. In the course of the poem, Achilles gains maturity and wisdom, and he sees that he does not have to spend the rest of his manhood as he and Patroclus spent the first part: "What pains they had suffered on the waves and in the hard wars of men" (*Iliad* 24.7–8). Achilles' vision clears and he recognizes the emptiness of heroic striving. But, though he can imagine a different way of life, he cannot grope his way toward it.

He stays in Troy to fight and die for the revenge he needs, but also for the glory that he claims no longer to want.

On a larger scale, on several occasions Trojans and Greeks futilely attempt to end the war so that they may enjoy the peace they all desire. Each time something stops them, sometimes a man, but more often a god. In book 3, Paris and Menelaus agree to settle their dispute in single combat to the death; why should all the men risk their lives when the two foes can settle things directly? The winner will claim Helen and, regardless of the outcome, the Greeks will go home to their wives and children, allowing the Trojans to rejoice in theirs. However, the gods intervene to save Paris' life, and the fighting resumes, bloodier than ever. Similarly, in book 22, Hector, great as he is, stands almost as helpless as a woman (22.125) before enraged, matchless Achilles. Hector is Troy's bulwark against massacre and rape, and he knows his death will seal the doom not only of his city but of his family: his brothers and brothers-in-law cut down in the last stand, his wife dragged off in rough Greek hands (6.450–55). By giving up Helen and Troy's vast wealth, he might yet save himself, his family, and his city (22.111–121). But the shame is too much, and he commits to a fight that he knows he cannot win; by Hector's own admission he is "weaker by far" (20.431–37).

If it is conventional to speak of the *Iliad* as a tragedy, it is almost as conventional to stress the comic aspects of the *Odyssey*.[16] Differences between the poems have inspired some interesting theories: that the *Iliad* was written by a man and the *Odyssey* by a woman; that the *Iliad* was the product of Homer's youth, and the *Odyssey* of his maturity; that, to the contrary, the *Iliad* was composed by a *mature* poet and the *Odyssey* by a youthful epigone; that Homer produced the *Iliad* for the men in the audience, and the *Odyssey* for the women.[17] These theories all arose from the same conviction: that differences in philosophy, tone, and outlook between the epics are so vast that a radical theory is needed to explain them. While the evidence for them is tenuous at best, they nonetheless reflect exaggerated versions of common sentiments among readers.

There are undeniably important differences between the poems. But I believe these are frequently overstated and that equally important commonalities are downplayed. To cite a particularly important instance of this tendency, it is sometimes argued that the conclusion of the *Odyssey* presages the development of a newer, gentler, moral order – the ethical world of the emerging *polis*, a world clearly at odds with what we see in the *Iliad*.[18] However, most of the evidence is set violently against this view. The final books of the *Odyssey* include the climactic massacre of 108 young men, Odysseus' cold rejection of their excuses and their desperate offers of huge compensation payments (worth more than 2,160 oxen; see 22.45–59), Telemachus' savage choice of a painful mode of execution for the twelve unfaithful slave women, Odysseus' killing of the relatively blameless Leodes before he can even finish begging for his life (22.310–29), the killing of the suitors' attendants, the bizarre cruelty of Odysseus' treatment of Laertes, and the deranged sadism of the torture and dismemberment of Melanthius.

In this last case, Odysseus instructs his swineherd *not* to immediately kill the traitorous goatherd Melanthius so that they may, at their leisure, fully satisfy their desire for revenge against him (22.164–77). As Davies writes of Melanthius' fate: "We have here a description not of a *killing* but of a *punishment* by maiming and mutilation. Melanthius, bereft of his extremities, is to be left a living corpse, legless and armless . . . This passage, standing as it does in a climactic position, is a useful antidote against the still common assumption that the *Odyssey* is more ethically advanced than the *Iliad* [emphasis in original]."[19]

In short, the *Odyssey* is a poem in which the hero triumphs, but the tone and texture of morality, philosophy and outlook are, for me, recognizably similar, recognizably Homeric. So, though it is much less central to the thematic heart of the poem, the notion that violent conflict is an inescapable facet of the human condition is also expressed in the *Odyssey*. And the suggestion is all the more powerful because the *Odyssey* is a portrait of a world at relative peace; there is no great conflict that men are drawn to participate in. Yet, after ten years of hand-to-hand battles, Odysseus has not had enough. Departing from Troy, holds straining with rich Trojan chattels, Odysseus' party still stops along the way home to rape and despoil (*Odyssey* 9.39–42). Later, when Odysseus journeys to the underworld, he is shocked to meet Agamemnon, not having heard of the great chief's murder. Odysseus' assumption that Agamemnon probably died in raids suggests that the life of the seafaring raider is the only one conceivable to him (*Odyssey* 11.397–403). Similarly, when the *psychai* of massacred suitors stream into the underworld, Agamemnon is waiting to greet them, and he jumps to exactly the same conclusion: these men must have been killed at sea or as they raided for flocks and women (*Odyssey* 24.109–13).

The epic of Odysseus' struggle to return home from the Trojan War, to reunite with his wife, and to put his house in order is as much a love poem as an adventure story. Thus it ends with the reunion of a long-divided family and the promise of future happiness and prosperity. But Homer's neat ending is "radically qualified" by hints of dark realities.[20] After twenty years of strife and struggle, Odysseus' battles are not yet at an end. As he tells Penelope, their trials are not over – measureless toil, long and hard, awaits them (23.248–50). Odysseus is bound by fate to embark on dangerous travels to far-flung lands as a missionary of Poseidon (*Odyssey* 23.264–84). Moreover, Odysseus, "raider of cities," is who he is: he will replenish his depleted flocks largely through aggressive raids (*Odyssey* 23.356–58). In this light, the words Odysseus speaks in the guise of his alter ego, the son of Castor, are almost ominous. Just like Odysseus, the pugnacious son of Castor finally returns home following the long ordeal of the Trojan War, but he is not the domestic type (*Odyssey* 14.216–28). He immediately yearns for the sea and the spear: "For wretched me, Zeus, the counselor, devised evil. For only a month I stayed, delighting in my children, my loyal wife, and my wealth. But then my heart urged me to sail on Egypt, to fit out good ships with godlike comrades in arms" (*Odyssey* 14.243–47).

Moreover, despite the *Odyssey*'s superficially optimistic conclusion, its philosophical mood is consistent with the *Iliad*'s, reflecting their common cultural (and perhaps authorial) origins. The twenty-four books of the *Odyssey*, like the books of the *Iliad*, contain salient interludes of joy and satisfaction. However, until the end of the poem, the dominant mood is one of suffering and futility. The bulk of the narrative features the main characters – Odysseus, Telemachus, and Penelope – in dismal straits, tearfully struggling with hopelessness and despair. The poem ends happily only through the intervention of gods (just the kind of *alogon* device, a veritable *deus ex machina*, that Aristotle loathed to see on stage). In blood-feuding Homeric society the calculated massacre of so many prominent men, each supported by formidable networks of kinsmen and allies, would result in massive retaliation.[21] But before the cycle of vengeance can begin its inexorable spin – before the town can cannibalize itself – Athena descends from Olympus to "purge the memories [of the suitors' kin] of the bloody slaughter of their sons and brothers" (*Odyssey* 24.484–85), and to establish "a solemn truce between the two sides" (*Odyssey* 24.546). Through the miracle of mass amnesia Homer succeeds in ending his story happily. But from a different perspective this ending is all the more dismal. Once violence breaks out, the only reprieve from a devastating series of reciprocal attacks is divine intervention.

WHY?

The tragic elements of the Homeric outlook are bitterly emphasized in his clashing juxtapositions of the horrors of conflict and the pleasures of peace. The blessings of peaceful existence are described with sweet intensity: there are the satisfactions of good marriage; the exuberance of boys destroying sand castles on the shore; the mental picture of a baby girl bawling on her mother's skirts until she is scooped up, or of a newborn infant set on his grandfather's knee to receive his name; the promise of young men; the disorienting beauty of young women; the never-cloying sweetness of "mingling in love"; the sleek power of horses; the love of song; the laughter of girls; the richness of red wine; and the savor of meat crusted in sea salt, roasted with fire, and consumed on the beach as the sun bleeds its last into the sea.

These images force on our minds what is, for me, the most profound and persistent question of the Homeric poems. Why? Why must they squander this beauty? Why, even when they seek out peace, do they so often find war?

The Homeric solutions to these enigmas are given in the nature of the gods and the sheer indifference of fate. The main reason for war is Olympian politics. The specific cause of the Trojan War is the ludicrous vanity of two enraged goddesses. Every time peace looms divinity intercedes. The massacre and mass rape of a city full of upright and pious people is all in revenge for one man's judgment in a beauty contest. In this we glimpse an attempt to conceive some rationale for the wasteful absurdity of Greek conflict – and fallout from a beauty contest, from a catfight, from the childish pique of gods, is a suitably *alogon* explanation. All of the fighting makes no sense unless forces this maniacal, capricious, and cruel control the universe.

In short, the Homeric worldview is reasonably based on the belief that the most irrationally painful aspects of the human condition must flow from irrational sources. Now we reach the core of my argument: While Homeric outcomes seemed irrational, they were driven by a clean, relentless, almost mathematical logic.

PRISONER'S DILEMMAS, VICIOUS CYCLES, AND TRAGEDY

But the most important thing for us is that we never end a war . . . it became known that you could win a war with the Yanomamö today, but your children's children would pay for it forever . . . Stopping fighting is not the Yanomamö way. (Jungleman, a Yanomamö shaman[22])

Perhaps the most striking thing about violence in warlike non-state societies is its vicious circularity. Violence begets violence, blood demands vengeance, in a self-reinforcing feedback loop.[23] As explained in the previous chapter, these patterns of conflict are particularly persistent in populations where operational and/or actual sex ratios are strongly "masculinized." Divale and Harris were the first to fully grasp that this engenders a vicious cycle: manipulation of the sex ratio in favor of males creates shortages of females, which creates an incentive to raid for women, which leads to violent retribution, which exacerbates the need for warriors, which increases pressures to manipulate the sex ratio in favor of males, which exacerbates the shortage of women, which increases incentive to raid, and on and on. The cycle can be summarized with this aptly circular formulation: parents bias their investment in favor of males largely because the world is violent; the world is violent largely because parents bias their investment in favor of males. We rebel against the senselessness of this tautology. But the tautology is appropriate in this case, paralleling the *alogon* absurdity of the situation it describes: the belligerents may all want peace, yet they find themselves trapped in conflict.[24]

As the anthropologist Azar Gat argues, violence in non-state societies often adheres to the tragic logic of the Prisoner's Dilemma.[25] The Prisoner's Dilemma describes a concept from game theory that has

		Prisoner Two	
		Cooperate (stay silent)	Defect (confess)
Prisoner One	Cooperate (stay silent)	1, 1	0, 30
	Defect (confess)	30, 0	15, 15

Figure 2. Payoff matrix for a standard game of Prisoner's Dilemma. The payoffs for Player One (the "row player" on the left) are represented to the left of the comma. The payoffs of Player Two (the "column player" across the top) are represented to the right of the comma. Outcomes always hinge on the other player's decisions, and all choices are made simultaneously.

become the classic example of a non-zero-sum game across the social, human, and life sciences. There is nothing frivolous about game theory, despite its name. Game theory was effectively invented in John von Neumann's 1928 paper on optimal strategies in parlor games. But von Neuman was interested in constructing a systematic theory of rational behavior, and he used games as a simple setting for the exercise of human rationality.[26] Game theory is the logical analysis of *any* situation of conflict and/or cooperation to determine how individual strategists should behave in order to achieve their best outcomes.

In the Prisoner's Dilemma two people have been accused of collaborating in a serious crime, and have been separated for interrogation (actually the dilemma still holds if the prisoners are allowed to communicate). The accused are both told exactly the same thing: if each of you confess (or "defect" in game theory terminology), you will both be sentenced to fifteen years in prison; if you both stay silent (or "cooperate") the prosecutor will convict you on a lesser charge, and you will both be sentenced to one year; if one confesses but the other does not, the confessor will make a deal with the prosecutor and go free while the other goes to jail for thirty years (see Figure 2). In sum, each prisoner is faced with the dilemma of how to achieve his best outcome: by cooperating with his partner in crime or defecting from him.

The dilemma is so devilishly frustrating because even though a reasonably desirable solution is in reach (only one year in jail if the prisoners silently cooperate with one another), the rational pursuit of self-interest compels them to defect, and to doom themselves to a much darker outcome. The Prisoner's Dilemma scenario, like all game theory scenarios, assumes players who are acting rationally to ensure their best outcomes. With this assumption in place, both prisoners *must* choose the option of defect (confess to the crime), because each is better off choosing that option *no matter what option the other chooses*. Prisoner One does best if he confesses (defects) and his partner remains stubbornly silent (cooperates). Whereas, in the event that his partner chooses to confess, Prisoner One had better confess too so as to avoid the worst outcome of thirty years in prison – in game-theory jargon, "the sucker's payoff." Precisely the same logic applies to Prisoner Two: no matter what his partner decides, he does best by defecting. The tragedy is that the prisoners fail to achieve their common interest of minimizing time served; if they had only cooperated, both would have been much better off.

The Prisoner's Dilemma is a game in which the playing field is slanted, by default, strongly in favor of the authorities and against the prisoners. As long as the prisoners behave rationally, seeking to maximize utility however they define it, they will always lose. In the Prisoner's Dilemma defection is a Nash Equilibrium – a stable strategy in which each player is making the best possible response to the other. There is no *rational* alternative to an equilibrium strategy. Of course, either player can choose to cooperate with their partner by remaining silent. But this is, in game-theory parlance, a "dominated" strategy that is apt to result in a sucker's reward.

The story of two prisoners faced with a terrible dilemma was devised by the mathematician Albert Tucker. The story was not meant to illustrate specific principles of crime, punishment, and dishonor among thieves. Rather, Tucker meant to provide one example of a pervasive class of competitive interactions – first described in mathematical terms by Melvin Dresher and Merrill Flood of the Rand Corporation[27] – in which the rational pursuit of self-interest leads to non-optimal outcomes for all. Tucker could have illustrated this conflict with any number of different scenarios, and since he first told the story of the Prisoner's Dilemma, many other theorists have done exactly that.[28] The Prisoner's Dilemma, at its core, describes a tragic paradox produced by the pursuit of individual good over collective good. In the end, individuals and groups faced with such dilemmas are prisoners of nothing so much as vaunted human rationality and natural self-interest.

Turning back to the anthropology of non-state violence, in many cases all sex-ratio-manipulating societies would be best served if the arms race to produce large numbers of warrior sons were ended. If all parties stood down, they would recoup the abominable waste of EFM while reaping the dividends of peace. In game-theory terms this is the substantial dividend that is paid if all parties choose the option of cooperation. However, the consequences of cooperating are staggering if other parties defect. So, in this viciously circular game of Prisoner's Dilemma, the only real option, both for societies and individual families, is to defect – to continue biasing sex ratios in favor of males so as to maintain a balance of power with neighbors. Unilaterally opting out of the race can lead to weakness within the group and to slaughter and rape in conflicts between groups.

THE SHADOW OF THE FUTURE

This explication requires caveats. First, the Prisoner's Dilemma is a behavioral model and, like all good models, it is useful precisely because it is simpler than what it represents. Of course, human behavior is not governed by logic alone. Social relationships, emotion, and other variables must be considered. For example, how would the outcomes change if the prisoners were brothers, if they were mother and child, or if one of them had powerful and vicious allies? Game-theory models are idealized, abstract, and artificial simulations of vastly complex real-world interactions. However, an enormous body of work in the life, human, and social sciences rests on the evidence that these models correspond to reality in important, concrete ways. Game theory is "the mathematical backbone" of the economic theory of competition; it is "one of the most important advances in evolutionary theory since Darwin"; and it has found extensive application in sociology, zoology, business, anthropology, philosophy, and other fields.[29]

Second, the above example is of a "one-shot" game of Prisoner's Dilemma. In a one-shot game – or in finite series of games – defection is the Nash Equilibrium; among rational and self-interested actors, cooperation cannot emerge. However, if the rules are modified so that prisoners play an open-ended sequence of games – where neither can confidently predict when the interaction will end – then cooperation can emerge in many (though not all) competitive milieus. In Robert Axelrod's nice phrase, cooperation is favored when "the shadow of the future" is long. When players expect an open-ended process of interaction the benefits of long-term cooperation can bulk larger than those of short-term defection. While purely cooperative strategies are defeated in almost every competitive environment, strategies based on the principle of "Tit For Tat" have achieved robust success in many competitive simulations.[30] Tit For Tat is not governed by the golden principle of "do unto others as you would *have them* do unto you"; rather, it does unto others *as others do unto it.* The Tit For Tat strategy is remarkably straightforward: on the first move cooperate; on all subsequent moves copy your opponent's previous move. Tit For Tat rewards cooperation with cooperation and punishes defection with defection.

Applying the Prisoner's Dilemma concept to Homeric conflict inspires a critical question: how long was the shadow of the future? When the shadow of the future is short, defection is the equilibrium strategy; when the shadow of the future is long, cooperation based on the principle of reciprocity can emerge. The arguments of this book suggest that, in Homeric society, the shadow of the future was relatively short and indistinct. Each *polis* existed precariously, and their interactions with most outsiders were relatively infrequent and marred by conflict. In other words, their environment was one in which future interaction and reciprocation of cooperation were not assured – precisely the type of environment, in other words, that rewards defection over cooperation.

However, from a different perspective, the question of whether the shadow of the future was long or short is immaterial. Tit For Tat is capable of playing nice, but it is also scarily provokable. The Tit For Tat strategy can quickly deteriorate into an unending spiral of defection and counter-defection – of plucking eyes for eyes and teeth for teeth – that is indistinguishable from the strategy of pure defection.

My argument is that the Prisoner's Dilemma captures, in a radically simplified form, the essence of many Homeric conflicts. What is important is the outcome: cycles of defection. Whether the cycles emerged through pure defection of through reciprocation is interesting, but less critical to the present discussion.

Homer's epics are about men who spend their childhoods preparing for conflict, and their manhoods killing or being killed as they fight for glory, wealth and women. And this is no quirk of the present generation, no passing blight of strife. Homer's Greeks are career warriors and raiders, following in the deeply impressed footprints of fathers, grandfathers, and older brothers who were themselves sackers of cities. Warrior panoply, craft, and pride are legacies passed from father to son. The Greeks of Achilles' generation fought a long, pyrrhic war at Troy. The Greeks of his father's generation fought a disastrous war at Thebes. And, while Homer invites us to imagine Troy in the "time of peace before the Achaians came" as tranquil and prosperous (e.g., *Iliad* 22.153–56), in the previous generation another bloody Greek, Heracles, sacked the city and "widowed her streets" (*Iliad* 5.642). For as long as anyone can remember, for as far back as any warrior can trace his family tree, the Greeks have supplemented their farming and husbandry with an economy of raiding and pillaging. Theirs has always been a violent way of life, as is indicated by the words of Odysseus: "We [the Greeks] are men to whom Zeus gave the fate of living through hard wars, from youth to old age, until we perish, each of us" (*Iliad* 14.85–87).

Odysseus' fatalistic resignation is typical of the philosophical mood of both poems. Homer's characters realize that they are spinning in a dizzy cycle of violence. And they believe, like Odysseus, that their way of life is the unavoidable issue of fate's decrees or some god's will. In either case, events are beyond their control; they are like delicate bubbles adrift on a wine-dark sea, helplessly tumbled by inscrutable forces.

The Prisoner's Dilemma captures the relentless logic behind many frustrating and seemingly illogical outcomes in human experience (famous examples include the tragedy of the commons and the nuclear arms race of the Cold War[31]), and it may help to illuminate the tragic elements of the Homeric worldview. Homer's epics reflect a world whose inhabitants were twirled by cycles of violence which, though they appeared *alogon*, actually followed the rigorous logic of the Prisoner's Dilemma. The rules of the game were slanted so that players were logically forced by greed and fear into mutually destructive outcomes. As in the classic game of Prisoner's Dilemma, Homeric conflicts tend to produce outcomes in which all sides lose. Through rational defection they may avoid the disastrous consequences of sucker's payoffs, but by failing to cooperate they fail to achieve not only what is best for the collectives, but also what is best for individuals.

The arms race to produce larger numbers of interest-asserting sons, at the expense of daughters – and its relationship to de facto Homeric polygyny – is only one of three situations described in this book that adhere to the logic of the Prisoner's Dilemma. The second is the cycle of "prudently bold" risk-taking behavior described in Chapter Five above. An entrenched system of social, material, psychological, and sexual rewards encourages and rewards competitive risk-taking. Once this system is in place, men who wish to achieve these rewards simply have no choice but to vigorously assert their interests within the group and to fight bravely when the community wages war. The cycle spins relentlessly in this direction: social and reproductive success is awarded to competitive risk-takers because the Homeric world is particularly dangerous; the world is particularly dangerous because a system of social and reproductive rewards favors competitive risk-taking.

Men in this situation can be envisioned as players in a game of Prisoner's Dilemma, where continuing to strive competitively is defined as defection and forsaking competitive striving is defined as cooperation. As in the classic formulation, each "player" achieves his best payoff through defection no matter how the other players behave. Because the other players cannot be counted on to "cooperate," those who forsake competitive risk-taking unilaterally are likely to be punished with the sucker's payoff – in this case, smaller payoffs of social, material and sexual rewards. The tragedy is that everyone incurs the steep costs of competitive striving in vain, because no one gets ahead. On the other hand, if players cooperated they would still be neck-and-neck, but they would have avoided the staggering and dangerous waste of continuously vying for hierarchical altitude. Like the Red Queen in Lewis Carroll's *Through the Looking-Glass*, then, Homeric men must run their hardest just to stay still.

Third, and finally, there is the vicious cycle generated by female mating preferences and male competitive and violent tendencies (see above, Chapter Six). Homeric women prefer men with a capacity for "demonism" because they inhabit a world populated with potentially dangerous men; the world is populated with highly competitive and potentially dangerous men, at least in part, because women consistently prefer such men as mates. And the cycle is difficult to disrupt. Individual men and women cannot safely behave differently. Men cannot choose the "cooperative" option of behaving angelically, and women cannot cooperate with their sisters by favoring angels, because they cannot trust other men and women to do the same. In these male and female dilemmas, behaving angelically (for men) and choosing a purely angelic mate (for women) are doomed strategies. To choose these strategies is to court the sucker's payoff: celibacy for men and, for women, incompetent male provisioning and protection.

EQUILIBRIUM

Homer's tragic vision of men fated to "live through hard wars" until they perish, no matter how much they might prefer peace, is a philosophy consistent with the logic of viciously circular violence in many non-state societies. The bitterness, pessimism, fatalism, and stoicism of the Homeric outlook may all be properties of the vicious cycles that rule their lives, that ruled the lives of their fathers and grandfathers, and that, they believe, will continue to rule the lives of their sons. Their vision of vain, petty, unbalanced gods randomly meting out good and bad fortune, whimsically razing cities – all in accord with the arbitrary dictates of fate – seems a groping attempt to explain the *alogon*: how can "terrible war" rage on and on in spite of the desirability of peace?

Of course, Homeric peoples may not have understood the complex relationship between perennial shortages of young women, volatile surpluses of young men, and unremitting warfare. They might not have grasped how female preferences for competitive and potentially dangerous men and violent tendencies among the males fed on one another like the ouroboros. They might not have fully seen the viciously escalating relationship between rich societal rewards for competitive risk-taking and a progressively more competitive and violent world. They would not have discerned how all of these cycles were ultimately rooted in competition for reproductive success in a specific, and highly competitive, physical and cultural ecology. And they certainly would not have understood that these cycles were governed by the vicious logic of the Prisoner's Dilemma. But they knew all too well that they were locked in relentless cycles of competition and conflict, and that it was all but futile to try to stop them. They knew they had reached a state of equilibrium, where their strategies – and their outcomes – could not change until the rules of the game did.

Conclusion: Between lions and men

The essence of the evolutionary approach to human behavior and psychology is that humans are animals, and, as a result, the tools we use to study animal behavior can be used to illuminate the human condition. *Homo sapiens* has complicated culture and stunning capacity to learn, but this does not change the fact that we are also animals, vertebrates, mammals, primates, great apes, and hominids. Aspects of our culture, intelligence, and symbolic behavior make us different from the other apes, but they do not emancipate us from our evolved biology or lift us above other animals onto an exalted link of the chain of being.

Evolutionary exploration of human behavior and psychology remains controversial for many reasons: the fear of biological fatalism and reductionism, the error of the naturalistic fallacy (the fallacious supposition that what is natural is therefore both "good" and inevitable) and, perhaps most importantly, the unquiet ghosts of Social Darwinism. But resistance to evolution is also a spasm against an approach that snatches humans from the top of the chain of being, and hurls us in the blood and filth to splash and gasp with the other animals. We are still assimilating Darwin's news that Adam and Eve were not molded lovingly from clay, inspired with life, and set apart by God as masters of His creation; Darwin argued, and subsequent research confirmed, that our progenitors were rude grandchildren of a "... hairy, tailed quadruped, probably arboreal in its habits, and an inhabitant of the Old World."[1]

But Homer would not have been scandalized by *The descent of man*.[2] The Homeric lifestyle of perennial warfare occasions an identity crisis that is fully expressed in the *Iliad*: What is a human being? What is this creature that adopts humane pretenses, and then wades into the melee to glut his spear with blood? While standing on the ramparts, trading soft words with his wife and joyfully dandling his fat baby boy, Hector is an incarnation of the humane ideal. But compare the gentle humanity of Hector, the family man, to the following description of Hector, the warrior:

> Hector, Priam's son, was himself very eager. And he was raging like Ares, who fights with the spear, or as destructive fire rages on the mountains and the thick forest. Foam appeared around his mouth and his eyes glowed under his shaggy brows, and around his temples the helmet of Hector shook terribly as he fought . . . [He] came against them like a destructive lion on cattle. (*Iliad* 15.604–30)

War can make the mildest man into a slavering animal. Hector's transformation is paralleled many times over in the description of other warriors as they take to the battlefield. Humane vestments fit loose, and fall away in the pitch and roll of battle. Consider, for instance, Homer's inspired description of Achilles' troops, the war-lusting Myrmidons:

> Achilles went here and there among the huts making all the Myrmidons don armor. And like wolves who eat raw flesh, in whose hearts the fury is boundless – who have killed a big horned stag in the mountains and lap the black surface of a deep and dark spring with their thin tongues, belching forth blood and gore, with the hearts in their chests dauntless and their bellies glutted – just so did the leaders and rulers of the Myrmidons rush out around the faithful retainer [i.e. Patroclus] of the swift-footed grandson of Aeacus [i.e. Achilles]. And among them stood Achilles urging on both the men who carry the shields and the horses. (*Iliad* 16.155–67)

The epics abound with short and extended similes of this type, juxtaposing the activities, behaviors, and mental states of men and animals; Homer anthropomorphizes animals and he zoomorphizes humans.[3] More than half (125:226) of the *Iliad*'s similes have an animal subject. The most frequent feature marauding lions; there are 50 such similes.[4] This is to say nothing of the many, many times where one hero or another is honored with leonine epithets like "lion-like" or "lion-hearted." The *Odyssey* is not a war poem, but when the plot turns violent, animal comparisons quickly emerge. For example, after Odysseus has massacred the suitors, the old slave woman Eurycleia finds him ". . . in the midst of the dead bodies, splattered with blood and gore like a lion coming from devouring an ox of the field, and both sides of his jaws and chest are streaked with blood, and he is terrible to behold – just so was Odysseus bespattered" (22.401–06). In short, Homer shows that men in combat stoop to a nearly quadrupedal level and concern themselves only with the animal processes of maintaining and destroying life.

But it is also through these comparisons that Homer explores entirely different dimensions of the human animal. When Homer seeks to do justice to the humane ties binding families he frequently relies on images of animals defending or fostering their young. The perfection of the similes – their nimble way of crossing species and leaping broad taxonomical chasms (mammals, birds, insects) – show deep appreciation for that which unites all life: the drive to produce and sustain progeny. The similes show that to condemn the animal in human nature is to condemn not only the marauding lion in man, but also the lion who loves his cubs, defends them, and laments their harms. They help us appreciate that the violence of men and lions is ultimately rooted in the love of cubs, in direct and indirect efforts to produce and sustain them. The irresistible emotional gravity of the *Iliad* and *Odyssey* emanates from brilliant depiction of hard struggles for survival and reproduction. Homer places sympathetic characters in conflict over the highest Darwinian stakes; they fight for life, vital resources, children, and to retain or wrest away mates. The tragedies of the poems focus on characters who have played for these high stakes – whether through choice or necessity – and lost: above all, Priam and Hector, but also Andromache, Hecuba, Briseis, Patroclus, Achilles and countless others bereaved of life or wealth or family or freedom. The poem's winners are men like Odysseus and Aeneas, men who somehow survive to enhance their standing and assure their posterity for generations to come (see *Odyssey* 14.323–26; *Iliad* 20.302–08; *Aeneid* 6.761–895). Homer's sensitive treatment of the central, universal theme of preservation of life and family helps to explain how the archaic songs of illiterate and obscure tribes have succeeded in touching all people always.

Michael Clarke's article "Between lions and men" argues that Homer's animal similes are intended to show that "we must do away with the assumption that men and beasts belong in different departments of creation, or that a resemblance between the two must be vague and superficial."[5] Clarke gleans the title of his study from Achilles' sharp rejection of Hector's proposal that the winner of their fight return the loser's undefiled corpse to his people. Achilles responds that as there can be no pacts "between lions and men" (22.262), there can be none between Hector and Achilles. But there is a purposeful double meaning in the title of Clarke's study, divorced, as it is, from context. It suggests that being a man is an unrealized ideal. Homer's men are works in progress, dwelling in limbo between the brute and the sublime human ideal, "between lions and men."

Homer's war epic is about the depredations of precocious killer apes who have applied their grand technologies and cooperative instincts to traverse broad seas and rob other men of all they hold precious: their wealth, their women, their lives. The *Iliad* is about the *menis* (rage) of Achilles "lionheart, breaker of men," the most violent man alive, a man with a body and heart of iron, a man who delights in slaughter and cruelty, a "raw meat eater" (*Iliad* 24.207), a lion loosed "against the flocks of men to make a feast" (*Iliad* 24.43), a man with hatreds so implacable that he contemplates devouring the flesh of his enemy (*Iliad* 22.345–48). But it is also about a quieter, gentler Achilles. We glimpse Achilles as a loving father (*Odyssey* 11.538–40), a conscientious son (*Iliad* 24.534–42), a singer of songs (*Iliad* 9.185–91), a teacher (*Iliad* 11.830), a devoted lover, and an intensely loyal friend. Homer's world is inhabited by men like Achilles – men who are gentle apes and killer apes, striving to accomplish, conquer, and possess, all in unconscious obedience to life's prime directive: be fruitful and multiply

As with Homeric critics who have coated the bitter pill of Homeric philosophy with the sugar of contrived optimism,[6] evolutionists have sometimes been loath to acknowledge (perhaps even to themselves) the challenges their perspective presents to universal hopes of human improvement. Books locating the fonts of human motivation in Darwinian selection often conclude with upbeat, almost conciliatory chapters, seeking to soften the bleaker implications of a Darwinian perspective on human behavior.[7] But critics of evolutionary study of human behavior and psychology have been right about at least one thing: the evolutionary view of human potential *is* appreciably more rigid than the liberal philosophical paradigms that have dominated intellectual life since the Enlightenment;[8] in place of utopian visions of infinitely malleable, potentially perfectible beings,[9] evolutionary theory offers only the hope of some unspecified level of diminishment in human suffering and malfeasance.

To be clear, the degree of hope is not inconsiderable. The Delphic imperative, know thyself!, rings as a great moral of evolutionary exploration of human nature.[10] Before we can change who we are, we must first understand *what* we are and how we got this way; we cannot understand human minds, much less persuade them to change, if we remain ignorant of biases and predispositions built into them by natural selection. As the biologist-philosopher Richard Alexander writes: "The value of an evolutionary approach to human sociality is not to determine the limits of our actions so that we can abide by them. Rather it is to examine our life strategies so that we can change them when we wish, as a result of understanding them."[11] Thus evolutionary study of human behavior and psychology is not – contrary to a common allegation[12] – an ideology of pessimism, defeatism, or conservative defense of the status quo. But even so, evolutionary thought *has*, as Peter Singer observes in *A Darwinian left*, "dashed the Left's great dream: The Perfectibility of Man," and replaced it with "a coolly realistic view of what may be achieved."[13]

In fact, if we search for lessons in the *Iliad* and in evolutionary study of human behavior and psychology, we find that they have much in common. Humans are animals, and it will be difficult for us to change behaviors that lead to our most pressing social problems, many of which are connected to the competitive tendencies of men. Despite the deeply prosocial elements of human nature (which are also a legacy of pitiless Darwinian selection[14]), and despite the fact that we can change ourselves and our societies for the better, the animal lives in us and cannot be extracted until we die. There is, then, a measure of determinism at the heart of the *Iliad* and of evolutionary studies of human nature; a fatal sense that we are what we are – magnificent, gentle, bloody-toothed – and there may be limits to how much we can change.

Perhaps just this idea is expressed in the final book of the *Iliad*. Achilles sits in his tent with his enemy, Priam, connecting with him on the basis of their common sufferings. Here we witness Achilles at his most humane and his most self-aware, displaying depths of empathy and hard-won wisdom that are the hope and hallmark of our species. He has swallowed his anger and harnessed his wild hatred. Wholesome cravings for food and lovemaking have blunted his appetite for blood. Treating Priam with due respect and kindness, he has agreed to release Hector's corpse. But even at this moment, when Achilles is at the apex of human sensitivity, he teeters and almost plummets to the nadir of savagery. Priam's lamentations finally provoke him, and he threatens to murder the old man where he sits. He restrains himself, bounding out of the hut "like a lion" (*Iliad* 24.572). But the poem ends with the burial of Hector, and the next day the fighting will begin again. In the morning Achilles will stride onto the plain to kill and kill and, soon, to be killed in the long shadow of the Trojan wall.

The *Iliad* tells the story of a man alienated from his society and himself, futilely groping for a different way to live. Though there is no way to escape the animal core of human nature, through self-knowledge Achilles is moving closer to his ideal self. But the road is very long and, for now, he is still "between lions and men." So it is with us as well.

Appendix: Dating Homeric society

The chronological setting of the Homeric world is an issue which during the last decades has almost reached the status of a new Homeric question. (Crielaard 1995, 201)

Crielaard's assessment is double-edged: it suggests that dating Homer is a research program of first importance, while also recalling, at least for me, all of the wasted effort of the war between analysts and unitarians. The controversy surrounding the date of Homer shares some fundamental properties with the original Homeric question: (1) a roaring, roiling mass of relevant but indecisive evidence; (2) a perfect void of decisive evidence; and (3) strong and varying opinions in the research community. This is a formula that almost guarantees a proliferation of competing scenarios, a wide field for confirmation biases to gambol,* and the drawing of battle lines. I have two reasons for believing that much of the effort currently being devoted to

* Homer's date is often explored not as an independent question but as an auxiliary support to larger arguments. A clear trend exists in which Homer scholars have tended to credit dating evidence that supports their scholarly agendas. To pluck a few examples, Burgess (2001) desires to show that the Epic Cycle was an authentic part of the pre-Homeric epic tradition and his tentative arguments for a relatively late Homer add heft to his case. West has long defended the lonely position that Hesiod came before Homer, and he has recently identified evidence which, he believes, decisively places Homer in the beginning of the seventh century at the earliest (1995). West's old rival on dating Homer, Janko, is not convinced; he continues to find evidence that is consistent with his own eighth-century estimates most compelling (Janko 1998, 1982). Powell believes that the Greek alphabet was invented/adapted as a "dedicated technology" for taking down hexameter verse: his argument for a confluence of evidence placing the primal Homeric texts around 800 BC is a prime strut to this main theory (2002). Finley (1954), Donlan (1980), and Dickinson (1986), among others, have argued for a Homeric society that is almost devoid of *polis* structures; they therefore credit evidence that places the poems between roughly 1000 and 800. My goal in producing this sample is not to impugn anyone's scholarship; confirmation bias is a pervasive scholarly problem, one to which my own study is surely not immune. Moreover, one of these theories may well be the

attempts to precisely date Homeric society – for all their resources of ingenuity, conspicuous erudition, and argumentative *aretē* – is being misplaced. First, no matter how earnestly the pile of available evidence – 28,000 lines of Homer and other early literary sources, artistic representations of epic subject matter, inscriptional evidence, potentially datable historical allusions, archaeological materials, quantitative linguistics, even astronomical data[1] – is rearranged and recombined, we will only leap forward in our understanding of this new Homeric question as we did with the old one: when new data, method, and theory radically change our understanding. Until then, we can weave ingenious, plausible, and interesting scenarios for when and how the primal Homeric texts were produced – "vivid screenplays"[2] starring a compiler, a guild of rhapsodes, a genius Semitic inventor of the Greek alphabet, an elite band of Euboean warriors, an amanuensis, a sixth-century Athenian festival organizer, or some combination of the above – but we will not be able to pinpoint Homer's location in time with any greater accuracy than a century or even two. This assessment would seem to be borne out by our present situation: different dating arguments by high authorities litter the time span of roughly 800–650 BC, with some contributors favoring dates in the ninth and sixth centuries.[3]

Second, while we are all very curious about Homer's date, this information has less relevance to debates about the nature of Homeric society than is generally assumed. A largely unexamined assumption forms the background to many discussions of Homer's date: if we knew the precise moment when the epics were composed, we could define the nature of the society that produced them. The inverse assumption is also widespread: if we could define the nature of Homeric society, we could pinpoint Homer's date. Both assumptions are false. Questions surrounding Homer's date and the nature of Homeric society are largely independent; answering one question provides only hints, not answers, to the other.

The issue of Homer's date is like scholarly quicksand: It is as hard to struggle out of this topic as it is easy to blunder in. Fortunately, for our purposes, it is only necessary to dip in our toes. I will focus on

right one. My point is that the current evidence is so malleable that it can support wide divergences of credible opinion among the most highly respected authorities. *What is the date of Homer's society? When do you need it to be?*

three currently insoluble difficulties that beset attempts to thin-slice Homer's date within a span of 25, 50 or even 100 years – problems of (1) variety across Greek communities; (2) the relatively incremental nature of change during the time period in question; and (3) unresolved questions about the nature of oral poetics.

Dating Homer is complicated by striking variation in the size, complexity, and organization of communities throughout Greek history. Classical Athens with its population in the tens of thousands shared the peninsula with sparsely populated territories (*ethnē*) employing loose political structures more characteristic of the Dark Age. Likewise, Dark Age Lefkandi – with a large population, impressive wealth, and cosmopolitan ways at least 200 years ahead of its time – coexisted alongside the simple, poor, insulated communities that were more typical of the period. So even in the highly unlikely event that we were able to conclude, definitively, that the Homeric poems as we know them reached relative fixity in 675, this would not decisively define Homeric society as mainly characteristic of the early Archaic period. This is partly because we have no firm idea where the Homeric poems were composed. Did our poet emerge from a cosmopolitan, rapidly progressing center or was he a product of one of the uncounted backwaters, where modes of life had been – and would yet be – more or less stable for generations? The latter scenario is not implausible: oral composition in hexameters was practiced in Greece down to the middle of the sixth century, and it continued in remote rural areas even longer.[4]

This leads into the second problem. There is no bright line separating the Early Archaic and Late Dark Ages. Rather the line is thin, filmy and nearly colorless. And it moves: different scholars draw it in different places, usually sometime between 800 and 700 BC, according to varying criteria. This period is often termed "the Greek renaissance," signaling the Aegean world's emergence from the long Dark Age. But nothing happened during this span of time – no cataclysm or pan-Aegean revolutionary movement – that signaled an immediate dislocation in the basic structures and modes of Greek life. For instance, the alphabet was a radical innovation indeed, and its development in Greece, c.800 BC, has been identified as the beginning of the Archaic Age.[5] But the alphabet's influence on Greek culture was initially all but undetectable, and the culture would remain mainly oral for hundreds of years. Similarly the radical innovation of the early city-state obviously did not come into existence overnight; to recruit biological vocabulary, it emerged by gradual evolution not saltation. This development cannot be precisely assigned to given decades or even to given half-centuries.

To be sure, many of the basic structures of Greek life *did* change dramatically, but the eighth-century archaeological evidence suggests the new era dawned gradually.[6] To extend this metaphor, every dawn is gradual. The sun crests the horizon and bathes the eastern frontiers in slanted light, before moving slowly upward and westward until a whole region radiates with its heat. From the long-range perspective of modern archaeology – from the distance of almost 3,000 years – transitions occurring over 100 or 150 years can be described as rapid. But from the perspective of actual Greek people living in and around the eighth century, change would have frequently come like the new day's sun: touching different places at different times, the heat and light increasing almost imperceptibly. In short, the fact that change around the eighth century was both relatively incremental and regionally variable, makes it impossible to confidently assign features of Homer's society to very small historical windows.

Third, there is still much that we don't understand about the nature of Homeric poetics. In this book I have suggested that Homer's epics present a reflected *picture* of life in the world that produced them. This invites analogy with the technology of photography. When we push the shutter release on a camera, the shutter blinks, briefly exposing the chemically treated film to light and searing a sharp image. A key to this process is the speed of the blink. If the camera malfunctions and the shutter remains open too long, information will flood into the camera with the light, and the resulting image will be a blurry and confusing record of change over time (unless the lens is trained on an unchanging subject). A serious problem with dating Homer's society is that we do not know, with precision, the shutter speed of the epic lens. True, much comparative analysis has documented the largely contemporary nature of the background picture of oral poetry; oral poetry cannot accurately preserve a coherent picture of culture or social life over spans of hundreds of years. This has pushed the idea that Homer's picture is a blurry mélange into the scholarly margins. But there are still legitimate debates about how rapidly the Homeric shutter opened and shut: Did the poems mainly absorb information from the immediate context in which they were composed? That is, was the blink of the poetic shutter almost instantaneous? Or was it pretty sluggish? For instance, could it be that the Homeric picture combines elements from several generations – that it pictures life "within the time span covered by the audience's collective memory"?[7]

Here I am dwelling very much on the negative: With current evidence precision dating of Homer is not possible, and even if it were possible this information alone could not define the nature of Homeric society. But there is a positive side to these debates. Recent discussions have led to healthy questioning of positions too lightly taken for granted, and they have led to progress in defining a ballpark estimate (c.800–650 BC) with good evidence and impressive – though not perfect – scholarly agreement. The once compelling Mycenaean time frame has been ruled out. Scenarios placing Homer as early as the tenth-century heart of the Dark Age are improbable for the same reason (among others):[8] without the technology of writing, which did not re-emerge until around 800, it is unlikely that a coherent portrait of life in tenth-century Greece could have been preserved over the many decades before the poems were finally written down. Likewise, scenarios suggesting that the primal texts were not produced until as late as the second half of the sixth century are also doubted by most – in this case, basic oral theory would lead us to expect much stronger evidence for contemporary political structures, military organization, material culture, and unmistakable references to the technology of writing. But we don't see this. In fact, several prominent commentators have argued that *no* aspect of Homeric culture can be confidently located after the year 700.[9]

The question of Homer's knowledge of writing is particularly important, and F. A. Wolf's assessment is almost as good today as it was more than two centuries ago:

> But not only is there no such testimony or trace of the device in Homer, no evidence of even the faintest beginnings of true writing . . . but what is by far the most important point, everything contradicts it. The word book is nowhere, writing is nowhere, reading is nowhere, letters are nowhere; nothing in so many thousands of verses is arranged for reading, everything for hearing; there are no pacts or treaties except face to face; there is no

source of report for old times except memory and rumor and monuments without writing . . . there is no inscription on the pillars and tombs that are sometimes mentioned; there is no inscription of any kind; there is no coin or fabricated money; there is no use of writing in domestic matters or trade; there are no maps; finally there are no letter carriers and no letters.[10]

There is only one reference to writing in Homer (*Iliad* 6.167–70), and whether or not it indicates Homer's knowledge of true alphabetic writing is hotly contested. Powell has argued, quite persuasively I think, that Homer's relative silence about writing is key to the dating controversies, and must define the Homeric world as overwhelmingly pre-literate. The composer of the epics could not have understood the historical importance of writing, and hence would not have excluded it for literary reasons (i.e., to artificially archaize his narrative world or to create "epic distance").[11]

Regarding Homer's date I am therefore content to remain agnostic within the space of a "long" eighth century. The coherent society I detect in the *Iliad* and *Odyssey* could have plausibly existed at any point during this period (though my societal model *does* become progressively less likely the deeper Homer's dates are pushed into the seventh century). As stated in chapter one, I *do* have leanings on this new Homeric question: I find arguments for an early eighth-century Homer most compelling.[12] But, like all other attempts to precisely situate Homer in time, this feeling is based as much on what Adam Parry called "intuitive calculus of probabilities"[13] as on scientific proof. When scholars debate Homer's historical epoch they are usually *really* arguing about different things. The date of Homer is, by itself, an alluring piece of trivia; it is not usually pursued as a question in its own right. Rather, it is frequently drafted into the service of different arguments – just to name a few, arguments about the history of Greece, the chronological ordering of Homer, Hesiod, and the Epic Cycle, or the nature of Homeric society. In this last category, the one under consideration here, arguments over dates frequently amount to proxy wars over where Homeric society sits on the continuum from very simple to very complex societies. Was Homer's world more like the relatively unstratified, pre-state chiefdoms of the late Dark Age or was it recognizably the world of the relatively advanced Archaic Greek *polis*. Those who argue for a relatively complex world have tended to also see evidence for a late date of Homeric composition; those who argue for relative simplicity have argued for correspondingly early dates. When I refer to my perspective on Homeric society as a "Late Dark Age" model – rather than, say, an "Early Archaic Age" model – I am taking a defined position in debates over the nature of Homeric society. I am siding with those who have stressed the relative simplicity of Homer's world.

Notes

INTRODUCTION

1. Myres 1958, 1.
2. Van Wees 1992, 2.
3. See van Wees 1992, 63–69. Van Wees is also the best source for vivid reconstructions of Homeric combat – of tactics, codes of behavior and so on (e.g., van Wees 1996, 2004; see below, Chapter Two).
4. For fine exposition of this view see Schein 1984.
5. For a history of the development of *Altertumswissenschaft* see Markner and Veltri 1999.
6. Wilamowitz-Moellendorff 1921 [1982], 1. Italics in original.
7. See also Blackwell 1736.
8. For example, Dodds 1951; Murray 1907; Kluckhohn 1961; Finley 1954; Donlan 1980, 1985, 1993, 1997a; Qviller 1981.
9. A. Parry 1971, xxxvii.
10. Unorthodox, but not unprecedented; see Burkert 1983; Fox 1995; Sallares 1991; Shay 2001.
11. See Keeley 1996; van Wees 1992.
12. For a recent and scalding expression of this criticism see Hanson and Heath 1998.
13. As the prominent nineteenth-century historian of Greece, George Grote, commented: "There is a tendency in critics, from Aristotle downwards, to invert the order of attributes in respect to the Homeric poems, so as to dwell on the most recondite excellences which escape the unaided reader, and which are even to a great degree disputable . . . [These critics forget that Homer is] intended for the feelings which the critic has in common with the unlettered masses. They are of all poems the most absolutely and unreservedly popular" (1872, 205–06).
14. Quoted in A. Parry 1971, lxii.
15. Adkins, 1960, vi.
16. See Darwin 1871, 1872, 1887. For accessible treatment of this vein in Darwin's thinking see Keynes 2002.

17. For first quote see Darwin 1871 [1998], 100, for second quote see Darwin 1859, ch. 6.
18. Some of the main theoretical works in this area include Darwin 1859, 1871, 1872; Williams 1966; Wilson 1975; Hamilton 1964; Dawkins 1976; Barkow, Tooby, and Cosmides 1992; Trivers 1971, 1972, 1974. The best general introduction to the field is to be found in Pinker 2002. Other serviceable introductions include Pinker 1995; Ridley 1993, 2003; Wright 1994. The most comprehensive and up-to-date surveys of research in the field are Buss 2005 and Dunbar and Barrett 2007.
19. Ridley 2003, 4.
20. This work is affiliated with an emerging research program – sometimes called "Literary Darwinism" – that seeks to illuminate traditional humanities subjects by calling upon scientific theory, data, and methods. For samples of current work, as well as reasonably up-to-date bibliographies, see Carroll 2004; Gottschall and Wilson 2005.
21. My phrasing is borrowed from Maurice Bowra who said that it is "not easy to say anything both new and true about the Greeks" (quoted in Kluckhohn 1961, 43).
22. See Sarah Pomeroy's argument that this "downplaying" tendency can be traced all the way back to Herodotus and Thucydides (1975, 16–18). See also Adkins (1982, 320) for ancient consternation that the Trojans did not send Helen back "on the next ship."

1 REBUILDING HOMER'S GREECE

1. For the mosaic/mélange view see Sherrat 1990; Coldstream 1977, 18; Geddes 1984; Whitley 1991, 34–39; and especially Snodgrass 1974. For some strong defenses of a historical and unitary Homeric society see Finley 1954; van Wees 1992; Osborne 2004; Raaflaub 1997a; and, especially, Morris 1986 and the contributors to Morris and Powell 1997.
2. For some serviceable overviews of the Homeric question see Davidson 1962a; Dodds 1968a, 1968b; A. Parry 1971; Turner 1997; Powell 2002, 2004; Fowler 2004.
3. Wood 1769 [1824], 276.
4. Josephus, *Against Apion*, 1.2.12.
5. Estimates of recitation times vary, depending as they do on individual rates of reading and speaking, as well as the stamina of singer and audience. The 24-hour figure is based on Davidson's (1962b, 255) estimate that it would take three eight-hour days to recite the *Iliad* aloud. Other scholars reach similar estimates: West, 2001, 19; and Janko 1982, 39.
6. Wood 1769 [1824], 259.
7. Wood 1769 [1824], 259–60.

8. In addition to Wood and Josephus, among those who had argued for an oral Homer before Wolf were the Italian philosopher Giambattista Vico (1668–1744), English philologist Richard Bentley (1662–1742), and the French writer Abbé D'Aubignac (1604–76).
9. Wilamowitz-Moellendorff 1884, 228.
10. Another scholar argued that the authentically Homeric "nucleus" of the *Iliad* consisted of just 1,500 lines, or 1/10th of its present length, with the rest representing late accretions (for discussion see Dodds 1968a, 3).
11. See Dodds 1968b, 11–12.
12. See Levin 1960, xv.
13. See Haslam 1997. West 2001 catalogs all 1,543 Homeric papyri so far discovered.
14. Lord 1960, 13.
15. Homeric descriptions of the experience of oral song are given in Phaiacia and Ithaca. For the classic description of the experience of Yugoslavian oral poetry see Lord 1960.
16. These include Uzbek, Karakirghiz (Bowra 1952, 354), and West African epic (e.g., *The Ozidi Saga, The Epic of Son-Jara*). Foley argues that the *Iliad* and *Odyssey* are "actually of middling length on an international scale" (2004, 181).
17. Porter 2004, 336.
18. On "fundamentalist faith" see Dodds 1968b, 11.
19. See Morris 2000.
20. Arthur Evans quoted in Gray 1968, 24.
21. Traill 1995.
22. See Allen 1999; Latacz 2004.
23. See Nilsson 1933 for a prime example.
24. See Finley 1957; Hansen 1997, 25; Pomeroy et al. 1999.
25. See Bowra 1952; Dickinson 1986; Lord 1960; Parry 1971; Rutherford 1996.
26. Raaflaub 1997a, 628.
27. For example, Bowra 1952; Rutherford 1996; Notopoulos 1960.
28. Finley 1957; for a recent view of the Mycenaean model see Bennet 1997.
29. Finley 1954, 153.
30. Drews 1993, 3; Hanson 2000, 29.
31. For what is probably the most highly regarded scenario for the Mycenaean collapse see Drews 1993. For an up-to-date overview and pluralistic assessment of the main competing theories for the collapse see Rutter 2000; Thomas and Conant 1999.
32. As regards available information, the Dark Age has brightened considerably since it was first given its name. For surveys of developments see Langdon 1997; Morris 2000; Thomas and Conant 1999.
33. See Van Wees 1992.

34. Finley 1954 [2002], xix.
35. See Geddes 1984, 16. While some archaeologists would bridle at this statement (e.g. Morris 2000), if we were to remove the *Iliad* and *Odyssey* as sources, Late Dark Age social history would not be merely dark, but quite black in its emptiness (see Van Wees 1992).
36. Finley's position represented a decisive return to a belief that had been embraced, even by many analysts, since the beginning of the modern era of Homeric scholarship in the late eighteenth century. Even Homerists who were skeptical of the poems' value as sources for historical reconstruction of Greek life at the time of the Trojan War frequently embraced the poems as guides "to the manners and principles of his [Homer's] age" (Mitford 1784, 85; see also Thirwall 1835. For other early sociologies of Homeric society see Buchkholz 1871–1885; Gladstone 1858; Jebb 1887; Keller 1902). For instance, George Grote, who drove the pre-Schliemann consensus that Homer was an unreliable guide to historical events at the time of the Trojan War, still relied on the *Iliad* and *Odyssey* to produce a long and accomplished – though now outdated– analysis of social customs in Homer's own age.
37. Havelock 1963, 87. Italics in original.

2 A SHORT ETHNOGRAPHY OF HOMERIC SOCIETY

1. Parry 1971 [1933], 377.
2. Hooper 1978, 7.
3. On the inappropriateness of these translations see Qviller 1981; Donlan 1993.
4. For a prime example of this confusion see Geddes 1984.
5. For detailed reconstructions of Homeric combat see Van Wees 1992, 1994, 1996, 1997, 2004. In general support of van Wees see Singor 1995.
6. Finley 1954 includes a good discussion of this issue; see also Van Wees 2002b.
7. But controversy persists for at least three reasons. First, the distinctions between bands, tribes, and chiefdoms are notoriously vague with much overlap; anthropologists have difficulty deciding how to classify many societies they have studied close-up in space and time (Johnson and Earle 1987, 314). The fact that the term "*basileus*" does not precisely mesh with definitions of the term "big man" or "chief" is hardly an argument against the poems' historicity or against the idea that they reflect a prestate society. Second, strictly speaking, there was no "Homeric *society*." There must have been, instead, a range of different *societies*, representing subtle variations in levels of social evolution from relatively complex "big man" societies, to different levels of chiefdoms, to societies

having more in common with the early *polis*. Third, differences between big man societies, chiefdoms, and early states are not strict demarcations of kind but subtle differences of degree. Almost all modelers of Ancient Greek political life agree that the structures of the early *polis* – like the assembly of males of fighting age and the council of elders – gradually evolved from more primitive structures already in place in the Dark Age.

8. Precise counts are not possible for the Late Dark Age, but the Greek world would eventually come to encompass more than 1,000 independent, self-governing *poleis* (Hansen 1997; Hansen and Nielsen 2004). About fifty of these were historically significant (Bryant 1996).
9. Geddes 1984, 26.
10. This is suggested among other places in Sarpedon's speech to Glaucus, *Iliad* 12.310–28, and in Hector's goading of fleeing Diomedes (*Iliad* 8.161–64). For further discussion of this issue see below, Chapter Five.
11. In his fury, Achilles accuses Agamemnon of exactly this behavior (1.225–31), but elsewhere in the *Iliad* Agamemnon is portrayed as among the most fearsome and valiant fighters (see especially *Iliad* 11). He is apparently considered to be the fourth most capable warrior by his peers, after Achilles, Ajax, and Diomedes (*Iliad* 7.179–80), and he is the best spear thrower (*Iliad* 23.890–94).
12. Donlan: "The common people are not regarded as social inferiors – there is, in fact, not birth or class nomenclature in Homer . . . It must be remembered that the rank and file are also given the epithet *aristoi* (best), and that they, too, are called 'heroes'" (1980, 19; for Homeric references in support see Donlan 187 n. 37).
13. Calhoun 1962; Geddes 1984.
14. Calhoun 1962; Geddes 1984.
15. This point is made by Kirk *et al.* 1985–93, 1:139.
16. The fact that Thersites is able to get away with abusing and harassing the top chiefs for years (until, according to tradition, Achilles finally kills him) also seems inconsistent with the idea that Thersites is a member of an inferior hereditary class.
17. Finley 1957. For comments on Finley see Yamagata 1997.
18. Bowra 1934, 60.
19. See also Yamagata 1997, who argues that there *are* consistent differences in the usages of the two words, but offers little support to the argument that the words signify differences in political power.
20. Calhoun 1962; Geddes 1984.
21. This significant stratification is, by the way, one of the primary factors behind my designation of Homeric societies as chiefdoms rather than more egalitarian big man societies. Another important factor is that paramount *basileis* usually transcend the big man's strictly local

autonomy and preside over multiple towns and territories (for example, see the Catalog of Ships, *Iliad* 2.484–877). Social organization is thus consistent with Carneiro's minimal definition of a chiefdom: "A chiefdom is an autonomous political unit comprising a number of villages or communities under the permanent control of a paramount chief" (1981, 45).

22. For the importance of the assembly and council see Geddes 1984; Glotz 1929; Hammer 1998; and, especially, Raaflaub 1997b. Finley argued that Homer conveys "no trace of the polis in a political sense" (1954 [2002], 27), minimizing to almost nothing the significance of the assembly (see also Adkins 1960). This position now enjoys little support. Most commentators take a position similar to Raaflaub's: "Homeric society reflects an early, not yet formalized, but clearly recognizable stage of [*polis*] development" (1997b, 23).
23. Raaflaub succinctly argues: "1) that the assembly and council were firmly established communal institutions, and 2) that opinions expressed in these institutions, individually and collectively, mattered" (1997b, 8).
24. For further elaboration and Homeric references suggesting community punishment of wayward chiefs see Raaflaub 1997b, 18–20.
25. Based in part on the epics and in part on anthropological analogies, Donlan argues that Dark Age leaders "had considerable authority but little power," meaning that they lacked the ability to compel compliance, but gained assent through persuasion and "charismatic authority" (1985, 39, 42). Osborne also expresses support for this view (2004, 212). For a defense of the traditional view – that the paramount *basileus* was a king – see van Wees 1992.
26. Another example is Nireus, mentioned in the Catalog of Ships. He is a rare example of a weak Homeric leader, but because of his weakness he has few followers (*Iliad* 2.671–75).
27. For example, Grote 1872.
28. The only prominent exception in the present generation is Locrian Ajax. Short of stature, he is still highly formidable owing to his foot speed and his outstanding skill as a spearman (*Iliad* 2.527–30). Also interesting is the minor figure Nireus (see above, n. 26). Odysseus is shorter than Menelaus and Agamemnon, but he is never described as short; further, Homer constantly stresses his stunning muscular bulk (see below, Chapter Seven). In the last generation, Tydeus, father of Diomedes, was both a great and a small warrior (*Iliad* 5.801).
29. See Dawson 1996; Ducrey 1986; Hanson 2000; Johnston 1998.
30. *Laws* 626a.
31. Finley 1954 [2002], 98.
32. Hanson 2000.

33. Adkins 1960.
34. See Seaford: "Homeric society is characterized by the solidarity of the household and by the near absence of collective organizations transcending households" (1994, 13).
35. However, Telemachus' attempt to do so fails miserably. Finley (1954) bases much of his case for the absence of the Homeric *polis* on the impotence of the Ithacan assembly.
36. This dynamic is clear, among other places, in the constant, crushing, and unreasonable pressure on young Telemachus – outnumbered 108 to 1 – to stand up and emulate Orestes' heroic killing of Aegisthus, the murderer of his father. It is also explicitly communicated by the bereaved kinsmen of the slaughtered suitors (*Odyssey* 24.426–37).
37. Van Wees 1992, 2.

3 WHY DO MEN FIGHT? THE EVOLUTIONARY BIOLOGY AND ANTHROPOLOGY OF MALE VIOLENCE

1. *Histories* 1.87.
2. See Jungleman's account in Ritchie 1996.
3. The words of the big man and accomplished warrior, Ongka (Strathern and Stewart 2000, 7).
4. Quoted in Keeley 1996, 144–46.
5. Thomas 1959.
6. Wrangham and Peterson 1996, 78.
7. Gat 2000c, 166.
8. For full description and analyses of these wars – including strong justifications for the use of the anthropocentric term "war" – see Ghiglieri (1999); Wrangham and Peterson (1996).
9. For this claim see Turney-High 1949; Wright 1942; Davie 1929; for refutation see Keeley 1996.
10. Keeley 1996.
11. Keeley 1996, 93.
12. Keeley 1996, 147.
13. For a native account see the personal history given by the New Guinean big man Ongka (Strathern and Stewart 2000).
14. See Gat 2000a.
15. Bower 1995; Kelly 2000, 148.
16. See Keeley 1996.
17. Robert Wright 1995, 71–72.
18. Daly and Wilson 1988, 274; see also Archer 1994.
19. See Mesquida and Wiener 1999; Wilson and Daly 1985; Hudson and den Boer 2002, 2005.

20. This mistaken notion was promulgated by Lorenz 1966; see also Ardrey 1966.
21. Williams 1988; Gould 1993.
22. Darwin 1871; Andersson 1994.
23. Mayr 2001, 276.
24. Trivers drew substantially on the insights of Bateman 1948 and Williams 1966.
25. In this discussion I have not found it necessary to distinguish between Trivers' model of sexual selection and the related arguments of Clutton-Brock and Parker 1992. The latter biologists identify the operational sex ratio (OSR) – the ratio of sexually available males to available females – as the most immediate determinant of which sex is more competitive. The OSR, in turn, is influenced by the potential reproductive rates of males and females. Since the potential reproductive rates of females are usually substantially lower than those of males, this typically results in more competitive males. Clutton-Brock and Parker offer a refinement, not refutation, of Trivers' original arguments. For my discussion, what is important is the simple, core insight these models share. Both are reducible to the logic of supply and demand: greater competitiveness in males stems from high demand for, and low supply of, female reproductive capacity.
26. Trivers 1972, 173.
27. For information on sexual selection see Andersson 1994; Cronin 1991; Darwin 1871; Trivers 1972; Clutton-Brock and Parker 1992; Miller 1998.
28. Jolly 1999, 77.
29. See Andersson 1994, 117.
30. For other important studies of reversed sex role species see Wallace 1867; Darwin 1871, ch. 16; Williams 1966; Bonduriansky 2001; Parker 1983.
31. A potentially important secondary cause of lower levels of female physical aggression has recently been proposed by Anne Campbell (2002). Campbell argues that, in ancestral human environments, the lives of most females were literally more important to their reproductive fortunes than were the lives of most males. Given the generally larger investments females made (and make) in rearing offspring, the death of a mother was more devastating to the fitness prospects of a child than the death of a father. When a man dies the main caretaker of his offspring lives on; the same is usually not true for women. Thus Campbell's argument is that death literally cost ancestral women more than it cost ancestral men, serving, over evolutionary timescales, to inhibit female aggressive tendencies.
32. For bottlenose dolphins see Ridley 1997, 160; for chimpanzees see Wrangham and Peterson 1996, 136–37; for lions see Pusey and Packer 1994.

33. Darwin 1871 [1998], 627.
34. For details of evidence see Murdock 1967; Daly and Wilson 1994; Alexander et al. 1979; Diamond 1992.
35. Pinker 2002, 347.
36. See literature review of Wood and Eagly 2002.
37. Cross-cultural sex differences in human competitiveness, especially in physically aggressive dimensions, are extremely well documented. For detailed overviews see Buss 2003; Geary 1998; Mealey 2000; Campbell 2002, 2005; Daly and Wilson 1988; Wrangham and Peterson 1996; Ghiglieri 1999; Archer 1994.
38. For cross-species surveys showing the pervasiveness of this relationship see Clutton-Brock 1988; Clutton-Brock and Harvey 1976; Cowlishaw and Dunbar 1991; Dewsbury 1982; Ellis 1995.
39. Herman 2004, 183. For more case studies see Daly and Wilson 1988. For more recent overviews of links between reproductive success and status see Geary 1998, 142–44; Barrett et al. 2002, 129–31; Cummins 2005.
40. Daly and Wilson 1988, 132.
41. See Low 2000, 64; for her sources see 271, n. 21
42. Pérusse 1993.
43. See Wilson and Daly 1997 for just such an example where an evolutionary explanation complements and enriches, rather than replaces, a strictly socio-economic explanation of urban violence.
44. Heolldobler and Wilson 1994. This, like so much else that is bizarre in ant social life, can ultimately be traced to the fact that females are more genetically related to their sisters than to their own offspring.
45. Darwin 1871 [1998], 581.
46. Chagnon 1968 [1992], 191–92.
47. Chagnon 1979b, 87.
48. Chagnon 1968 [1992], 95.
49. Chagnon 1968 [1992].
50. See also Ferguson 1995.
51. See Betzig 1986, 21.
52. Similar patterns of raid and counter-raid are commonly found among other swidden agriculturalists and hunter-gatherers (Robarchek and Robarchek 1992).
53. Chagnon 1979b.
54. See Keeley 1996, 68.
55. Gat 2000c.
56. Gat 2000c, 167; see also Lowe's conclusion based on a survey of case studies and large-scale statistical analyses of world ethnography: "The broad cross-cultural data suggest . . . reproductive matters lie at the root of war in most traditional societies" (2000, 227; see also ch. 13).

57. See also Hrdy 1999; Allen and Smith 1994; Betzig 1986; Boehm 1999; Darwin 1871; Divale and Harris 1976; Gat 2000a, 2000b, 2000c; Hewlett 1991; Knauft 1991; Otterbein 1994; Turney-High 1949, 151; Warner 1931; Wrangham and Peterson 1996. Even Chagnon's arch-critic, Brian Ferguson, does not disagree that conflict over women was a significant source of violence among the Yanomamö and other prestate societies (1995, 344, 355).
58. For this assessment of Chagnon's early presentation of results see Gat 2000a.

4 WHAT LAUNCHED THE 1,186 SHIPS?

1. For ancient discussion see Herodotus *Histories*, 2.112–20. For recent discussion see Meagher 1995.
2. Apollodorus, *Library and Epitome* 3.10.8–9.
3. For discussion of this matter see Pomeroy 1975, 17–18.
4. Felson and Slatkin 2004, 95, 96.
5. Van Wees 1992, ch. 4, section two (italics mine).
6. For "defeat and humiliation" see Pomeroy et al., 1999, 62.
7. Donlan 1993, 159. Also representative, the jacket copy for the Loeb Classical Library edition of the *Iliad* (1999) says that the poem revolves around Achilles' anger "over a grave insult to personal honor," with no mention of Briseis.
8. See Redfield 1975, 15–16.
9. Donlan: "What is required by custom, let us be clear, is for him to return Briseis with a public apology and a fitting compensatory gift. Instead, what follows is a gift-attack against Achilles" (1993, 164). This argument is based on anthropological inference and two scenes where men in the wrong give gifts and make a public display of contrition (*Iliad* 23.566–616; *Odyssey* 8.396–415). Many other commentators attribute Achilles' rejection of the compensation to the lack of an apology (e.g., Kirk et al. 1985–93, 4:309; 5:244; Heubeck et al. 1988–1992, 3:79–80).
10. Donlan also notes that Agamemnon's offer would place Achilles not only in the subordinate position of son-in-law, but in the subordinate-obligated position of the son-in-law who has not paid a bride price.
11. Donlan 1993, 170.
12. The genuineness of Achilles' epiphany seems to be verified at *Odyssey* 11.488–503, where he fiercely asserts that the most abject condition in life is far superior to the most glorious condition in death.
13. Most prominently Finley, who wrote that the "prerogative" of choosing a new ruler "mysteriously belonged to Penelope" (1954 [2002], 90–91). See also Carlier 1984, 206–07; Cobet 1981, 28.

14. For analysis of Eurymachus' and Antinous' motives see Van Wees 1992, 288–89.
15. In the same way, while the details are foggy, it is at least suggested that Aegisthus comes to lead the Mycenaeans through the murder of Agamemnon; it is not suggested that he does so through his marriage to Clytemnestra (*Odyssey* 3.303–05).
16. For similar arguments see Van Wees: "The traditional notion that they court Penelope because whomever she chooses to wed will be the new monarch, is mistaken. This view would give her a surprising amount of power, and in any case it is not borne out by the evidence" (1992, 288; see also 288–90). See also Halverson 1986, 121–22, 126; Deger 1970, 143–50.
17. Van Wees concludes: "Thus those who court Penelope are not expecting any gain from the marriage as such, other than a beautiful wife of a good family, the prestige of having beaten more than a hundred rivals for her hand, and perhaps a tenuous family-connection with the previous ruler" (1992, 289).
18. For a review of the literary evidence on ages of females at first marriage see Golden 1981, 322.
19. In the same way, the manly strength and athleticism of Odysseus, who would be at least forty upon his return to Ithaca, is depicted as undiminished. This is despite the fact that both poems instruct us – as if we needed instructing – that younger men make more formidable fighters and athletes.
20. Three ancient authors tell the story of the wooing of Helen: Apollodorus, the pseudo-Hesiod (*Catalog of women*), and Hyginus. They disagree on the number of suitors. Apollodorus' account includes, at thirty, the largest number of suitors (Apollodorus, *Library and epitome* 3.10.8).
21. It is not clear if Odysseus condemned the raped women to the same fate as the consenting.
22. I would therefore question Van Wees' conclusion that, "In the epics, anger, not sex, is the dangerous, uncontrollable drive that rules men's lives. Anger, if anything, is what the epics are all about" (126). This statement overlooks proliferating instances where sex plays a leading role in the instigation of anger. In fact, the epics testify to a primal interrelationship between sex and anger.
23. Questions of what we consider beautiful and why represent a booming field of inquiry in the human sciences. The most impressive finding: the age-old wisdom that "beauty is in the eye of the beholder" is almost certainly wrong. Across diverse cultures and ethnicities people agree just as well about what is attractive as they agree within the same culture/ethnicity. This finding, based on extremely robust meta-analysis of a large number of studies, calls "seriously [into] question the common

assumption that attractiveness ratings are culturally unique" and suggests "a possibly universal standard by which attractiveness is judged" (Langlois, Kalakanis, Rubenstein et al. 2000). Focusing on females, where do apparently universal preferences for youth, health, face and body symmetry, facial averageness and neoteny, and a low waist-to-hip ratio come from? Many researchers believe that human attractiveness preferences, like those of other organisms, emerged for non-arbitrary reasons: they convey reliable information about mate quality. That female beauty is highly correlated with fertility is most obvious in the way that the curve of female fertility (rising in the mid-teens, peaking in the early twenties, dipping through the thirties, and usually tailing away to nothing through the forties) closely parallels the curve of ratings of female physical attractiveness (rising in the teens, peaking in the late-teens and early twenties, declining through the thirties and forties). Other aspects of women's faces and figures – for example, a low waist-to-hip ratio, a low waist-to-bust ratio, gracile jaws, pert and symmetrical breasts – are also widely believed to convey reproductively significant information about age, hormonal health, pregnancy status, and general reproductive condition. While the empirical research remains at an early stage, some of these hypotheses are substantiated by fertility studies showing that women with lower waist-to-hip and waist-to-bust ratios get pregnant faster than women with higher ratios (Jasienska, Ziomkiewicz, Ellison, Lipson, and Thune 2004; Zaastra, Seidell, Van Noord et al. 1993). Cues like the bilateral symmetry of bodies and faces are also proposed to convey information about genetic quality. The literature in this area is already vast and growing quickly. For good overviews of theory and research see Langlois et al. 2000; Rhodes and Zebrowitz 2002; Symons 1995, 1979; Sugiyama 2005; Etcoff 1999.

24. Chagnon 1988, 1990.
25. See Betzig 1986, 33.
26. Zerjal et al. 2003. Geneticists have recently found further genetic evidence of a link between "profligacy and power" in a study of the Y-chromosomes of men from Northern Ireland (Moore et al., 2006). The study shows that a single early medieval ancestor is the forebear of approximately one in twelve Irishmen and nearly 3 million men worldwide.
27. Quoted in Man 2005, 251.
28. For literature review see McCarthy 1994.
29. For arguments based on a large-scale statistical study see Divale and Harris 1976. For a recent survey of the literature see Low 2000, ch. 13.
30. Ogden 1996.
31. For Shinbone see Chagnon 1968 [1992]. For similar findings see Divale and Harris 1976; Betzig 1986; Gat 2000a, 2000b.

32. Ogden 1996, 21–22.
33. See Ogden 1996.
34. Burgess argues that the Cycle poems were, in the early Archaic Age, more prominent than the Homeric epics: "If the tradition of the Trojan War were a tree, initially the *Iliad* and *Odyssey* would have been a couple of small branches, whereas the Cycle poems would be somewhere in the trunk" (Burgess 2001, 1).
35. See West 2003, 35.
36. For all of these attitudes in one place see Davies 1989. For inferior artistic quality see Griffin 1977. For counter-arguments on all scores see Burgess 2001.
37. Burgess 2001.
38. Burgess 2001, 170.
39. For argument that Homer's reference to Aithra indicates his knowledge of Helen's first abduction see Gantz 1993, 289.
40. The earliest sources for these stories are the summaries of the lost Cycle by Proclus, the pseudo-Hesiod's *Catalogue of Women*, and the mythographer Apollodorus. For a comprehensive handbook of early Greek myth see Gantz 1993.
41. See Redfield 1975, 161; Schein 1984, 9; Vermeule quoted in Schein 1984; Nagler 1974, 49.
42. This list is drawn from the following sources: Amnesty International 1997, 1998, 2000; Barstow 2000, 3; Brownmiller 1975; Chelela 1998; Ghiglieri 1999, 90; Littlewood 1997; Menon 1998; Neier 1998, 172–91; Oosterveld 1998, 64–67; Swiss and Giller 1993; Tanaka 1998, 174–76; Thomas and Regan 1994.
43. This partial list is drawn from the following sources: Littlewood 1997; Meron 1993; Brownmiller 1975, 35; Hanson 2000, 188; Karras 1990; Ghiglieri 1999, 90; Finley 1954.
44. For overviews see Boehm 1999; Chagnon 1968 [1992]; Divale and Harris 1976; Gat 2000a, 2000b.
45. Strathern and Stewart 2000, 41.
46. For some native accounts see Ritchie 1996; Strathern and Stewart, 2000; Valero and Biocca 1969. See also below, Chapter Seven.
47. Thornhill and Palmer's book is the best-known. For similar arguments see contributors to Buss and Malamuth 1996; Jones, 1999; Mealey 2000; Shields and Shields, 1983; Thornhill and Thornhill, 1983; Malamuth, Huppin, and Paul 2005. Lalumiere et al. (2005) provide the most recent, and perhaps the most comprehensive treatment of the subject.
48. See Wrangham and Peterson 1996.
49. For surveys of the relatively common phenomenon of sexual coercion in other species see Clutton-Brock and Parker 1992; Palmer 1989b; and especially Lalumiere et al. 2005. Lalumiere et al. survey dozens of highly

diverse species and conclude that sexual coercion, particularly in the form of forced copulation, is without exception perpetrated by males, and "is a tactic used by some males under some conditions to increase reproduction" (5).

50. Palmer 1989b.
51. Malamuth, Huppin, and Paul 2005, 401.
52. For representative samples of this literature see contributors to Barstow 2000; contributors to Dombrowski 1999; contributors to Sajor 1998; contributors to Stiglmayer 1994.
53. Brownmiller 1975, 13–15.
54. Gottschall 2004.
55. See Siefert 1994, 36.
56. Palmer 1989a.
57. Agamemnon's taunting words to Chryses regarding his lecherous plans for the latter's daughter unmistakably convey the menace of sexual coercion.
58. For multiple examples see Apollodorus' *Library and epitome*; Gantz 1993.
59. Pomeroy et al. 1999, 62.

5 STATUS WARRIORS

1. "The touchiness of men is their most striking trait of character. Touchiness consists in responding immediately and aggressively to a perceived lack of deference" (Van Wees 1992, 109).
2. Knox 1996, 38.
3. Van Wees 1992, 155.
4. See Cummins 2005, 677.
5. Hrdy 1981, 1999.
6. See Campbell 2002; Hrdy 1981, 1999; Low 2000.
7. See Daly and Wilson 1988, 132; Pérusse 1993; Betzig 1986; Irons 1979. See above, Chapter Three, for fuller argument and documentation.
8. Daly and Wilson 1988, 127.
9. Daly and Wilson 1988, 146.
10. Gat 2000b, 75.
11. Griffin 1980, 73.
12. Donlan 1980, 20.
13. Finley 1954 [2002], 124
14. For example, Antonaccio 1995; Qviller 1981; Jackson 1993 gives limited support to this view.
15. Finley 1954 [2002], 59.
16. Gallant 1991, 110.
17. For discussion see Bryant 1996, 24.
18. Finley 1954 [2002], 60.

19. See Antonaccio 1995; Qviller 1981.
20. Malinowski 1929, 319.
21. For India see Dickemann 1979; Miller 1981. Finley 1954 [2002], 87.
22. See Snodgrass 1974; Sherratt, 1990; Coldstream 1977, 18.
23. Morris 1986, 66.
24. Murdock's comprehensive *Ethnographic Atlas* found that 66 percent of ethnographical societies practiced bride price and only 3 percent practiced dowry. See also Birkhead 2000; Low 2000; Buss 1999, 104. For discussion of special conditions that give rise to dowry see Alcock 1998, ch. 15.
25. Kirkpatrick and Ryan 1991, 361.
26. See Buss 1989. See also Gottschall et al. 2004 for another cross-cultural study and up-to-date references.
27. Historical and anthropological studies suggest that women who win high-status mates have more children, and more surviving children than average. For discussion and overview of evidence see Low 2000; Barret, Dunbar, and Lycett 2002, 126–31.
28. Ritchie 1996, 217.
29. Fisher 1958, 265.
30. Fisher 1958, 265.
31. Hamilton 1964.
32. See Schein 1984.
33. Van Wees 1996.
34. Van Wees 1996, 49; for support of Van Wees see Osborne 2004.
35. Again, for copious argumentation and textual support see Van Wees 1996.

6 HOMERIC WOMEN: RE-IMAGINING THE FITNESS LANDSCAPE

1. For overview of female competitive strategies see Campbell 2002. The main difference between female and male strategies is that males are more likely to employ direct confrontation while females are more likely to employ indirect strategies (e.g., spreading derogatory rumors about rivals or seeking to exclude or socially isolate them) (see also Cummings 2005).
2. See Hrdy 1981, 1999.
3. Samuel Butler's *The Authoress of the Odyssey* (1897) proclaimed that the *Odyssey* was composed by a woman. This argument is without foundation and universally discredited. Both evidence internal to the poems and the cross-cultural study of heroic oral epics suggest that the composers of Greek epic were men.
4. Although we cannot quite take this conclusion quite for granted, as in some warrior societies a high proportion of women suffer rape at some point in their lives. To call again on the example of the Yanomamö, after living with the tribe for many years – and taking a native wife – the

anthropologist Kenneth Good wrote in harrowing detail about the prevalence of rape, saying, "I know there isn't a Yanomamö woman who hasn't been raped" (Good and Chanoff 1991, 199).

5. For reputational damage and abandonment see the story of Aphrodite's adulterous tryst with Ares (*Odyssey* 8.266–369), see also Nausicaa's words at *Odyssey* 6.273–88. For physical abuse see *Iliad* 1.565–67; 15.16–22. For murder see the execution of Odysseus' slave women. For discussion of these potentially grave sanctions, including murder, see Fulkerson 2002. This pattern of grave sanctions for female sexual transgression extends to the summaries of the Epic Cycle.
6. For Homeric women bridling against philandering husbands see *Iliad* 9.444–53, *Odyssey* 1.429–33. See especially Hera, who is consistently portrayed, in Homer and elsewhere, as vigilantly policing Zeus and cruelly harassing his bastards, paramours, and even his rape victims. For wives being supplanted by younger and more beautiful slaves see *Iliad* 9.444–53, 1.113–15; for the diversion of resources to bastards see above, Chapter Four; Ogden 1996.
7. See *Odyssey* 11.427–39. While the sentiments in this passage are reminiscent of Hesiod's misogynous outbursts, the general attitude of the Homeric poems is not one of misogyny but of ambivalent philogyny.
8. Hera is a good example of such a woman (e.g., *Iliad* 18.364–67), as is Arete. See also *Odyssey* 6.298–315 and *Iliad* 21.498–501.
9. See "Princess" Nausicaa doing laundry (*Odyssey* 6.85–96) and the "princess" of the Laestrygonians hauling heavy buckets of water from the spring back to town (*Odyssey* 10.105–08).
10. For review of research of the role of physical attractiveness in the formation of female hierarchies, see Campbell 2002.
11. Trans. H. G. Evelyn-White 1982.
12. Thematically parallel episodes include the story of Aphrodite's cuckolding of Hephaestus. In this episode, Hermes says that he would gladly suffer the ridicule of all the gods to lie in Aphrodite's bed (*Odyssey* 8.339–42). Similar dynamics are also at play in stories of men who take on great physical risks for the sake of marrying a particularly desirable bride (*Odyssey* 11.281–91; *Iliad* 13.361–82).
13. For Troy and Trojans as Zeus' favorites see *Iliad* 4.43–49; for Sarpedon as Zeus's favorite son see *Iliad* 16.433–34.
14. Smuts 1991, 1995a; Good 1991.
15. For a classic study of the violence of stepfathers see Daly and Wilson 1988. Daly and Wilson found that a child living with a step-parent was 70 times as likely to be abused and 100 times as likely to be fatally abused. The risks were highest for children living with stepfathers. See also Daly and Wilson 1999; Hrdy 1999. For similar findings in non-human organisms see

Parmigiani and Vom Saal 1994; Wrangham and Peterson 1996; Hausfater and Hrdy 1984.

16. Pomeroy 1975, 44.
17. Eagly and Wood 1999; Wood and Eagly 2002. Anthropologist Kenneth Good wrote of the Yanomamö, "They have to eat. And for this a man needs a woman, a woman needs a man, and children need their parents" (Good and Chanoff 1991, 73).
18. This sense of partnership is amply conveyed at *Odyssey* 6.180–85.
19. Two large-scale statistical studies illustrate this cross-cultural trend (Broude and Greene 1983; Small 1992). Both studies examined ethnographical material from scores of traditional cultures and found that women usually had a significant role in decisions about their marriages, almost always in negotiation with their kin. Even in societies with arranged marriage, girls frequently had influence, even veto power, over their partners. Moreover, Small 1992 stresses that in many cases girls and their families preferred the same sort of mates (for further information see Geary 1998, 124–26).
20. See previous note.
21. Geary 1998, 125–26.
22. Hrdy 1981, 18.
23. Pers. comm. quoted in Batten 1992, 22.
24. For sexual selection see Andersson 1994; Darwin 1871; Miller 1998; Cronin 1991.
25. The claim that Homeric women place a premium on the physical appearance of their mates may seem out of step with well-publicized research suggesting that, across a wide cross-section of societies, women tend to place greater emphasis on a potential mate's wealth and social status while men tend to place more emphasis on youth and beauty (Buss 1989; Gottschall et al. 2004). While this appears to be a consistent cross-cultural trend, there is nothing in this substantial body of research to suggest that physical appearance is an unimportant factor in female mate selection decisions; the research suggests male physical appearance is an important variable for women, just not as important as it is for men.
26. For a seminal study of cross-cultural tendencies in women's mate preferences see Buss 1989; for a relatively current review see Buss 2003.
27. For a review of historical and anthropological studies indicating that tall men enjoy, on average, higher status, pay, and reproductive success see Sugiyama 2005, 315–21; see also Barrett et al. 2002, 106–07.
28. For an anthropological and historical overview of infanticide by warriors see Hrdy 1999, 237–44, 413. For a harrowing first-person account among the Yanomamö see Valero and Bioca 1969.
29. *Erotikos* 761d.

30. The only other exception I can recall is Nireus, who is very briefly described in the Catalog of Ships as a strikingly handsome weakling (*Iliad* 2.671–75).
31. This relationship is articulated by Wrangham and Peterson 1996 and also by Smuts 1991, 1995b.

7 HOMER'S MISSING DAUGHTERS

1. For instance, Gat 2000a.
2. Darwin 1871 [1998], 614.
3. Mesquida and Wiener 1996, 1999.
4. Hudson and Den Boer 2002, 12; for the most comprehensive review and analysis of this subject see Hudson and Den Boer 2005.
5. Hudson and Den Boer 2002, 24. The behavioral ecologists Mesquida and Weiner agree that high-sex-ratio societies are more likely to engage in aggressive war, but they sharply question the conclusion, favored by Hudson and Den Boer, that young men are sent to fight in these conflicts against their interests and wishes: "Currently we have a tendency, at least in the western world, to assume that young men are essentially unwilling participants in armed conflicts. We tend to see such participation as a consequence of manipulation and coercion, and we often make the assumption that a special interest group or class is promoting or financing, in its own interest, the young male coalition . . . But it is probably because we have no recent experience with territorial expansion that we fail to appreciate the fact that whenever a population has an over-abundance of well armed and organized young men, pure exploitation and coercion are extremely difficult to implement . . . we would like to propose that . . . intergenerational competition for reproductive resources, when exacerbated by the presence of a relatively large number of resourceless young males, might result in the emergence of male collective aggression, which occasionally expresses itself as expansionist warfare" (1996, 286–87).
6. Mesquida and Wiener 1996, 1999.
7. Courtwright 1996.
8. Allen and Smith 1994.
9. Quoted in Allen and Smith 1994, 607.
10. Chagnon 1979a, 1979b.
11. For review and references to specific studies see Hudson and Den Boer 2005, 33.
12. Divale and Harris 1976, 521.
13. Kruger and Nesse 2004.
14. Divale and Harris 1976, 528.
15. Divale and Harris 1976, 526.

16. Divale and Harris 1976, 526.
17. Hewlett 1991, 26.
18. Hudson and Den Boer 2005, 201.
19. Guttentag and Secord 1983; Pomeroy 1975, 45–46.
20. Fragment 11 in T. Koch, *Comicorum atticorum fragmenta*, 3 vols. (Leipzig: Teubner, 1880–88).
21. Excellent and comprehensive reviews of the main arguments of the nineteenth and twentieth centuries can be found in Oldenziel 1987; Patterson 1983; Rousselle 2001. Other prominent contributors to the literature include Cameron 1932; Engels 1984; Glotz 1929; Golden 1981, Golden 1990; Langer 1974–75; Pomeroy 1975, 1983; Van Hook 1920.
22. Among other sources, Plato's *Theaetetus* strongly supports the conclusion that exposure was relatively common. New comedy is one source of evidence in favor of preferential female exposure; the fragment of Poseidippus which comprises the epigraph to this section is a particularly compelling – if controversial – piece of evidence.
23. Gallant 1991; Rousselle 2001; Patterson 1983; Blundell 1995, 131; Garland 1998, 57, 60.
24. Major contributors to this literature include Cameron 1932; Engels 1984; Golden 1981, 1990; Langer 1974–75; Patterson 1983; Glotz 1929; Oldenziel 1987; Pomeroy 1983; Van Hook 1920.
25. Patterson, who is skeptical of much of the evidence for preferential female exposure, writes: "Nonetheless, an unequal sex ratio (favoring males) seems to me quite likely in ancient Greece" (1983, 120). And "Taken together, such considerations suggest that the life expectancy of female infants in ancient Greece *was* less than that of the male . . ." (121). Sallares (1991, 130) expresses a similar view.
26. The arch-skeptic Bolkenstein wrote, "No one will be able to deny that, both in this territory and in the rest of the Greek world, in the subsequent centuries, exposure was a means, frequently employed by parents, of getting rid of undesired children, especially when the latter were girls" (1922). Another important skeptic, Van Hook, wrote: "It is doubtless true that in the vast majority of cases of exposure girls and not boys were the victims. I fail, however, to find any evidence of frequency of their exposure in Athens in the fifth and fourth centuries" (1920, 136).
27. Pomeroy describes Dark Age cemetery evidence as consistent with the hypothesis of sex-ratio manipulation in favor of males, but she acknowledges that the data are meager and inconclusive (1975, 44–45). It should also be noted that excavations of cemeteries in the Late Cypriot and Cypro-Geometric periods reveal a scarcity of female remains; archaeologists have advanced the possibility of preferential female infanticide and neglect as a plausible explanation (Bright 1995).

28. On genealogical information as source see Pomeroy 1975, 70; Stark 1997, 97.
29. Agamemnon with three daughters is one example; see also *Iliad* 10.317.
30. Minturn and Stashak 1982; Hrdy 1999, 321; Divale and Harris 1976, 525.
31. Schein 1984, 72; Vermeule 1979, 113; Finley 1954 [2002], 130–31.
32. The arguments of this chapter are inspired by the "differential payback hypothesis" of sex-ratio manipulation, which suggests that parents will invest preferentially in the sex that produces greater returns on parental investment measured, ultimately, in the currency of parental inclusive fitness (Cronk 1993). However, as I have argued elsewhere, there are also reasons, based on both historical and anthropological precedent and biological theory (see Trivers and Willard 1973), to suspect that sex-ratio manipulation in favor of Homeric sons may have been particularly pronounced among Homeric elites (see Gottschall 2003).
33. Cronk 1993.
34. On "most prestate societies" see Betzig 1986, 22; see also Chagnon 1990, 90. Finley wrote of Homeric society that "kinship thinking permeated everything" (1954 [2002], 81).
35. This is at least implied by Finley: "personal power meant the strength of the household and the family" (1954 [2002], 94).
36. While Hector has forty-nine brothers at the beginning of the Trojan War and almost ten by the end of the *Iliad*, Kirk et al. 1985–93 suggest that the pathos of the *Iliad*'s final books is partly generated by Hector's standing as a symbolic only son (6:324, 326, 518–51). Priam tells Achilles that the death of Hector has left him without sons ("not one is left") and that Hector was the "only one" he had standing between Troy's people and grievous calamity (24.493–501).
37. See Donlan 1985, 299; Donlan 1997a, 658, 1997b; Pomeroy et al. 1999, 66.
38. Otterbein 1994, 148.
39. See also *Iliad* 24.725–34 where Andromache worries that Astyanax will be murdered by a Greek in revenge for Hector's slaying of a kinsman.
40. See Davies 1989, 49.
41. This Hobbesian assessment is perhaps most prominent in the writings of Adkins (e.g., 1960, 1966). As described by Van Wees, Adkins describes a Homeric world where "innate egoism and aggression are allowed and even encouraged to express themselves" (1992, 66). For analysis of Adkins' views and full references see Van Wees 1992, 63–69.
42. Boehm 1999; for discussion and examples of community uprisings against powerful Homeric individuals see Raaflaub 1997b.
43. For discussion see Davies 1989, 43.
44. Bryant 1996, 26.
45. Golden 1990.

46. "Many so-called egalitarian societies include individuals who vary along an axis of 'funds of kinship power' that has enormous implications for their survival and reproduction . . . The age and sex of one's relatives are also important. Someone with many adult male relatives has an advantage in some contexts compared to another with many adult female relatives . . . Among the Yanomamö, virtually every village I have studied is led by headmen who invariably come from the largest descent groups in the village" (Chagnon 1990, 90). See also Betzig's analysis of cross-cultural ethnography: "Very generally, where there is no arbitrating authority, amassed strength determines the outcomes of conflicts, and strength is almost invariably determined by one's own physical prowess, and that represented by the aggregated force of one's kinship and alliance network" (1986, 22).
47. See Harris 1982; Hudson and Den Boer 2005, 205.
48. See Johansson 1979; Dickemann 1979; Bugos and McCarthy 1984; contributors to Parmigani and Vom Saal 1994; contributors to Hausfater and Hrdy 1984.
49. Hewlett 1991, 23; see also Alexander et al. 1979; Allen and Smith 1994, 612; for review of evidence and case studies of rare societies with excess mortality of juvenile *males* see Cronk 1993.
50. Allen and Smith 1994.
51. Knud Ramsen quoted in Allen and Smith 1994.
52. Allen and Smith 1994.
53. See Hudson and Den Boer 2005 for review of cross-cultural data suggesting relationship between low female economic productivity (relative to male) and high rates of EFM. See also Dickemann 1979; Guttentag 1983.

8 THE PRISONER'S DILEMMA AND THE MYSTERY OF TRAGEDY

1. Aristotle says that the tragic outcome arises because of a *hamartia*. In earlier interpretations this difficult term was often rendered as "tragic flaw." However, most modern scholars argue that Aristotle is not attributing blame. *Hamartia* is more accurately understood as a simple mistake or error (the word was originally used in archery to describe an errant shot). See, for example, House 1956; Lucas 1968; Von Fritz 1962.
2. Aristotle, *Poetics*, 24, trans. Preston Epps.
3. Modern commentators widely treat the *Iliad* as a tragic poem (for discussion and criticism of this trend see Silk 1989). Plato considered Homer to be the first and best of the tragedians. And Aeschylus is reputed to have said that his plays were "slices from the banquet of Homer."
4. These facts are consistent with more recent pronouncements on the nature of tragedy. Subsequent writers have argued that tragedies express the

"sadness and wretchedness" of the human condition. And most germane to our purposes here, they have shown that the tragic hero's situation is defined by *hopelessness* (for overview see Cuddon 1991, 983–91). The tragic hero's situation is both intolerable and inescapable. The more he struggles to escape, the more helplessly he is ensnared.

5. Griffin 1976 shows that pathos was recognized as a special Homeric quality in ancient criticism.
6. See Halliwell 1986, 264 for multiple *Poetics* references suggesting Aristotle's quasi-tragic view of the *Odyssey*. Also see Kirk et al. 1985–1993, 6:272: The *Odyssey*'s plot "is just the sort recommended for tragedy."
7. Halliwell expresses a similar sentiment. For Halliwell, one reason that the *alogon* is acceptable in epic but not drama is that "... epic is not performed on stage, so that anomalies which might show up in the theatre, but do not in recitation or reading, therefore become permissible" (1986, 259).
8. I am not alone in feeling that this sense of the *alogon* is conveyed in *Poetics* (e.g., Else 1957, 624–25). If I am mischaracterizing Aristotle's perspective, then I join those many who have already charged that Aristotle has imperfectly characterized the genre of tragedy.
9. I know of just one precedent for the application of game theory to the literature of antiquity, Lowe's *The classical plot and the invention of western narrative* (2000).
10. Weil 1956.
11. For "poem of death" see Reinhardt 1960, 13. For 250 named warriors see Basset cited in Emily Vermeule 1979, 96.
12. For instance, Homer knows sixty ways to say "X died."
13. For more on this contrast see Taplin 1980.
14. On psychological traumas see Shay 1994.
15. See Weil 1956.
16. It is inappropriate to lightly describe the *Odyssey* as a comedy because (1) delivering few laughs, it does not fit well with modern ideas of the comic, and (2) it is unclear how it should be classified within a formal Aristotelian framework. A drama in which a disastrous outcome was averted at the end could still be classified among the "ideal" tragedies, so long as it met the other criteria of tragedy (e.g., arousing pity and fear). Aristotle's theory of tragedy readily accommodated happy endings, and there is ambiguity in the *Poetics* about which form of tragedy is superior: the type that ends happily or the type that concludes in disaster. A defensible case could be made for aligning the *Odyssey* with the former type of ideal tragedy.
17. On the *Odyssey* by a woman see Butler 1897 [1922]; On the *Iliad* by mature poet and the *Odyssey* by youthful epigone see Heubeck 1988, 13.

Longinus wrote, in *On The Sublime*, that the *Iliad* was by a youthful poet and the *Odyssey* by the same poet in his maturity.

18. For the ending of the *Odyssey* symbolizing the establishment of "a new moral order" see Heubeck et al. 1988–1992, 3:406; see also Finley 1954 [2002], 146. For similar arguments about the *Iliad* see Nagy 1997, 194.
19. Davies 1994, 535–36.
20. Felson and Slatkin 2004, 113. Also: "Although the *Odyssey* might be seen to offer a kind of 'comedy of remarriage,' it also intermittently posits ominous narrative alternatives – its own shadows" (Felson and Slatkin 2004, 113).
21. Before receiving assurances from Athena, Odysseus himself assumes that it will be necessary to flee after killing the suitors and that escaping will be more difficult than the actual slaughter (*Odyssey* 20.40–43).
22. Ritchie 1996, 44, 105.
23. For broad anthropological overviews see Otterbein 1994; Gat 2000b, 2000c; Divale and Harris 1976. For illuminating single-culture case studies see Chagnon 1968 [1992]; Smith and Smith 1994.
24. See Gat 2000c.
25. Gat 2000b.
26. See also von Neumann and Morgenstern 1944.
27. For a detailed, lively history of the conception of the Prisoner's Dilemma scenario see Poundstone 1992.
28. See Poundstone 1992 for a number of illustrative scenarios demonstrating the applicability of the Prisoner's Dilemma model to diverse competitive situations.
29. For "mathematical backbone" see Hammerstein 1998 (also Myerson 1999); for "one of the most important advances in evolutionary theory since Darwin," see Dawkins 1976 (see also M. Smith 1982; Axelrod 1984; contributors to Dugatkin and Reeve 1998); for serviceable overviews of the field see Axelrod 1984; Barash 2003; Colman 1995; Straffin 1993; and, especially, Poundstone 1992.
30. For a classic exposition of these simulations see Axelrod 1984; see also Smith and Price's "Retaliator" strategy, M. Smith 1982.
31. For tragedy of the commons see Hardin 1968; for arms races in the context of superpower conflict see Brams 1985.

CONCLUSION: BETWEEN LIONS AND MEN

1. Darwin 1871 [1998], 632.
2. See Gottschall 2001.
3. Animals are frequently imputed with human qualities: nobility, guile, rationality, loyalty etc. Achilles' famous horses are, perhaps, the best example. They

are, practically, human beings encased in horse flesh. They are capable of rational even eloquent speech, the elation of battle, deep mourning, and dogged loyalty. Antilochus' horses are similar. Their master gets them to run faster through threats, appeals to their vanity, and encouraging them to imagine the shame of being surpassed by a female horse (*Iliad* 23.407–13).

4. On similes see Lonsdale 1990, 10, 39.
5. Clarke 1995, 145; see also Schein 1984, 79.
6. For vigorous discussion of this sugar-coating tendency see Johnston 1988, ch. 7. See also Finley: "The *Iliad* is saturated in blood, a fact which cannot be hidden or argued away, twist the evidence as we may in a vain attempt to fit archaic Greek values to a more gentle code of ethics" (1954 [2002], 121). See above, Chapter Eight, for similar arguments about the *Odyssey*.
7. See, for instance, final chapters of Dawkins 1976; Johnston 1997. This tendency can be traced back to the final chapter of the first work of what would come to be known as evolutionary psychology, Darwin's *The descent of man* (1871).
8. See Pinker 2002 on contrast between the "tragic" and "utopian" (or constrained and unconstrained) views, ch. 16.
9. Margaret Mead, for instance, argued that human nature was "almost unbelievably malleable" (1935 [1963], 260), "the rawest, most undifferentiated of raw material" (quoted in Freeman 1983, 101).
10. See Alexander 1987.
11. Alexander 1987, 9.
12. This allegation is at the heart of much criticism of sociobiology and evolutionary psychology. For representative examples of this criticism see Rose, Kamin, and Lewontin 1985; contributors to Rose and Rose 2000. This class of criticism has been painstakingly addressed in publications too numerous to comprehensively cite. For a small sample, see Alcock 2001; Alexander 1979, 1987; Dawkins 1985; Dennett 1995; Ridley 2003. Pinker 2002 is more up-to-date and especially accessible.
13. Singer 2000, first quote, p. 24, second quote, p. 62.
14. While this book focuses on competition, exploration of the cooperative elements of human nature is currently fueling some of the most promising and original research in the field of evolution and human behavior. For diverse analyses of this subject consult Alexander 1987; Boehm 1999; De Waal 1996; Gintis 2000; Gintis et al. 2005; Kropotkin 1904; Ridley 1997; Singer 2000; Sober and Wilson 1998; Wilson 2002.

APPENDIX: DATING HOMERIC SOCIETY

1. Heubeck et al. (1988–1992, 1:276) give astronomical data in support of an eighth-century Hesiod.

2. West 1995 applies this term to Burkert's argument for a *terminus post quem* for the *Iliad* of 663. Nagy, without abusiveness, has called different scenarios for text fixation "myths" (1996, 93).
3. The closest approximations to censuses of current scholarly opinion are to be found in Morris' and Powell's *A new companion to Homer* (1997) and in Fowler's *Cambridge companion to Homer* (2004). With rare exceptions, contributors to the former volume express support for eighth-century dates, while contributors to the latter almost uniformly date Homer to "around 700." Other recent and significant statements on Homer's date include West 1995; Van Wees 2002a; Nagy 1995, 1996; Burgess 2001; Burkert 1976; Powell 2002, 2004; Janko 1982, 1998; Raaflaub 1997a; Crielaard 1995; Ruijgh 1995; Donlan 1985.
4. See Janko 1998. The plausibility of this scenario is further boosted by analogies with well-studied traditions of oral poetry that continued to thrive in isolated, illiterate regions long after literacy had elsewhere prevailed (e.g., Lord 1960).
5. Powell 2002.
6. Coldstream argues that the "real dawn came in the middle of the eighth century, and gradually illumined the whole Greek world" (1977, 367); Snodgrass 1971 also argues in favor of a renaissance beginning in the middle of the eighth century (see also Starr 1961). For an up-to-date overview of the evidence in favor of the eighth-century transitions see Morris (forthcoming).
7. Raaflaub 1997b, 9.
8. For instance, Finley 1954; Dickinson 1986.
9. Powell examined thirteen Homeric details claimed to be post-700 elements of Greek material and social culture. His conclusion: "No object or social reality is necessarily later than 700 BC, an extraordinary fact when we consider how many have assumed, and assume, the poems to be rife with interpolations" (1991, 206). Silk (1989, 4) agrees with Powell, and Kirk had already reached the same conclusion: "Post-Homeric details, later than around 700 BC, whether of language or content, are virtually absent" (Kirk et al. 1985–1993, 1:10).
10. Wolf 1795 [1985], 101.
11. See Powell 2002; for arguments that *Iliad* 6.167–70 may *not* indicate knowledge of true alphabetic writing see Powell 1991.
12. Evidence for the eighth-century view is well marshaled by Morris 1986; Powell 1991, 2002, 2004; Janko 1982; see also most contributors to Morris and Powell 1997.
13. A. Parry 1989, 112.

Works cited

Adkins, A. W. H. 1960. *Merit and responsibility; A study in Greek values.* Oxford: Clarendon Press.

1966. Basic Greek values in Euripides' *Hecuba* and *Hercules. Classical Quarterly* 19:20–33.

1982. Values, goals, and emotions in the *Iliad. Classical Philology* 77:292–326.

Alcock, J. 1998. *Animal behavior: An evolutionary approach.* Sunderland, MA: Sinauer.

2001. *The triumph of sociobiology.* Oxford: Oxford University Press.

Alexander, R. D. 1979. *Darwinism and human affairs.* Seattle: University of Washington Press.

1987. *The biology of moral systems: Foundations of human behavior.* Hawthorne, NY: Aldine de Gruyter.

Alexander, R. D., J. Hoogland, R. Howard, K. Noonan, and P. Sherman. 1979. Sexual dimorphisms and breeding systems in pinnipeds, ungulates, primates, and humans. In Chagnon and Irons 1979, 402–35.

Alexander, R. D., and K. Noonan. 1979. Concealment of ovulation, parental care, and human social evolution. In Chagnon and Irons 1979, 436–53.

Allen, E. A., and S. A. Smith. 1994. Inuit sex ratio variation: Population control, ethnographic error, or parental manipulation? *Current Anthropology* 35:595–624.

Allen, S. H. 1999. *Finding the walls of Troy: Frank Calvert and Heinrich Schliemann at Hisarlik.* Berkeley: University of California Press.

Amnesty International. 1997. Zaire: Rape, killings and other human rights violations by the security forces, (cited February 19, 1997). Available from http://web.amnesty.org/library/Index/engAFR620061997.

2003a. Democratic Republic of Congo: War against unarmed civilians, November 23, 1998 (cited April 15, 2003). Available from http://web.amnesty.org/library/Index/engAFR620361998.

2003b. Sierra Leone: Rape and other forms of sexual violence must be stopped, June 30, 2000 (cited April 20, 2003). Available from http://www.amnestyusa.org/news/2000/15104800.htm.

Andersson, M. B. 1994. *Sexual selection*. Princeton, NJ: Princeton University Press.

Antonaccio, C. 1995. Lefkandi and Homer. In *Homer's world: Fiction, tradition, reality*, ed. O. Andersen and M. Dickie, 5–27. Papers from the Norwegian Institute at Athens 3.

Apollodorus. 1997. *The library of Greek mythology*. Trans. Robin Hard. Oxford: Oxford University Press.

Archer, J., ed. 1994. *Male violence*. London: Routledge.

Ardrey, R. 1966. *The territorial imperative: A personal inquiry into the animal origins of property and nations*. New York: Atheneum.

Aristotle. 1942. *The Poetics of Aristotle*. Trans. P. H. Epps. Chapel Hill, NC: University of North Carolina Press.

Axelrod, R. M. 1984. *The evolution of cooperation*. New York: Basic Books.

Barash, D. P. 2003. *The survival game: How game theory explains the biology of human cooperation and competition*. New York: Times Books.

Barkow, J., L. Cosmides, and J. Tooby, eds. 1992. *The adapted mind: Evolutionary psychology and the generation of culture*. Oxford: Oxford University Press.

Barrett, L., R. Dunbar, and J. Lycet. 2002. *Human evolutionary psychology*. Princeton: Princeton University Press.

Barstow, A. L. 2000. *War's dirty secret: Rape, prostitution, and other crimes against women*. Cleveland, Ohio: Pilgrim Press.

Bateman, A. 1948. Intra-sexual selection in Drosophila. *Heredity*: 2: 349–68.

Batten. M. *Sexual strategies: How females choose their mates*. New York: Putnam, 1992.

Bennet, J. 1997. Homer and the bronze age. In Morris and Powell 1997, 511–33.

Betzig, L. L. 1986. *Despotism and differential reproduction: A Darwinian view of history*. New York: Aldine.

Birkhead, T. R. 2000. *Promiscuity: An evolutionary history of sperm competition*. Cambridge, MA: Harvard University Press.

Blackwell, T. 1736 [1976]. *An enquiry into the life and writings of Homer*. Philadelphia: Coronet Books.

Blundell, S. 1995. *Women in ancient Greece*. Cambridge, MA: Harvard University Press.

Boehm, C. 1999. *Hierarchy in the forest: The evolution of egalitarian behavior*. Cambridge, MA: Harvard University Press.

Bolkenstein, H. 1922. The exposure of infants at Athens and the *Egchutristriai*. *Classical Philology* 17:222–39.

Bonduriansky, R. 2001. The evolution of male mate choice in insects: A synthesis of ideas and evidence. *Biological Review* 76:305–39.

Bower, B. 1995. Seeds of warfare precede agriculture. *Science News* 147:4.

Bowra, C. M. 1934. Homeric words in Cyprus. *Journal of Hellenic Studies* 54:54–74.

1952. *Heroic poetry*. London: Macmillan.

Brams, S. J. 1985. *Superpower games: Applying game theory to superpower conflict*. New Haven and London: Yale University Press.

Bright, L. 1995. A possible case of the practice of abandonment during the Late Cypriot and Cypro-Geometric periods. In *Klados: Essays in honor of J. N. Coldstream*, ed. C. Morris, 35–43. London: University of London, Institute of Classical Studies.

Broude, G. J., and S. Greene. 1983. Cross-cultural codes on husband–wife relationships. *Ethnology* 22:263–80.

Brown, Donald E. 1991. *Human universals*. Philadelphia: Temple University Press.

Brownmiller, S. 1975. *Against our will: Men, women, and rape*. New York: Simon and Schuster.

Bryant, J. M. 1996. *Moral codes and social structure in ancient Greece: A sociology of Greek ethics from Homer to the Epicureans and Stoics*. Albany, NY: State University of New York Press.

Buchholz, E. 1871–75. *Die homerischen Realien*. Leipzig: W. Engelmann.

Bugos, P., and L. McCarthy. 1984. Ayoreo infanticide: A case study. In Hausfater and Hrdy 1984, 503–20.

Burgess, J. 2001. *The tradition of the Trojan War in Homer and the epic cycle*. Baltimore, MD: Johns Hopkins University Press.

Burkert, W. 1976. Das hunderttorige Theben und die Datierung der Ilias. *Wiener Studien* 10:5–21.

1983. *Homo necans: The anthropology of ancient Greek sacrificial ritual and myth*. Berkeley: University of California Press.

Buss, D. M. 1989. Sex differences in human mate preferences: Evolutionary hypothesis testing in 37 cultures. *Behavioral and Brain Sciences* 12:1–49.

1999. *Evolutionary psychology: The new science of the mind*. Boston: Allyn and Bacon.

2000. *The dangerous passion: Why jealousy is as necessary as love and sex*. New York: Free Press.

2003. *The evolution of desire: Strategies of human mating*. New York: Basic Books.

ed. 2005. *The Handbook of evolutionary psychology*. New York: Wiley.

Buss, D. M., and N. M. Malamuth. 1996. *Sex, power, conflict: Evolutionary and feminist perspectives*. New York: Oxford University Press.

Butler, S. 1897 [1922]. *The authoress of the Odyssey*. London: J. Cape.

Calhoun, G. 1962. Polity and society: The Homeric picture. In Wace and Stubbings 1962, 431–52.

Cameron, A. 1932. The exposure of children and Greek ethics. *Classical Review* 46:105–14.

Campbell, A. 2002. *A mind of her own: The evolutionary psychology of women.* Oxford: Oxford University Press.

2005. Aggression. In Buss 2005, 628–52.

Carlier, P. 1984. *La Royauté en Grèce avant Alexandre.* Strasbourg: Université des Sciences Humaines de Strasbourg.

Carneiro, R. 1981. The chiefdom: Precursor of the state. In *The transition to statehood in the new world*, ed. Grant Jones and Robert Kautz, 37–79. Cambridge: Cambridge University Press.

Carroll, J. 2004. *Literary Darwinism.* London: Routledge.

Chagnon, N. A. 1968 [1992]. *Yanomamö.* San Diego: Harcourt Brace Jovanovich.

1979a. Is reproductive success equal in egalitarian societies? In Chagnon and Irons 1979, 379–401.

1979b. Mate competition, favoring close kin, and village fissioning among the Yanomamö Indians. In Chagnon and Irons 1979, 86–131.

1988. Life histories, blood revenge, and warfare in a tribal population. *Science* 239:985–993.

1990. Reproductive and somatic conflicts of interest in the genesis of violence and warfare among tribesmen. In *The anthropology of war*, ed. J. Haas, 77–104. Cambridge: Cambridge University Press.

Chagnon, N. A., and W. Irons, eds. 1979. *Evolutionary biology and human social behavior: An anthropological perspective.* North Scituate, MA: Duxbury Press.

Chelala, C. 1998. Algerian abortion controversy highlights rape of war victims. *Lancet* 351:1413–14.

Chung, C. S. 1995. Korean women drafted for military sexual slavery by Japan. In *True stories of the Korean comfort women*, ed. Keith Howard, 11–31. London: Cassell.

Clarke, M. 1995. Between lions and men: An image in the *Iliad. Greek, Roman and Byzantine Studies* 36:137–59.

Clutton-Brock, T. 1988. Reproductive success. In *Reproductive Success*, ed. T. Clutton-Brock, 472–85. Chicago: University of Chicago Press.

Clutton-Brock, T., and P. Harvey. 1976. Evolutionary rules and primate societies. In *Growing points in ethology*, ed. P. Bateson and R. Hinde, 195–238. Cambridge: Cambridge University Press.

Clutton-Brock, T., and G. Parker. 1992. Sexual coercion in animal societies. *Animal Behaviour* 49:1345–65.

Cobet, J. 1981. König, Anführer, Herr; Monarch, Tyrann. In *Soziale Typenbegriffe im alten Griechenland*, ed. E. Welskopf, 9–66. Berlin: Akademic-Verlag.

Coldstream, J. N. 1977 [2003]. *Geometric Greece: 900–700 BC*. London: Routledge.

Colman, A. M. 1995. *Game theory and its applications in the social and biological sciences*. Oxford: Butterworth-Heinemann.

Courtwright, D. T. 1996. *Violent land: Single men and social disorder from the frontier to the inner city*. Cambridge, MA: Harvard University Press.

Cowlishaw, G., and Dunbar, R. 1991. Dominance rank and mating success in male primates. *Animal Behaviour* 41:1045–56.

Crielaard, J. P. 1995. Homer, history, and archaeology: Some remarks on the date of the Homeric world. In *Homeric questions: Essays in philology, ancient history and archaeology, including the papers of a conference organized by the Netherlands Institute at Athens (15 May 1993)*, ed. Jan Paul Creilaard, 201–88. Amsterdam: J. C. Gieben.

Cronin, H. 1991. *The ant and the peacock: Altruism and sexual selection from Darwin to today*. Cambridge: Cambridge University Press.

Cronk, L. 1993. Parental favoritism toward daughters. *American Scientist* 81:292–99.

Cuddon, J. 1991. *The Penguin dictionary of literary terms and literary theory*. New York: Penguin.

Cummins, D. 2005. Dominance, status, and social hierarchies. In Buss 2005, 676–97.

Daly, M., and M. Wilson. 1988. *Homicide*. New York: Aldine de Gruyter.

1992. The man who mistook his wife for a chattel. In Barkow, Cosmides, and Tooby 1992, 289–322.

1994. The evolutionary psychology of male violence. In Archer 1994, 253–88.

1999. *The truth about Cinderella: A Darwinian view of parental love*. New Haven and London: Yale University Press.

Darwin, C. 1859. *On the origin of species by means of natural selection*. London: J. Murray.

1871 [1998]. *The descent of man, and selection in relation to sex*. New York: Prometheus Books.

1872. *The expression of the emotions in man and animals*. London: J. Murray.

1887 [1958]. *Autobiography. With original omissions restored*. London: Collins.

Davidson, J. A. 1962a. The Homeric question. In Wace and Stubbings 1962, 234–68.

1962b. The transmission of the text. In Wace and Stubbings 1962, 215–33.

Davie, M. R. 1929. *The evolution of war; A study of its rôle in early societies.* New Haven: Yale University Press.

Davies, M. 1989. *The Greek epic cycle.* Bristol: Bristol Classical Press.

1994. *Odyssey* 22.474–7: Murder or mutilation? *Classical Quarterly* 44:534–36.

Dawkins, R. 1976. *The selfish gene.* Oxford: Oxford University Press.

1985. Sociobiology: The debate continues. *New Scientist*, January 24.

Dawson, D. 1996. *The origins of Western warfare: Militarism and morality in the ancient world, history and warfare.* Boulder, CO: Westview Press.

Deger, S. 1970. *Herrschaftsformen bei Homer.* Vienna: Notring.

Dennett, D. C. 1995. *Darwin's dangerous idea: Evolution and the meanings of life.* New York: Simon & Schuster.

Dewsbury, D. 1982. Dominance rank, copulatory behavior and differential reproduction. *Quarterly Review of Biology* 57:135–59.

Diamond, J. M. 1992. *The third chimpanzee: The evolution and future of the human animal.* New York: HarperCollins.

Dickemann, M. 1979. Female infanticide, reproductive strategies, and social stratification. In Chagnon and Irons 1979, 321–67.

Dickinson, O. T. P. K. 1986. Homer, The poet of the Dark Age. *Greece and Rome* 33:77–86.

Divale, W., and M. Harris. 1976. Population, warfare, and the male supremacist complex. *American Anthropologist* 78:521–38.

Dodds, E. R. 1951. *The Greeks and the irrational.* Berkeley: University of California Press.

1968a. Homer and the analysts. In *Fifty years (and twelve) of classical scholarship*, ed. M. Platnauer, 1–8. New York: Barnes & Noble.

1968b. Homer and the unitarians. In *Fifty years (and twelve) of classical scholarship*, ed. M. Platnauer, 8–13. New York: Barnes & Noble.

Dombrowski, N. 1999. *Women and war in the twentieth century: Enlisted with or without consent.* New York: Garland.

Donlan, W. 1980. *The aristocratic ideal in Ancient Greece: Attitudes of superiority from Homer to the end of the 5th century BC.* Lawrence, KS: Coronado Press.

1985. The social groups of Dark Age Greece. *Classical Philology* 80:293–309.

1993. Dueling with gifts in the *Iliad*: As the audience saw it. *Colby Quarterly* 29:155–72.

1997a. The Homeric economy. In Morris and Powell 1997, 649–67.

1997b. The relations of power in the pre-state and early state polities. In *The development of the polis in archaic Greece*, ed. L. G. Mitchell and P. J. Rhodes, 39–48. London: Routledge.

Drews, R. 1993. *The end of the Bronze Age: Changes in warfare and the catastrophe ca. 1200 BC.* Princeton, NJ: Princeton University Press.

Ducrey, P. 1986. *Warfare in ancient Greece*. New York: Schocken Books.

Dugatkin, L. A., and H. Kern Reeve. 1998. *Game theory and animal behavior*. New York: Oxford University Press.

Dunbar, R., and L. Barrett. 2007. *The Oxford handbook of evolutionary psychology*. Oxford: Oxford University Press.

Eagly, A., and W. Wood. 1999. The origins of sex differences in human behavior: Evolved dispositions versus social roles. *American Psychologist* 54:408–23.

Ellis, L. 1995. Dominance and reproductive success among nonhuman animals: A cross-species comparison. *Ethology and Sociobiology* 16:257–333.

Else, G. 1957. *Aristotle's Poetics*. Harvard.

Engels, D. 1984. The use of historical demography in ancient history. *Classical Quarterly* 34:386–93.

Etcoff, N. 1999. *Survival of the prettiest: The science of beauty*. New York: Anchor.

Evelyn-White, H. G. 1982. *Hesiod, the Homeric hymns, and Homerica*. Cambridge, MA: Harvard University Press.

Felson, N., and L. Slatkin. 2004. Gender and Homeric epic. In Robert Fowler 2004, 91–114.

Ferguson, R. Brian. 1995. *Yanomami warfare: A political history*. Sante Fe, NM: School of American Research Press.

Fields, N. 2004. *Troy: c. 1700–1250 BC*. Oxford: Osprey Publishing.

Finkleman, P., and J. Miller, eds. 1998. *Macmillan encyclopedia of world slavery*. New York: Simon & Schuster.

Finley, M. I. 1954 [2002]. *The world of Odysseus*. New York: Viking Press.

1957. Homer and Mycenae: Property and tenure. *Historia* 6:133–59.

Fisher, R. A. 1958. *The genetical theory of natural selection*. New York: Dover Publications.

Foley, J. 2004. Epic as genre. In Fowler 2004, 171–87.

Fowler, R. 2004. The Homeric question. In Fowler 2004, 220–32.

ed. 2004. *The Cambridge companion to Homer*. Cambridge: Cambridge University Press.

Fox, R. 1995. Sexual conflict in the epics. *Human Nature* 6:135–44.

Freeman, D. 1983. *Margaret Mead and Samoa: The making and unmaking of an anthropological myth*. Cambridge, MA: Harvard University Press.

Fulkerson, L. 2002. Epic ways of killing a woman: Gender and transgression in the *Odyssey* 22.465–472. *Classical Journal* 97:335–50.

Gallant, T. W. 1991. *Risk and survival in ancient Greece: Reconstructing the rural domestic economy*. Stanford, CA.: Stanford University Press.

Gantz, T. 1993. *Early Greek myth*. Baltimore, MD: Johns Hopkins University Press.

Garland, R. 1998. *Daily life of the Ancient Greeks*. Westport, CN: Greenwood Press.

Gat, A. 2000a. The human motivational complex: Evolutionary theory and the causes of hunter-gatherer fighting. Part I. Primary somatic and reproductive causes. *Anthropological Quarterly* 73:20–34.

2000b. The human motivational complex: Evolutionary theory and the causes of hunter-gatherer fighting, Part II. Proximate, subordinate, and derivative causes. *Anthropological Quarterly* 73:74–88.

2000c. The causes and origins of "primitive warfare": Reply to Fergusen. *Anthropological Quarterly* 73:165–68.

Geary, D. 1998. *Male, female: The evolution of human sex differences.* Washington, DC: American Psychological Association.

Geddes, A. G. 1984. Who's who in Homeric society? *Classical Quarterly* 34:17–36.

Ghiglieri, M. P. 1999. *The dark side of man: Tracing the origins of male violence.* Reading, MA: Perseus Books.

Gintis, H. 2000. Strong reciprocity and human sociality. *Journal of Theoretical Biology* 206:169–79.

Gintis, H., S. Bowles, R. Boyd, E. Fehr, eds. 2005. *Moral sentiments and material interests: The foundations of cooperation in economic life.* Cambridge, MA: MIT Press.

Gladstone, W. E. 1858. *Studies on Homer and the Homeric age.* Oxford: Oxford University Press.

Glotz, G. 1929. *The Homeric city.* Trans. N. Mallison and K. Paul. London: A. Knopf.

Golden, M. 1981. Demography and the exposure of girls at Athens. *Phoenix* 35:316–31.

1990. *Children and childhood in classical Athens.* Baltimore, MD: Johns Hopkins University Press.

Good, K. and D. Chanoff. 1991. *Into the heart: One man's pursuit of love and knowledge among the Yanomama.* New York: Simon & Schuster.

Gottschall, J. 2001. Homer's human animal: Ritual combat in the *Iliad. Philosophy and Literature* 26:278–94.

2003. An evolutionary perspective on Homer's invisible daughters. *Interdisciplinary Literary Studies* 4:36–55.

2004. Explaining wartime rape. *Journal of Sex Research* 41:129–36.

Gottschall, J., J. Martin, J. Rea, and H. Quish. 2004. Sex differences in mate choice criteria are reflected in folk tales from around the world and in historical European literature. *Evolution and Human Behavior* 25:102–12.

Gottschall, J., and D. S. Wilson, eds. 2005. *The literary animal: Evolution and the nature of narrative.* Evanston, IL: Northwestern University Press.

Gould, S. 1993. Ten thousand acts of kindness. In S. Gould, *Eight little piggies*, 275–83. New York: Norton.

Gray, D. 1968. Homer and the archaeologists. In *Fifty years (and twelve) of classical scholarship*, ed. Maurice Platnauer, 25–28. New York: Barnes & Noble.

Griffin, J. 1976. Homeric pathos and objectivity. *Classical Quarterly* 24:161–87.

1977. The epic cycle and the uniqueness of Homer. *Journal of Hellenic Studies* 97:39–53.

1980. *Homer on life and death*. Oxford: Oxford University Press.

Grote, G. 1872. *A history of Greece; From the earliest period to the close of the generation contemporary with Alexander the Great*. 4th edn. London: J. Murray.

Guttentag, M., and P. F. Secord. 1983. *Too many women? The sex ratio question*. Beverly Hills: Sage Publications.

Halliwell, S. 1986. *Aristotle's Poetics*. Chapel Hill, NC: University of North Carolina Press.

Halverson, J. 1986. The succession issue in the *Odyssey*. *Greece and Rome* 33:119–28.

Hamilton, W. D. 1964. The genetical evolution of social behaviour I and II. *Journal of Theoretical Biology* 7:1–16 and 17–52.

Hammer, D. 1998. The politics of the *Iliad*. *Classical Journal* 94:1–30.

Hammerstein, P. 1998. What is evolutionary game theory? In Dugatkin and Reeve 1998, 3–15.

Hansen, H. 1997. The Copenhagen inventory of *poleis* and the *Lex Hafniensis De Civitate*. In *The development of the polis in archaic Greece*, ed. L. G. Mitchell and P. J. Rhodes, 9–23. London: Routledge.

Hansen, H., and T. Heine Nielsen. 2004. *An inventory of Archaic and Greek poleis: An investigation conducted by The Copenhagen Polis Centre for the Danish National Research Foundation*. Oxford: Oxford University Press.

Hanson, V. D. 2000. *The Western way of war: Infantry battle in classical Greece*. Berkeley: University of California Press.

Hanson, V. D., and J. Heath. 1998. *Who killed Homer? The demise of classical education and the recovery of Greek wisdom*. New York: Free Press.

Hardin, G. 1968. The tragedy of the commons. *Science* 162:1243–48.

Harris, W. V. 1982. The theoretical possibility of extensive infanticide in the Greco-Roman World. *Classical Quarterly* 32:114–16.

Haslam, M. 1997. Homeric papyri and transmission of the text. In Morris and Powell 1997, 55–100.

Hausfater, G., and S. B. Hrdy. 1984. *Infanticide: Comparative and evolutionary perspectives*. New York: Aldine.

Havelock, E. A. 1963. *Preface to Plato: A history of the Greek mind*. Cambridge: Belknap Press, Harvard University Press.

Hèolldobler, B., and E. O. Wilson. 1994. *Journey to the ants: A story of scientific exploration*. Cambridge, MA: Belknap Press of Harvard University Press.

Herman, E. 2004. *Sex with Kings: Five hundred years of adultery, rivalry, and revenge*. New York: Harper Perennial.

Herodotus. 1998. *The Histories*. Trans. R. Waterfield. Oxford: Oxford University Press.

Heubeck, A. 1988. Introd. to Heubeck et al. 1988–92, vol. 1, 3–23.

Heubeck, A., S. West, and J. Hainsworth, eds. 1988–92. *A commentary on Homer's Odyssey*. 3 vols. Oxford: Oxford University Press.

Hewlett, B. S. 1991. Demography and childcare in pre-industrial societies. *Journal of Anthropological Research* 47:1–37.

Hooper, F. 1978. *Greek realities: Life and thought in ancient Greece*. Detroit: Wayne State University Press.

House, H. 1956. *Aristotle's Poetics*. London: Rupert Hart-Davis.

Hrdy, S. B. 1981. *The woman that never evolved*. Cambridge, MA: Harvard University Press.

1994. Fitness tradeoffs in the history of mothering. In *Infanticide and parental care*, ed. S. Parmigiani and F. S. Vom Saal, 3–42. Langhorne, PA: Harwood Academic Publishers.

1999. *Mother nature: A history of mothers, infants, and natural selection*. New York: Pantheon Books.

Hudson, V., and A. Den Boer. 2002. A surplus of men, a deficit of peace: Security and sex ratios in Asia's largest states. *International Security* 26:5–38.

2005. *Bare branches: The security implications of Asia's surplus male population*. Cambridge, MA: MIT Press.

Irons, W. 1979. Cultural and biological success. In Chagnon and Irons 1979, 257–72.

Jackson, A. 1993. War and raids for booty in the world of Odysseus. In *War and society in the Greek world*, ed. J. Rich and G. Shipley, 64–76. London: Routledge.

Janko, R. 1982. *Homer, Hesiod, and the Hymns: Diachronic development in epic diction*. Cambridge: Cambridge University Press.

1998. The Homeric poems as oral dictated texts. *Classical Quarterly* 48:1–13.

Jasienska, G., A. Ziomkiewicz, P. Ellison, S. Lipson, and I. Thune. 2004. Large breasts and narrow waists indicate high reproductive potential in women. *Proceedings of the Royal Society of London B* 271:1213–17.

Jebb, R. C. 1887. *Homer: An introduction to the Iliad and Odyssey*. Glasgow: J. Maclehose.

Johansson, S. R. 1979. Deferred infanticide: Excess female mortality during childhood. In Chagnon and Irons 1979, 463–85.

Johnson, A. W., and T. K. Earle. 1987. *The evolution of human societies: From foraging group to agrarian state*. Stanford, CA: Stanford University Press.

Johnston, I. C. 1988. *The ironies of war: An introduction to Homer's* Iliad. Lanham, MD: University Press of America.

Johnston, V. 1997. *Why we feel: The science of human emotions*. Cambridge, MA: Harvard, University Press.

Jolly, A. 1999. *Lucy's legacy: Sex and intelligence in human evolution*. Cambridge, MA: Harvard University Press.

Jones, O. D. 1999. Sex, culture, and the biology of rape: Toward explanation and prevention. *California Law Review* 87:827–941.

Karras, R. M. 1990. Concubinage and slavery in the Viking age. *Scandinavian Studies* 62:141–62.

Keeley, L. H. 1996. *War before civilization*. New York: Oxford University Press.

Keller, A. G. 1902. *Homeric society: A sociological study of the Iliad and Odyssey*. New York: Longmans, Green & Co.

Kelly, R. C. 2000. *Warless societies and the origin of war*. Ann Arbor, MI: University of Michigan Press.

Keynes, R. 2002. *Darwin, his daughter, and human evolution*. New York: Riverhead Books.

Kirk, G. S., M. Edwards, B. Hainsworth, R. Janko, and N. Richardson. 1985–93. *The Iliad: A commentary*. 6 vols. Cambridge: Cambridge University Press.

Kirkpatrick, M., and M. J. Ryan. 1991. The evolution of mating preferences and the paradox of the lek. *Nature* 350: 33–38.

Kluckhohn, C. 1961. *Anthropology and the classics*. Providence: Brown University Press.

Knauft, B. 1991. Violence and sociality in human evolution. *Current Anthropology* 32:391–428.

Knox, B. 1996. Introd. to the *Odyssey*. Trans. R. Fagles, 3–64. New York: Viking.

Kropotkin, P. A. 1904. *Mutual aid, a factor of evolution*. London: W. Heinemann.

Kruger, D. J., and R. M. Nesse. 2004. Sexual selection and the male:female mortality ratio. *Evolutionary Psychology* 2:66–77.

Lalumiere, M., G. Harris, V. Quinsey, and M. Rice. 2005. *The causes of rape: Understanding individual differences in male propensity for sexual aggression*. Washington, DC: American Psychological Association.

Langdon, S. H., ed. 1997. *New light on a dark age: Exploring the culture of geometric Greece*. Columbia, MO: University of Missouri Press.

Langer, W. L. 1974–75. Further notes on the history of infanticide. *History of Childhood Quarterly* 2:129–34.

Langlois, J., L. Kalakanis, A. Rubenstein, A. Larson, M. Hallam, and M. Smoot. 2000. Maxims or myths of beauty? A meta-analytic and theoretical review. *Psychological Bulletin* 126:390–423.

Latacz, J. 2004. *Troy and Homer: Toward a solution of an old mystery*. Trans. Kevin Windle and Rosh Ireland. Oxford: Oxford University Press.

Lerner, G. *The creation of patriarchy*. New York: Oxford University Press, 1986.

Levin, H. 1960. Preface to Lord 1960, xxxi–xxxiv.

Littlewood, R. 1997. Military rape. *Anthropology Today* 13:7–17.

Lonsdale, S. H. 1990. *Creatures of speech: Lion, herding, and hunting similes in the Iliad*. Stuttgart: Teubner.

Lord, A. B. 1960. *The singer of tales*. Cambridge: Harvard University Press.

Lorenz, K. 1966. *On aggression*. London: Methuen.

Low, B. S. 2000. *Why sex matters: A Darwinian look at human behavior*. Princeton, NJ: Princeton University Press.

Lucas, D. 1968. *Aristotle's Poetics*. Oxford: Oxford University Press.

Malamuth, N., M. Huppin, and B. Paul. 2005. Sexual coercion. In Buss 2005, 394–418.

Malinowski, B. 1929. *The sexual life of savages in north-western Melanesia*. New York: Halcyon House.

Man, John. 2005. *Ghengis Khan: Life, death and resurrection*. New York: Thomas Dunne Books.

Markner, R., and G. Veltri, eds. 1999. *Friedrich August Wolf: Studien, Dokumente, Bibliographie, Palingenesia*. Stuttgart: Franz Steiner.

Maschner, H., and K. Reedy-Maschner. 1998. Raid, retreat, defend (repeat): The archeology and ethnohistory of warfare on the north pacific rim. *Journal of Anthropological Archaeology* 17:19–52.

Mayr, E. 2001. *What evolution is*. New York: Basic Books.

McCarthy, B. 1994. Warrior values: A socio-historical survey. In Archer 1994, 105–20.

Mead, M. 1935 [1963]. *Sex and temperament in three primitive societies*. New York: William Morrow.

Meagher, R. E. 1995. *Helen: Myth, legend, and the culture of misogyny*. San Diego: Academic Press.

Mealey, L. 2000. *Sex differences: Developmental and evolutionary strategies*. Boston: Wiley.

Menon, R. 1998. Borders and bodies: Recovering women in the national interest. In Sajor 1998, 301–38.

Meron, T. 1993. *Henry's wars and Shakespeare's laws*. Oxford: Oxford University Press.

Mesquida, C., and N. Wiener. 1996. Human collective aggression: A behavioral ecology perspective. *Ethology and Sociobiology*, 17:247–62.

1999. Male age composition and severity of conflicts. *Politics and the Life Sciences* 18:181–89.

Miller, B. D. 1981. *The endangered sex: Neglect of female children in rural North India*. Ithaca, NY: Cornell University Press.

Miller, G. 1998. How mate choice shaped human nature: A review of sexual selection and human evolution. In *Handbook of evolutionary psychology: Ideas, issues, and applications*, ed. C. Crawford and D. Krebs, 87–130. London: Lawrence Erlbaum Associates.

Minturn, L., and J. Stashak. 1982. Infanticide as a terminal abortion procedure. *Behavior Science Research* 17:70–90.

Mitford, W. 1784. *History of Greece*. London: J. Murray and J. Rolsson.

Mokdad, A. H., J. Marks, D. Stroup, and J. Gerberding. 2004. Actual causes of death in the United States, 2000. *Journal of the American Medical Association* 291:1238–45.

Moore, L., B. McEvoy, E. Cape, K. Simms, and D. Bradley. 2006. A Y-chromosome signature of hegemony in Gaelic Ireland. *American Journal of Human Genetics* 78:334–38.

Morris, I. 1986. The uses and abuses of Homer. *Classical Antiquity* 5:81–138.

2000. *Archaeology as cultural history: Words and things in Iron Age Greece*. Oxford: Blackwell.

forthcoming. The eighth-century revolution. In *A Companion to Archaic Greece*, ed. K. Raaflaub and H. van Wees. Oxford: Blackwell.

Morris, I. and B. Powell, eds. 1997. *A new companion to Homer*. Leiden: Brill.

Murdock, G. 1967. *Ethnographic atlas*. Pittsburgh, PA: University of Pittsburgh Press.

Murray, G. 1907. *The rise of the Greek epic*. Oxford: Clarendon Press.

Myerson, R. 1999. Nash equilibrium and the history of economic theory. *Journal of Economic Literature* 37: 1067–82.

Myres, J. L. 1958. *Homer and his critics*. London: Routledge & Kegan Paul.

Nagler, M. N. 1974. *Spontaneity and tradition: A study in the oral art of Homer*. Berkeley, University of California Press.

Nagy, G. 1995. An evolutionary model for the making of Homeric poetry: Comparative perspectives. In *The Ages of Homer: A tribute to Emily Townsend Vermeule*, ed. Jane Carter and Sarah Morris, 163–79. Austin: University of Texas Press. 163–180.

1996. *Homeric questions*. Austin: University of Texas Press.

1997. The shield of Achilles: Ends of the *Iliad* and beginnings of the *polis*. In Langdon 1997, 194–208.

Neier, A. 1998. *War crimes: Brutality, genocide, terror, and the struggle for justice*. New York: Random House.

Nilsson, M. P. 1933. *Homer and Mycenae*. London: Methuen.

Notopoulos, J. 1960. The genesis of an oral Greek poem. *Greek, Roman and Byzantine Studies* 3:135–44.

Ogden, D. 1996. *Greek bastardy in the classical and Hellenistic periods.* Oxford: Oxford University Press.

Oldenziel, R. 1987. The historiography of infanticide in antiquity: A literature stillborn. In *Sexual asymmetry: Studies in ancient society*, ed. J. Blok and P. Mason, 87–107. Amsterdam: J. C. Gieben.

Oosterveld, V. 1998. When women are the spoils of war. *UNESCO Courier* 51:64–67.

Osborne, R. 2004. Homer's society. In Fowler 2004, 206–19.

Otterbein, K. F. 1994. *Feuding and warfare: Selected works of Keith F. Otterbein*. Langhorne, PA: Gordon and Breach.

Palmer, C. 1989a. Is rape a cultural universal? *Ethnology* 28:1–16.

1989b. Rape in nonhuman species: Definitions, evidence, and implications. *Journal of Sex Research* 26:353–74.

Parker, G. A. 1983. Mate quality and mating decisions. In *Mate choice*, ed. P. Bateson, 181–210. Cambridge: Cambridge University Press.

Parmigiani, S., and F. Vom Saal, eds. 1994. *Infanticide and parental care.* Langhorne, PA: Harwood Academic Publishers.

Parry, A. 1971. Introd. to Parry and Parry 1971, ix–lxxi.

1989. *The language of Achilles and other papers*. Oxford: Oxford University Press.

Parry, M., and A. Parry. 1971. *The making of Homeric verse: The collected papers of Milman Parry*. Oxford: Clarendon Press.

Patterson, C. 1983. "Not worth rearing": The causes of infant exposure in Ancient Greece. *Transactions of the American Philological Association* 115:103–23.

Pérusse, D. 1993. Cultural and reproductive success in modern societies: Testing the relationship at the proximate and ultimate levels. *Behavioral and Brain Sciences* 16:267–322.

1994. Mate choice in modern societies: Testing evolutionary hypotheses with behavioral data. *Human Nature* 5:225–78.

Pinker, S. 1995. *How the mind works.* New York: Norton.

2002. *The blank slate: The modern denial of human nature.* New York: Viking.

Plato. 2000. *Laws*. Trans. B. Jowett. New York: Prometheus Books.

Pomeroy, S. B. 1975. *Goddesses, whores, wives, and slaves: Women in classical antiquity*. New York: Schocken Books.

1983. Infanticide in Hellenistic Greece. In *Images of women in antiquity*, ed. A. Cameron and A. Kuhrt. Detroit: Wayne State University Press.

Pomeroy, S. B., S. Burstein, W. Donlan, and J. Tolbert Roberts. 1999. *Ancient Greece: A political, social, and cultural history*. Oxford: Oxford University Press.

Porter, J. 2004. Homer: The history of an idea. In Fowler 2004, 324–43.

Poundstone, W. 1992. *Prisoner's dilemma: John von Neuman, game theory, and the puzzle of the bomb*. New York: Anchor Books.

Powell, B. 1991. *Homer and the origin of the Greek alphabet*. Cambridge: Cambridge University Press.

1997. Homer and writing. In Morris and Powell 1997, 3–32.

2002. *Writing and the origins of Greek literature*. Cambridge: Cambridge University Press.

2004. *Homer*. Oxford: Blackwell.

Pusey, A., and C. Packer. 1994. Infanticide in lions: Consequences and counterstrategies. In Parmigiani and Vom Saal 1994, 277–330.

Qviller, B. 1981. The dynamics of Homeric society. *Symbole Osloenses* 56:109–55.

Raaflaub, K. A. 1997a. *Homeric society*. In Morris and Powell 1997, 624–48.

1997b. Politics and interstate relations in the world of early Greek poleis: Homer and beyond. *Antichthon* 31:1–27.

Redfield, J. M. 1975. *Nature and culture in the Iliad: The tragedy of Hector*. Chicago: University of Chicago Press.

Reinhardt, K. 1960. *Tradition und Geist: Gesammelte Essays zur Dichtung*. Göttingen: Vandenhoeck & Ruprecht.

Rhodes, J., and L. Zebrowitz. 2002. *Facial attractiveness: Evolutionary, cognitive, and social perspectives*. Westport, CN: Ablex Publishing.

Ridley, M. 1993. *The Red Queen: Sex and the evolution of human nature*. London: Viking.

1997. *The origins of virtue: Human instincts and the evolution of cooperation*. New York: Viking.

2003. *Nature via nurture: Genes, experience, and what makes us human*. New York: HarperCollins.

Rihll, Tracey. 1993. War, slavery, and settlement in early Greece. In *War and society in the Greek world*, ed. J. Rich and G. Shipley. London: Routledge.

Ritchie, M. A. 1996. *Spirit of the rainforest: A Yanomamö shaman's story*. Chicago: Island Lake Press.

Robarchek, C. A., and C. J. Robarchek. 1992. Cultures of war and peace: A comparative study of Waorani and Semai. In *Aggression and peacefulness in humans and other primates*, ed. J. Silverberg and J. Gray, 189–213. Oxford: Oxford University Press.

Rose, H., and S. Rose, eds. 2000. *Alas, poor Darwin: Arguments against evolutionary psychology*. New York: Harmony.

Rose, S., L. Kamin, and R. Lewontin. 1984. *Not in our genes: Biology, ideology and human nature*. New York: Pantheon Books.

Rousselle, R. 2001. "If it is a girl, cast it out": Infanticide/exposure in Ancient Greece. *Journal of Psychohistory* 28:303–33.

Ruijgh, C. 1995. D'Homère aux origines proto-mycéniennes de la tradition épique: Analyse dialectologique du langage homérique, avec un *excursus* sur la création de l'alphabet grec. In *Homeric questions: Essays in philology, ancient history and archaeology, including the papers of a conference organized by the Netherlands Institute at Athens (15 May 1993)*, ed. J. P. Crielaard, 1–96. Amsterdam: J. C. Gieben.

Rutherford, R. 1996. *Homer*. Greece and Rome: New surveys in the classics no. 26. Oxford: Oxford University Press.

Rutter, J. 2000. *The Prehistoric Archaeology of the Aegean* (cited May 15 2006). http://projectsx.dartmouth.edu/history/bronze_age/lessons/les/28.html

Sajor, I. L., ed. 1998. *Common grounds: Violence against women in war and armed conflict situations*. Quezon City, Philippines: Asian Center for Women's Human Rights.

Sallares, R. 1991. *The ecology of the ancient Greek world*. London: Duckworth.

Schein, S. L. 1984. *The mortal hero: An introduction to Homer's Iliad*. Berkeley: University of California Press.

Seaford, R. 1994. *Reciprocity and ritual: Homer and tragedy in the developing city-state*. Oxford: Oxford University Press.

Shay, J. 1994. *Achilles in Vietnam: Combat trauma and the undoing of character*. New York: Atheneum.

2001. Killing rage: *Physis* or *nomos* – or both? In *War and violence in Ancient Greece*, ed. H. van Wees, 31–56. London: Duckworth and the Classical Press of Wales.

Sherratt, E. 1990. Reading the texts: Archaeology and the Homeric question. *Antiquity* 64:807–24.

Shields W., and L. Shields. 1983. Forcible rape: An evolutionary perspective. *Ethology and Sociobiology* 4:115–36.

Siefert, R. 1994. War and rape: A preliminary analysis. In Stiglmayer 1994, 54–72.

Silk, M. 1989. *Homer: The Iliad*. Cambridge: Cambridge University Press.

2004. The *Odyssey* and its explorations. In *The Cambridge companion to Homer*, ed. Robert Fowler, 31–44. Cambridge: Cambridge University Press.

Singer, P. 2000. *A Darwinian left: Politics, evolution, and cooperation*. New Haven and London: Yale University Press.

Singor, H. W. 1995. *Eni Prōtoisi Machesthai*: Some remarks on the Iliadic image of the battlefield. In *Homeric questions: Essays in philology, ancient history and archaeology, including the papers of a conference organized by the Netherlands Institute at Athens (15 May 1993)*, ed. J. P. Crielaard, 183–200. Amsterdam: J. C. Gieben.

Small, M. 1992. The evolution of female sexuality and mate selection in humans. *Human Nature* 3:133–56.

Smith, E. and S. Smith. 1994. Inuit sex ratio variation: Population control, ethnographic error, or parental manipulation? *Current Anthropology* 35: 595–624.

Smith, M. 1982. *Evolution and the theory of games*. Cambridge: Cambridge University Press.

Smuts, B. 1991. Male aggression against women: An evolutionary perspective. *Human Nature* 3: 1–44.

1995a. Apes of wrath. *Discover*, August, 103–05.

1995b. The evolutionary origins of patriarchy. *Human Nature* 6:1–32.

Snodgrass, A. M. 1971. *The Dark Age of Greece*. Edinburgh: Edinburgh University Press.

1974. An historical Homeric society? *Journal of Hellenic Studies* 94:114–25.

Sober, E., and D. S. Wilson. 1998. *Unto others: The evolution and psychology of unselfish behavior*. Cambridge, MA: Harvard University Press.

Stark, R. 1997. *The rise of Christianity: How the obscure, marginal Jesus movement became the dominant religious force in the Western world in a few centuries*. San Francisco: HarperCollins.

Starr, C. 1961. *The origins of Greek civilization*. New York: Knopf.

Stiglmayer, A., ed. 1994. *Mass rape: The war against women in Bosnia-Herzegovina*. Lincoln: University of Nebraska Press.

Straffin, P. D. 1993. *Game theory and strategy*. Washington: Mathematical Association of America.

Strathern, A., and P. Stewart. 2000. *Collaborations and conflicts: A leader through time*. Fort Worth, TX: Harcourt College.

Sugiyama, L. 2005. Physical attractiveness in adaptationist perspective. In Buss 2005, 292–343.

Swiss, S., and J. Giller. 1993. Rape as a crime of war: A medical perspective. *Journal of the American Medical Association* 270:612–15.

Symons, D. 1979. *The evolution of human sexuality*. New York: Oxford University Press.

1995. Beauty is in the adaptations of the beholder: The evolutionary psychology of human female sexual attractiveness. In *Sexual nature sexual culture*, ed. P. R. Abramson and S. D. Pinkerton, 80–118. Chicago: University of Chicago Press.

Tanaka, Y. 1998. Rape and war: The Japanese experience. In Sajor 1998, 174–76.

Taplin, O. 1980. The shield of Achilles within the *Iliad*. *Greece and Rome* 27:1–21.

Thirwall, C. 1835. *A History of Greece*. London: Longman.

Thomas, C. G., and C. Conant. 1999. *Citadel to city-state: The transformation of Greece, 1200–700 BC*. Bloomington: Indiana University Press.

Thomas, D., and R. Regan. 1994. Rape in war: Challenging the tradition of impunity. *SAIS Review* 14:81–99.

Thomas, E. 1959. *The harmless people*. New York: Knopf.

Thornhill, R., and C. Palmer. 2000. *A natural history of rape: Biological bases of sexual coercion*. Cambridge, MA: MIT Press.

Thornhill R., and N. Thornhill. 1983. Human rape: An evolutionary analysis. *Ethology and Sociobiology* 4:137–73.

Tierney, P. 2000. *Darkness in El Dorado: How scientists and journalists devastated the Amazon*. New York: Norton.

Tooby, J., and L. Cosmides. 1988. The evolution of war and its cognitive foundations. *Institute for Evolutionary Studies Technical Report* 88:1–5.

Traill, D. A. 1995. *Schliemann of Troy: Treasure and deceit*. New York: St. Martin's Press.

Trivers, R. 1971. The evolution of reciprocal altruism. *Quarterly Review of Biology* 46:35–57.

1972. Parental investment and sexual selection. In *Sexual selection and the Descent of Man 1871–1971*, ed. B. Campbell, 136–207. Chicago: Aldine.

1974. Parent–Offspring Conflict. *American Zoologist* 14:249–64.

Trivers, R., and D. Willard. 1973. Natural selection of parent ability to vary the sex ratios of offspring. *Science* 179:90–92.

Turner, F. 1997. The Homeric question. In Morris and Powell 1997, 123–45.

Turney-High, H. H. 1949. *Primitive war, its practice and concepts*. Columbia: University of South Carolina Press.

Valero, H., and E. Biocca. 1969. *Yanomama: The story of a woman abducted by Brazilian Indians*. London: Allen & Unwin.

Van Hook, L. 1920. The exposure of infants at Athens. *Transactions of the American Philological Association* 51:134–45.

Van Wees, H. 1992. *Status warriors: War, violence, and society in Homer and history*. Amsterdam: J.C. Gieben.

1994. The Homeric way of war: The *Iliad* and the hoplite phalanx. *Greece and Rome* 41:1–18.

1996. Heroes, knights, and nutters. In *Battle in antiquity*, ed. A. Lloyd, 1–86. London: Duckworth.

1997. Homeric warfare. In Morris and Powell 1997, 668–93.

2002a. Greed, generosity and gift-exchange in early Greece and the Western Pacific. In *After the past*, ed. W. Jongman and M. Kleijwegt. Leiden: Brill.

2002b. Homer and early Greece. *Colby Quarterly* 32:94–117.

2004. *Greek warfare: Myths and realities*. London: Duckworth.

Vermeule, E. 1979. *Aspects of death in early Greek art and poetry*. Berkeley: University of California Press.

Von Fritz, K. 1962. *Antike und moderne Tragödie*. Berlin: De Gruyter.

Von Neumann, J., and O. Morgenstern. 1944. *Theory of games and economic behavior*. Princeton: Princeton University Press.

Waal, F. B. M. de. 1989. *Chimpanzee politics: Power and sex among apes.* Baltimore: Johns Hopkins University Press.

1996. *Good natured: The origins of right and wrong in humans and other animals.* Cambridge, MA: Harvard University Press.

Wace, A. J. B., and F. H. Stubbings. 1962. *A companion to Homer.* London: Macmillan.

Wallace, A. R. 1867. *Westminster Review.* July.

Warner, W. L. 1931. Murngin warfare. *Oceania* 1:457–94.

Weil, S. 1956. *The Iliad; The poem of force.* Wallingford, PA: Pendle Hill.

West, M. 1995. The date of the *Iliad. Museum Helveticum.* 52:203–19.

2001. *Studies in the text and transmission of the Iliad.* Munich: K. G. Saur.

2003. *Greek epic fragments.* Cambridge, MA: Harvard University Press.

Whitley, J. 1991. *Style and Society in Dark Age Greece: The changing face of a preliterate society.* Cambridge: Cambridge University Press.

Wiedemann, Thomas. 1981. *Greek and Roman Slavery.* Baltimore: Johns Hopkins University Press.

Wilamowitz-Moellendorff, U. von. 1884. *Homerische Untersuchungen.* Berlin: Weidmann.

1921 [1982]. *History of classical scholarship.* Trans. Alan Harris. London: Duckworth.

Williams, G. C. 1966. *Adaptation and natural selection; A critique of some current evolutionary thought.* Princeton: Princeton University Press.

1988. Huxley's evolution and ethics in sociobiological perspective. *Zygon* 23:383–407.

Wilson, D. S. 2002. *Darwin's cathedral: Evolution, religion, and the nature of society.* Chicago: Chicago University Press.

Wilson, E. O. 1975. *Sociobiology: The new synthesis.* Cambridge, MA: Belknap Press, Harvard University Press.

1978. *On human nature.* Cambridge: Harvard University Press.

Wilson, M., and M. Daly. 1985. Competitiveness, risk-taking, and violence: The young male syndrome. *Ethology and Sociobiology* 6:59–73.

1993. An evolutionary perspective on male sexual proprietariness and violence against wives. *Violence and Victims* 8:3–16.

1997. Life expectancy, economic inequality, homicide, and reproductive timing in Chicago neighborhoods. *British Medical Journal* 314:1271–74.

Wolf, F. A. 1795 [1985]. *Prolegomena to Homer,* trans. A. Grafton, G. Most, and J. Zetzel. Princeton: Princeton University Press.

Wood, R. 1769 [1824]. *An essay on the original genius and writings of Homer.* London.

Wood, W., and A. H. Eagly. 2002. A cross-cultural analysis of the behavior of women and men: Implications for the origins of sex differences. *Psychological Bulletin* 128:699–727.

Wrangham, R W., and D. Peterson. 1996. *Demonic males: Apes and the origins of human violence*. Boston: Houghton Mifflin.

Wright, Q. 1942. *A study of war*. Chicago: University of Chicago Press.

Wright, R. 1994. *The moral animal: The new science of evolutionary psychology*. New York: Pantheon Books.

1995. The biology of violence. *The New Yorker* March 10, 68–77.

Yamagata, N. 1997. *Anax* and *basileus* in Homer. *Classical Quarterly* 47:1–14.

Zaastra, B., J. Seidell, P. Van Noord, E. te Velde, D. Habbema, B. Vrieswijk, and J. Karbaat. 1993. Fat and female fecundity: Prospective study of effect of body fat distribution on conception rates. *British Medical Journal* 306:484–88.

Zerjal, T., and 15 co-authors. 2003. The genetic legacy of the Mongols. *American Journal of Human Genetics* 72:717–21.

Index